Publisher's Acknowledgements
Special thanks to **Renee McKee** and **Kendra McLaughlin**, New York. We would also like to thank the following authors and publishers: ART Press, New York; **Art Resources Transfer, Inc.**, New York; **Chuck Close**, New York; **New Directions Publishing Corporation**, New York, and **Pollinger Limited and the proprietor**, London. Thanks to the following for lending reproductions: **Institute of Contemporary Art**, London; **McKee Gallery**, New York. Photographers: **Eric Baum**, **John Bigelow Taylor, Geoffrey Clements, Edward Cornachio, Susan Cooder, James Dee, Sydney B. Felsen, Leo Holub, Jan Jedlička, Michael Korol, Renee McKee, Robert E. Mates, Josh Nefsky, Richard Nicol, Frank A. Thomas, Susan Titelmanm, Sarah Wells.**

Artist's Acknowledgements
I would like to thank the publishers and staff who contributed to making this book, and especially Gilda Williams and John Stack for their patience and guidance. Also thanks to the McKee Gallery staff: Kendra McLaughlin, Anders Bergstrom and Angela Boulart. A special thanks to Renee McKee for her relentless hard work to make this book possible.
Thank you to Briony Fer and Lane Relyea for giving some interesting insights and perspective on the work. I would also thank Bob Gober, who agreed to come to my house in Sag Harbor to see my garden, eat lunch, and talk a little about making art and what it might mean to make it.

All works are in private collections unless otherwise stated.

Phaidon Press Limited
Regent's Wharf
All Saints Street
London N1 9PA

Phaidon Press Inc.
180 Varick Street
New York, NY 10014

www.phaidon.com

First published 2004
Reprinted 2010

ISBN 9 780 7148 4264 6

A CIP catalogue record of this book is available from the British Library.

Printed in Hong Kong
Designed by Onespace – Ben Dale and Andrew Beattie

cover, front, **Untitled (Web)** (detail)
2000
Oil on canvas
38.5 × 45.5 cm
15.25 × 18 in

cover, back, **House #2** (detail)
1965
Oil on wood with cardboard
30.5 × 25 × 18 cm
12 × 9.75 × 7 in

page 4, **Soup** (detail)
1964
Oil on canvas
46.5 × 41 cm
18.25 × 16.125 in

page 6, **Vija Celmins**
Artist's studio, SoHo, New York, 1987

page 44, **Untitled (Ocean)** (detail)
1968
Graphite on acrylic ground on canvas
35 × 47 cm
13.75 × 18.5 in

page 100, **Night Sky #19** (detail)
1998
Charcoal on paper on acrylic ground
48.5 × 58.5 cm
19.125 × 23 in

page 108, **Web #3** (detail)
1999
Charcoal on paper
48.5 × 57 cm
19 × 22.438 in

page 144, Artist's studio, New York, 2003

Lane Relyea Robert Gober Briony Fer

Vija Celmins

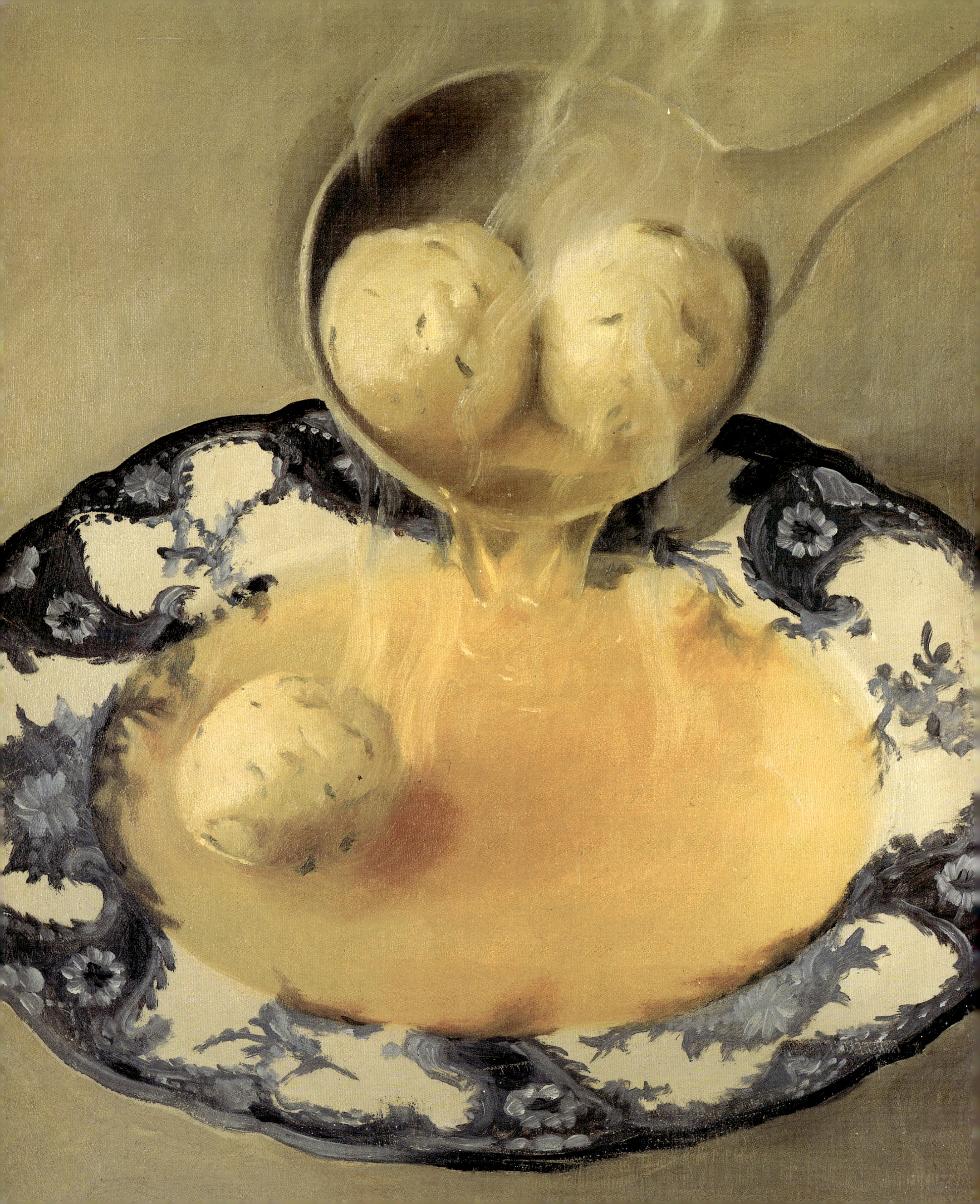

Contents

Interview **Robert Gober** in conversation with **Vija Celmins, page 6**.

Survey **Lane Relyea** Vija Celmins' Twilight Zone, **page 44**.

Focus **Briony Fer** *Night Sky #19*, 1998, **page 100**.

Artist's Choice **Jorge Luis Borges** Funes the Memorious (extracts), 1941, **page 108**.

Artist's Writings **Vija Celmins** Interview with Chuck Close (extracts), 1991, **page 116**.

Chronology **page 144** & Bibliography, List of Illustrations, **page 158**.

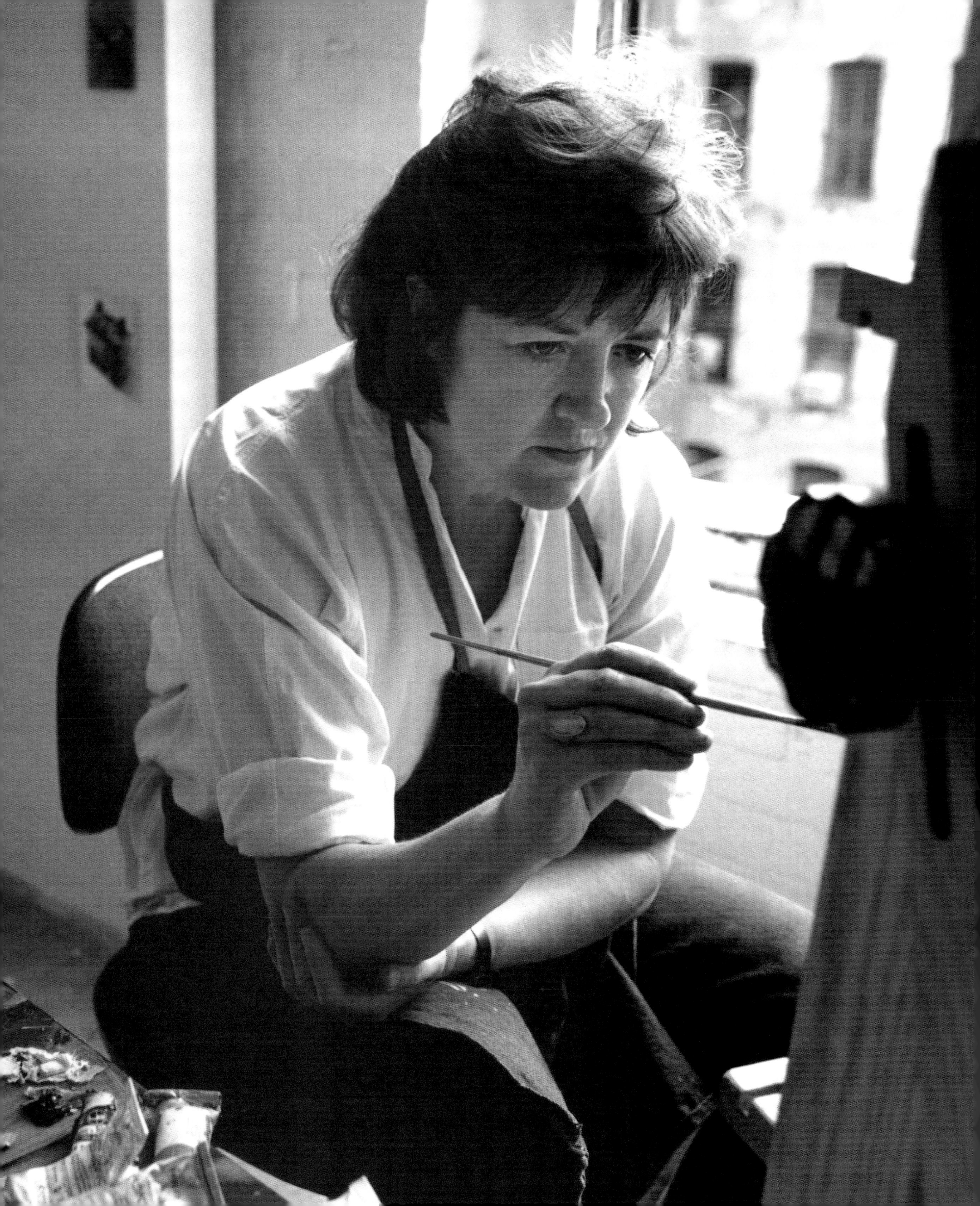

Contents

Interview **Robert Gober** in conversation with **Vija Celmins, page 6.**

Survey Lane Relyea Vija Celmins' Twilight Zone, page 44.

Focus Briony Fer *Night Sky #19*, 1998, page 100.

Artist's Choice Jorge Luis Borges Funes the Memorious (extract), 1941, page 108.

Artist's Writings Vija Celmins Interview with Chuck Close (extracts), 1991, page 116.

Chronology page 144 & Bibliography, List of Illustrations, page 158.

Since 1980 Vija Celmins has lived and worked in New York City. About four years ago she purchased a small house on a corner lot in a seaside town on the east end of Long Island. I visited her there on a sultry afternoon in August 2002. She loves her garden and I was introduced to almost every plant, bush and tree. She showed me the grave of her dog, picked beans for lunch and sat me down for our conversation in her living room.

Vija Celmins **(*laughing*) So Bob – where's your notebook with questions?**

Robert Gober I don't have any.

Celmins **Oh, you must have some.**

Gober I started writing down questions and they were really stupid, they were so self-conscious. I have a question to start though, about how you work. Do you work every day?

Celmins **No, I don't work every day. I have always had a very complicated relationship with working – stopping and starting. I can see by your catalogues that you're much more workman-like, maybe that's because you have people working for you whom you have to feel responsible for.**

Gober Yeah, I come in at a certain hour and leave at a certain hour.

Celmins **So in a way, you're engaged in a little community that works with you, where I tend to be always alone in my studio.**

Gober Well, that's why for the last four years I've worked in my garage out on Long Island, so that I could be by myself again. So I could do nothing and get bored all day if I wanted to, or work right out of bed at six in the morning. I needed that kind of freedom.

Celmins **So do I. I am now at a point where I have to re-establish that, because I have been making prints, where there's all those people around all the time, and expectations and deadlines and so forth. And when I do that so much, I lose my sense of self. I have to kind of rebuild myself in the studio again. When I was younger I used to have a lot of problems working. I would spend many days anguishing. Do you ever do that?**

Gober I haven't really worked for the last year and a half.

Celmins **Oh, how could you say that!**

Gober Because it's true. I haven't made a new sculpture in a year and a half.

Celmins **See, now when I don't do something that is real to me – like work, of course – I start feeling incredibly anxious. And then when I fall into finally making the stuff and being in my studio … that's the best. Well, so anyway, you know I'm not that happy with a lot of my work. I tend to beat up my work a lot …**

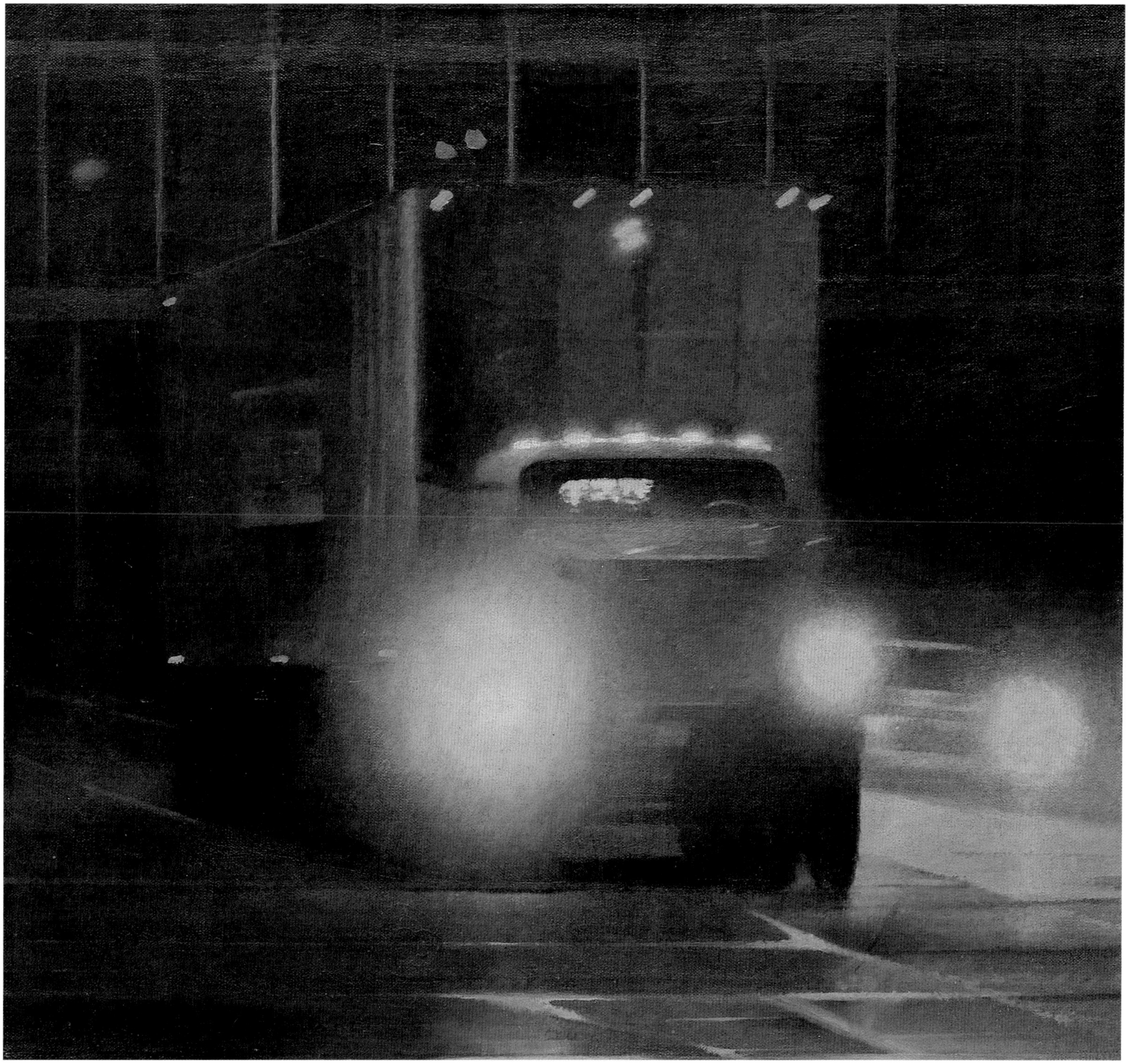

Truck
1966
Oil on canvas
51 × 55 cm
20 × 21.75 in

Gober Mentally?

Celmins **Yes, with a kind of relentless questioning and criticizing of everything. Lately I have been painting a work over and over … sanding it off and painting it again on top of itself. Same image over and over. Actually, I tend to end up with a simple-looking single image that may have six months of work under it. It begins to have this strange quality when you get to a certain point, you can actually … it lets you in for a little bit and you think you may be seeing something that isn't there. The black night sky paintings are especially hard to penetrate … yet I think you get the feeling of a fuller space and some solid structure underneath. I mean one of the things that painting does is … it's quite difficult to react to verbally, even though many try, don't they? They're all out there with their pencils and things.**

Gober I was reading all the essays about you, in which so many talented writers have really seriously taken on the challenge of trying to contribute to an understanding of your work, but after I read them all there was – for me anyway – a threadbare feeling. I think that what's just missing is the experience of the object, and there's no replacing that.

Celmins **Of course. The early work, which had more of a dramatic narrative, like the *Freeway* painting (1966) or the *Burning Man* (1966) or the aeroplanes (i.e., *German Plane*, 1966), they're easier to see in reproduction and to talk about, but the late work isn't. It's more about experience.**

Gober That's why I think that seeing in reproduction images of the later work, the oceans or the galaxies, is deceptive. Because I don't think the paintings themselves are 'images' of the ocean, or 'images' of stars.

Celmins **No. The recognizable image is just one element to consider. The paintings seem more a record of my grappling with how to transform that image into a painting and make it alive. I mean, dead *and* alive, since in the end the paintings (at least lately) have become so restrained and still … the paint and the image packed tightly together. The surface is very closed and flat, but the feeling of the painting (I hope) is full and dense – like a chord of music, maybe. Hard to talk about it; it's sort of difficult to figure out how to make a painting interesting. One of the things I like about painting is that it is so slight a presence … you can't trip over it like any object. You turn away and it disappears immediately, you know?**

Gober People always approach the earlier work through autobiography. I was wondering if the changes in the work might not be some kind of reaction to that, or against that. Of course art comes directly out of who we are, but it's –

Celmins **Well, I believe that the early work *was* kind of autobiographical. But you can only say that looking back, because when I was doing the work I had a million things I was interested in, like depth and flatness. Somehow I fell in love with that, depth and flatness. Rummaging through memories, trying to find out who I was … My work now seems more abstract.**

Gober But then you stopped painting.

German Plane
1966
Oil on canvas
40.5 × 66 cm
16 × 26 in
Collection Modern Art Museum of Fort Worth, Texas

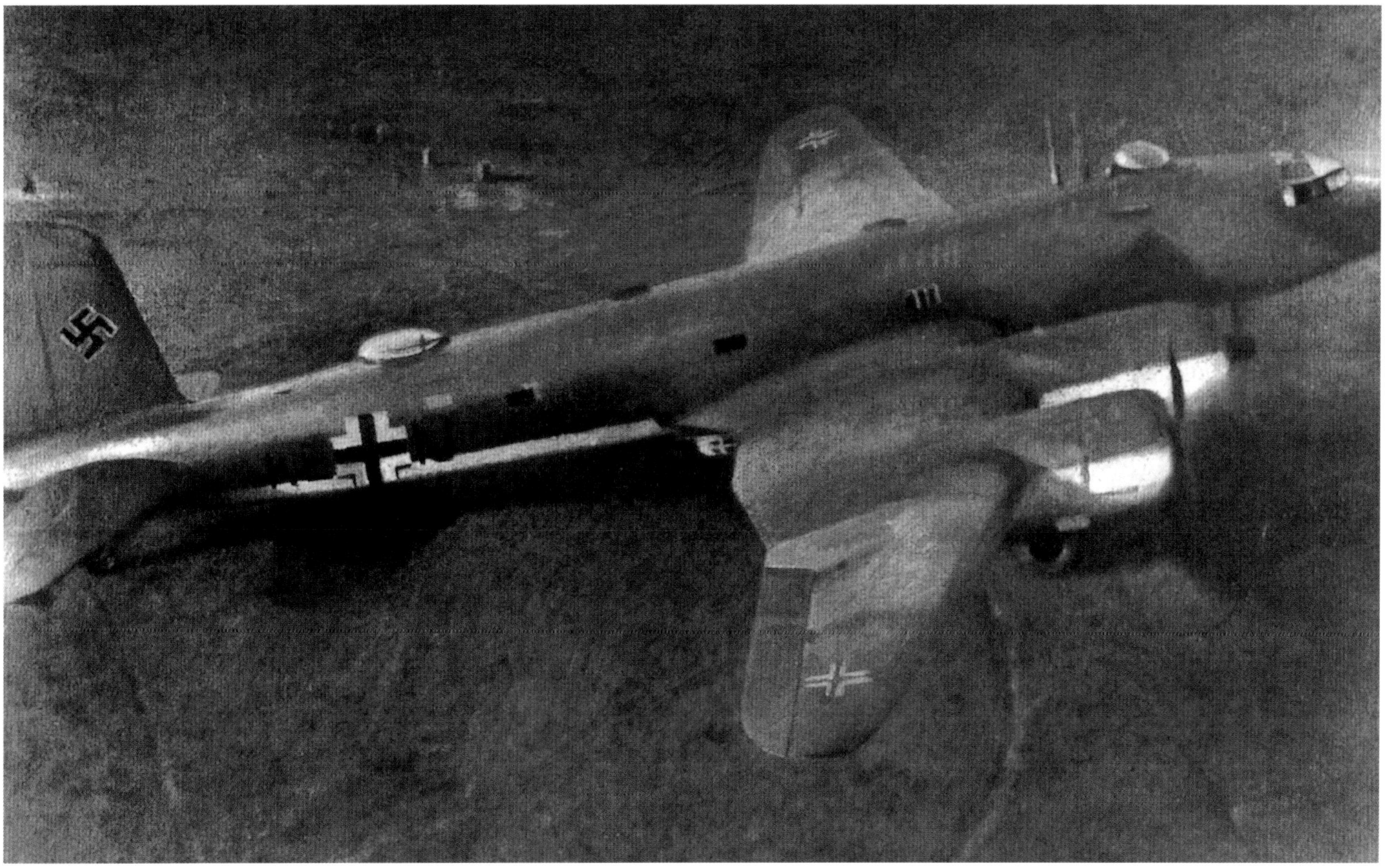

Celmins **Well, I did do some painted objects in the late 1960s, early 1970s; then I switched to drawing only, using a pencil. More clear, I thought at the time. But basically the work stayed flat.**

Gober I get very frustrated when people ask me, 'What does your sculpture mean?' I respond by talking about what it's made of and they get impatient, as though I'm avoiding the question. But I feel that unless you know what it's physically made of, you can't begin to understand it. A lot of times the metaphors are embedded right in the medium and the way that you work.

Celmins **That's true, I'm always talking about 'making' as if that is the only thing there is to it. I think that you, Bob, build more meaning in. You don't think so? I think that your work fits different interests in your life – political, social, personal. My work seems to communicate less about what I think and is more ambiguous. Sometimes I think the meaning is only in the material – I guess you said that already. At any rate, we leave the material there as evidence.**

I generally start a painting after obsessing on an image, or the look of a printed image I've found somewhere in a book or remembered from somewhere. I fall for it, carry it around in my head, sort of fall in love with it. I like scientific images, they're so anonymous, and I like the printing quality of certain images. I have collections of many clippings stuffed in drawers. I don't know, do you collect images too?

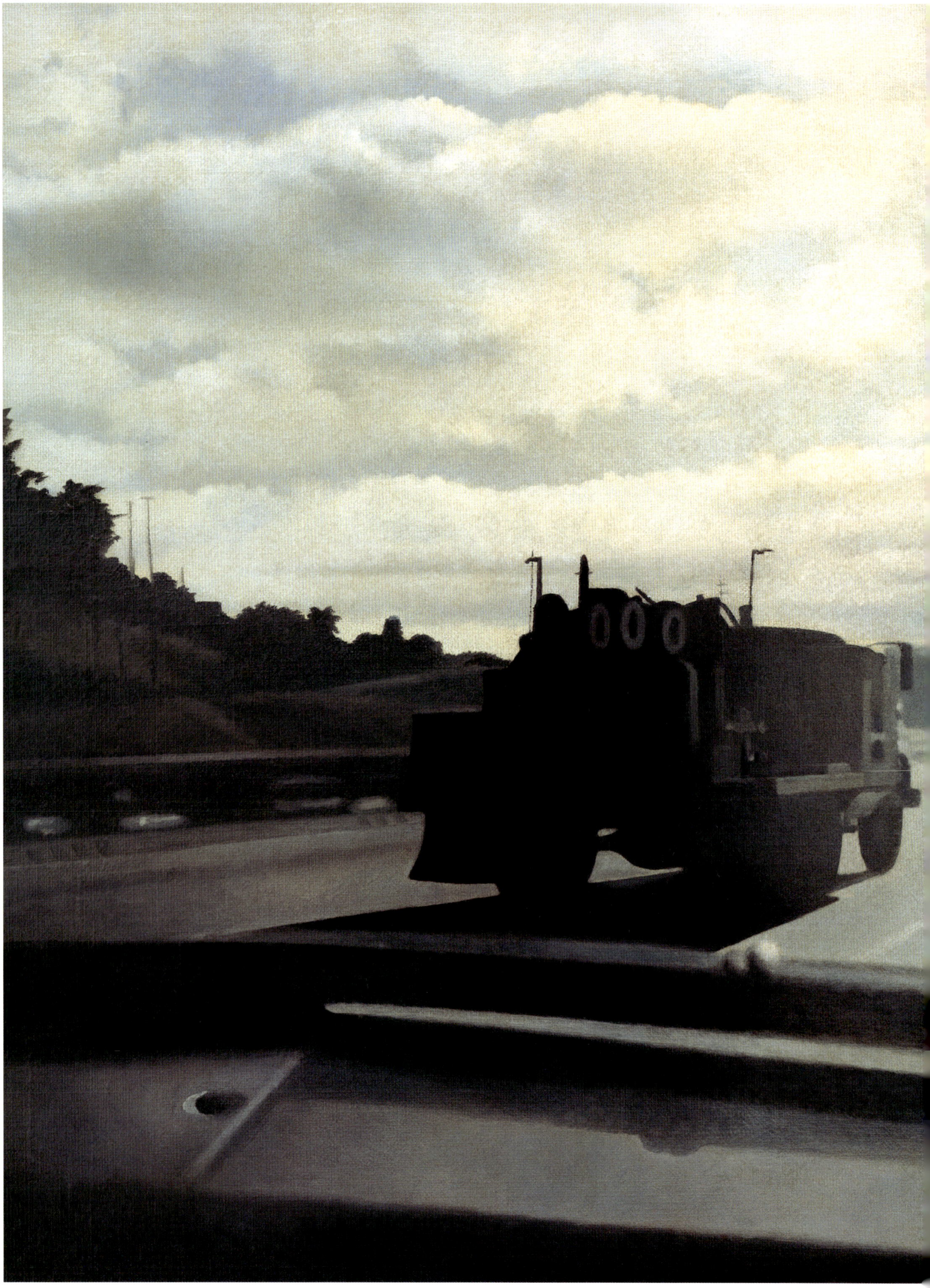

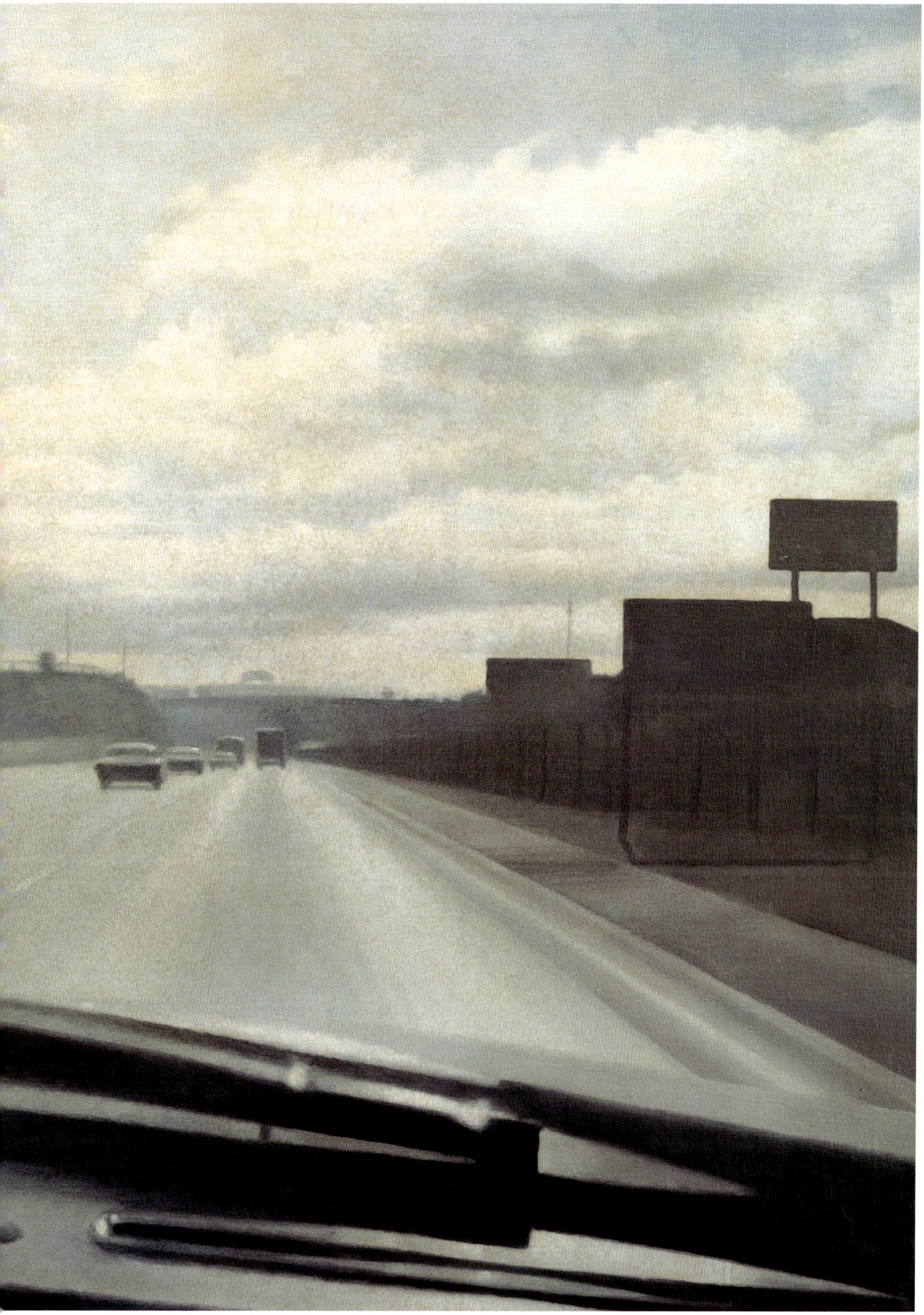

Freeway
1966
Oil on canvas
44.5 × 67.5 cm
17.5 × 26.5 in

Gober I do, but I think maybe you were right in pointing out one of our differences, because what I'll collect is more word- than image-based, like clippings from a newspaper. I feel that that content shouldn't be lost – the way it is, because a new newspaper comes the next day.

Celmins **Yes! See, but that is such a beautiful thought to me, and it never occurred to me to do that. Even though sometimes I cut out a thing and send it to a friend, saying, 'Isn't this outrageous?' or something. But, what I do is I fall for the look. I mean it's so stupid, really. I fall in love with the look. Then the problem is, how to send it through my system, and pack it into this flat thing that I'm going to bring to life in another way.**

Gober That's very familiar to me, because I'll see an image in the world that I also blindly need. I don't know why, necessarily. But then I have the problem of how to make an interesting sculpture out of it, which is a whole other problem.

Celmins **Well, that's your problem. I don't have that problem! (*laughs*)**

Gober Right, you have the problem of painting.

Celmins **I have the painting problem, although I did do a lot of objects too, the comb (*Comb*, 1970), the pencil (*Pencil*, 1967), puzzles (*WWII Puzzle Toy*, 1965) and the houses (*House #1* and *#2*, both 1965). I think they were probably pretty much images of my childhood. See, I think ... obviously we're very different artists, but we have a few things which I think we've both tapped**

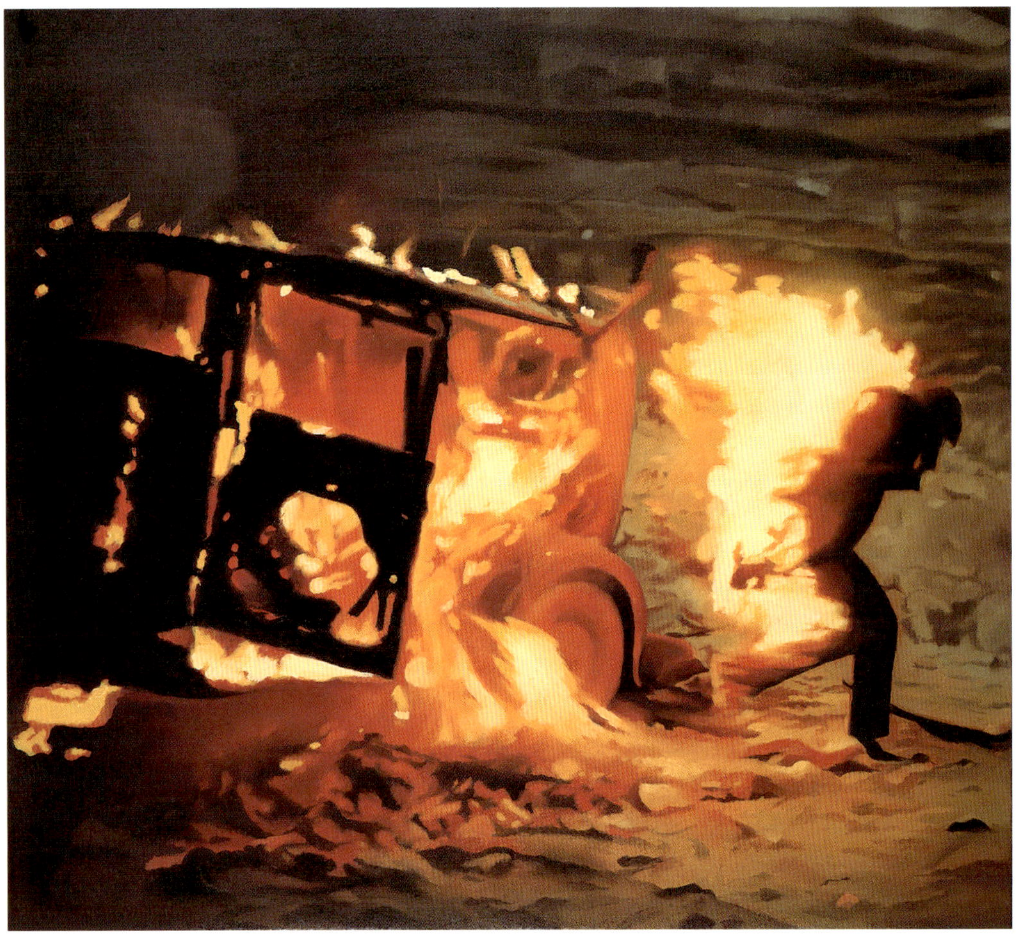

left, **Burning Man**
1966
Oil on canvas
51 × 57 cm
20 × 22.5 in

opposite, **House #1**
1965
Oil on wood with metal, fur and plastic
19 × 26.5 × 24 cm
7.5 × 10.5 × 9.5 in

into, and one of them is childhood. And I'm not sure that many artists don't live their whole lives from that childhood.

Gober Not just artists; most people.

Celmins **Yes, maybe most people. Yeah. I don't know a lot of people, I just know mostly artists. Your work may have been coloured by your religious experience, or whatever, and I think mine was coloured mostly by the chaos of my early childhood in the war. Not that I knew what it was, or that I understood it in any way. Nobody ever talked about it. It was like, this is it, you're born, you're here, you have to deal with it. I was so afraid of being abandoned and lost in it. But later, in the studio, I think I relived all these things, the burning houses, the aeroplanes, the Latvian school in Germany, my eraser, my little pencils. Kind of like sewing this big thing – like the way that you Robert put different images together in one piece. I, too, am not bad at picking images, but mine dribble out one by one over a long time. I touch on one thing, and another, done totally like you were saying, in a blind way at the time. Like a kind of desire to see something come up, and then a kind of desire to try to make a painting out of it. Then when the painting got so, you know, tedious, really, I would make a piece that was dimensional. Not uninfluenced by maybe Pop art, except done in a maybe more meticulous manner. Not using Pop's commercial techniques either, but a more tender touch. I developed a touch that you could hardly tell was a touch.**

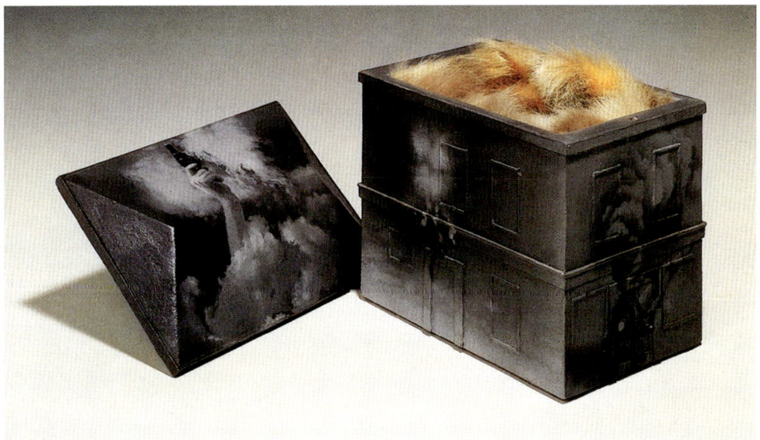

Gober I think my hands are too big to do that. I can't do such detailed work.

Celmins **What is your problem? You do the most detailed, gorgeous work ...**

Gober Maybe it's the physical tininess of some of your gestures which add up to the larger images that I don't think I could do. I was looking at those drypoint marks on your plates; there are so many nearly infinitesimal marks.

Celmins **I know. Can you imagine that the eyes can still do it? I'm in my sixties, you know?**

Gober Do you wear glasses?

Celmins **I have contacts on. And I wear glasses.**

Gober I have a question a little far afield. One of your early sculptures was a huge tortoise shell *Comb*. And when I was in your bathroom just now, I noticed you use the exact same tortoise shell comb. That was really interesting to me; I, for instance, could never live with a white porcelain sink in my kitchen.

Celmins **Well, you're more perverse than I am!**

Gober Are you aware that that's the comb from your early sculpture? Do you like it because of that? Or don't you even think about it?

Celmins **No, I sort of remember a comb somewhere. Maybe my mother had, maybe my father had, maybe I had, maybe Magritte had. I mean, obviously,**

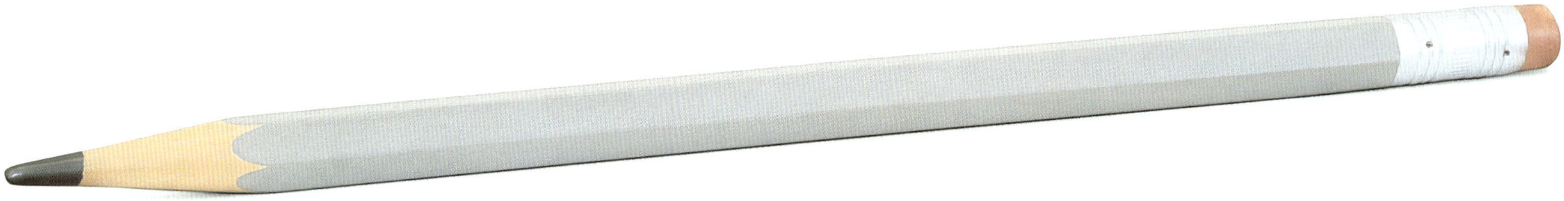

nobody could look at that comb that I made and not think of Magritte. You know when you're young ... I don't know whether you had influences like this?

Gober Yes.

Celmins **I had influences that lasted, like, for two months. And I would run through one artist and be seduced by another.**

Gober And did you know you were doing it? Because sometimes I didn't even know I was doing it.

Celmins **No.**

Gober Until later, people would point it out.

Celmins **I'm telling you now all of these memories, and I'm remembering that I once painted a train on one of those little houses I made. Now, where would that train be from? Except, of course, I lived on trains when I was little. A lot of trains, with the smoke coming out. But I think it's probably Magritte's train that got in there. And, of course, Magritte's comb. Not that I was aware of it ... I had seen that painting, *Personal Values* (1952), but had I seen it in real life? Or in a book? I think in a book, maybe. I saw the painting later.**

Gober When did you start to see real art?

Celmins **Well, I saw real art, of course, as a youngster in Indiana, but I think my biggest turn-on was when I went to Europe with my boyfriend, in 1962. Quite late.**

Gober Do you remember your first reactions to particular works when you went to your first museum?

Celmins **I remember first seeing the Giotto frescos at the Arena Chapel in Padua. We had to wait to have someone open the door for us and we were the only ones there. What a surprise inside! We were just beside ourselves. So very excited and running back and forth from one panel to another. I had**

above, **Pencil**
1968–70
Acrylic on canvas on wood
L. 167.5 cm, ∅ 7.5 cm
L. 66 in, ∅ 3 in

opposite, **House #2**
1965
Oil on wood with cardboard
30.5 × 25 × 18 cm
12 × 9.75 × 7 in

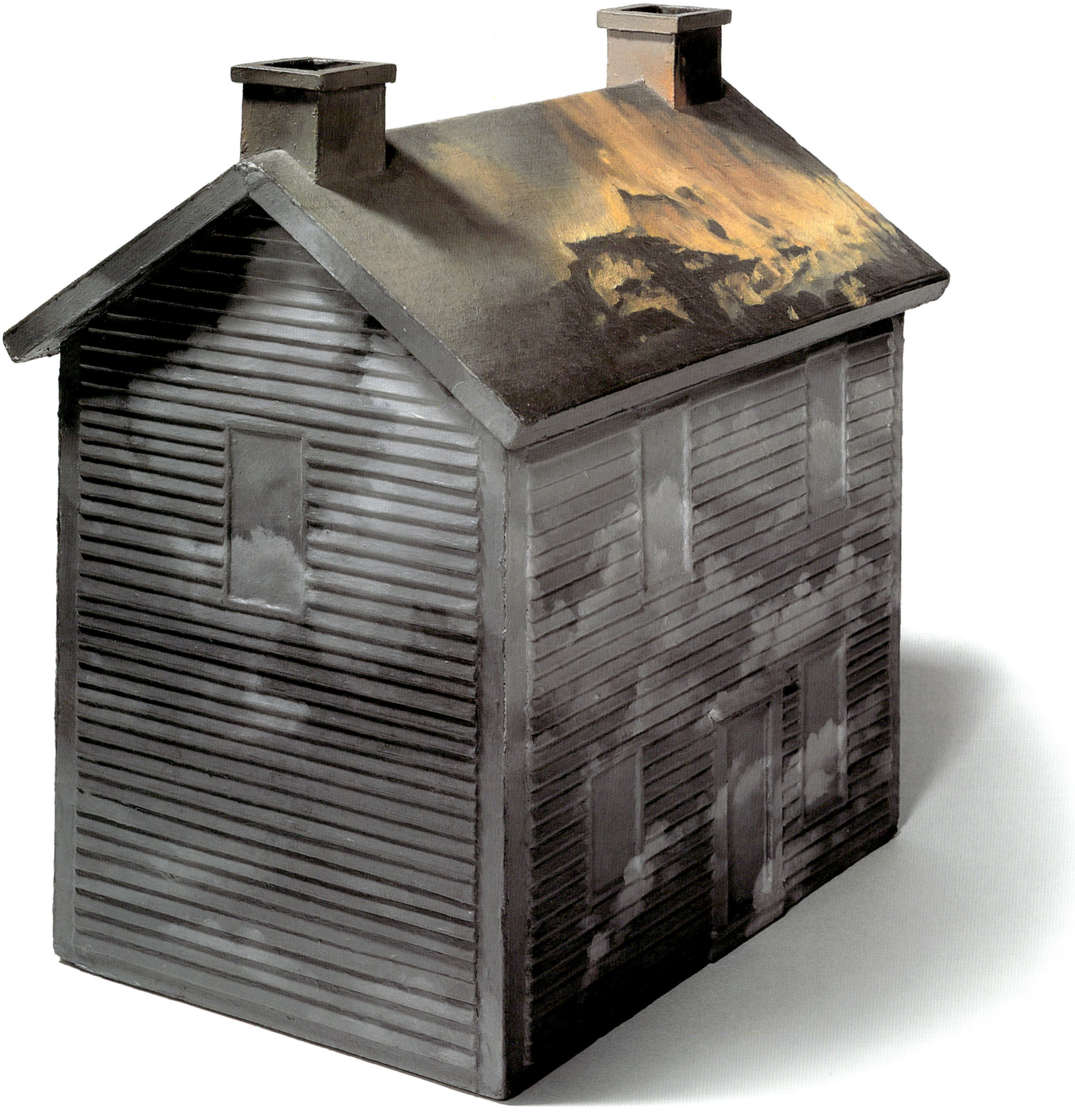

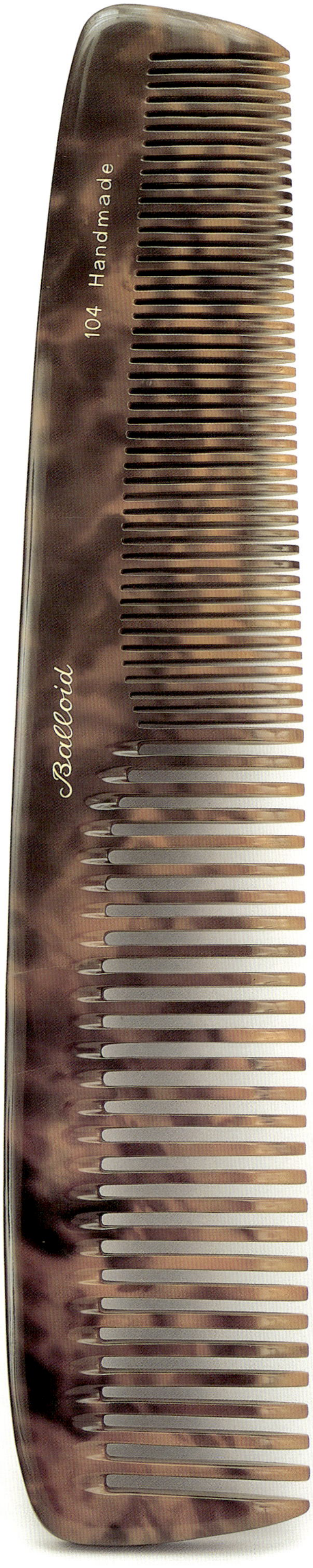
104 Handmade
Balloid

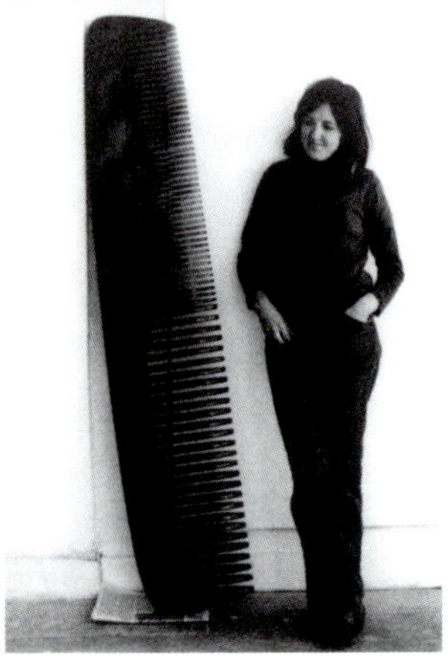

opposite, **Comb**
1969–70
Lacquer and epoxy on wood
195.5 × 61 × 7.5 cm
77 × 24 × 3 in
Collection Los Angeles County Museum of Art

opposite, below,
the artist with *Comb*,
c. 1970–71

right, **Train**
1965–66
Oil on canvas
30 × 30 cm
11.75 × 11.75 in

below, top to bottom,
René Magritte
Time Transfixed
1938
Oil on canvas
146 × 97.5 cm
57.5 × 38.375 in

René Magritte
Personal Values
1952
Oil on canvas
80 × 100 cm
31.5 × 39.375 in
Collection San Francisco Museum of Modern Art

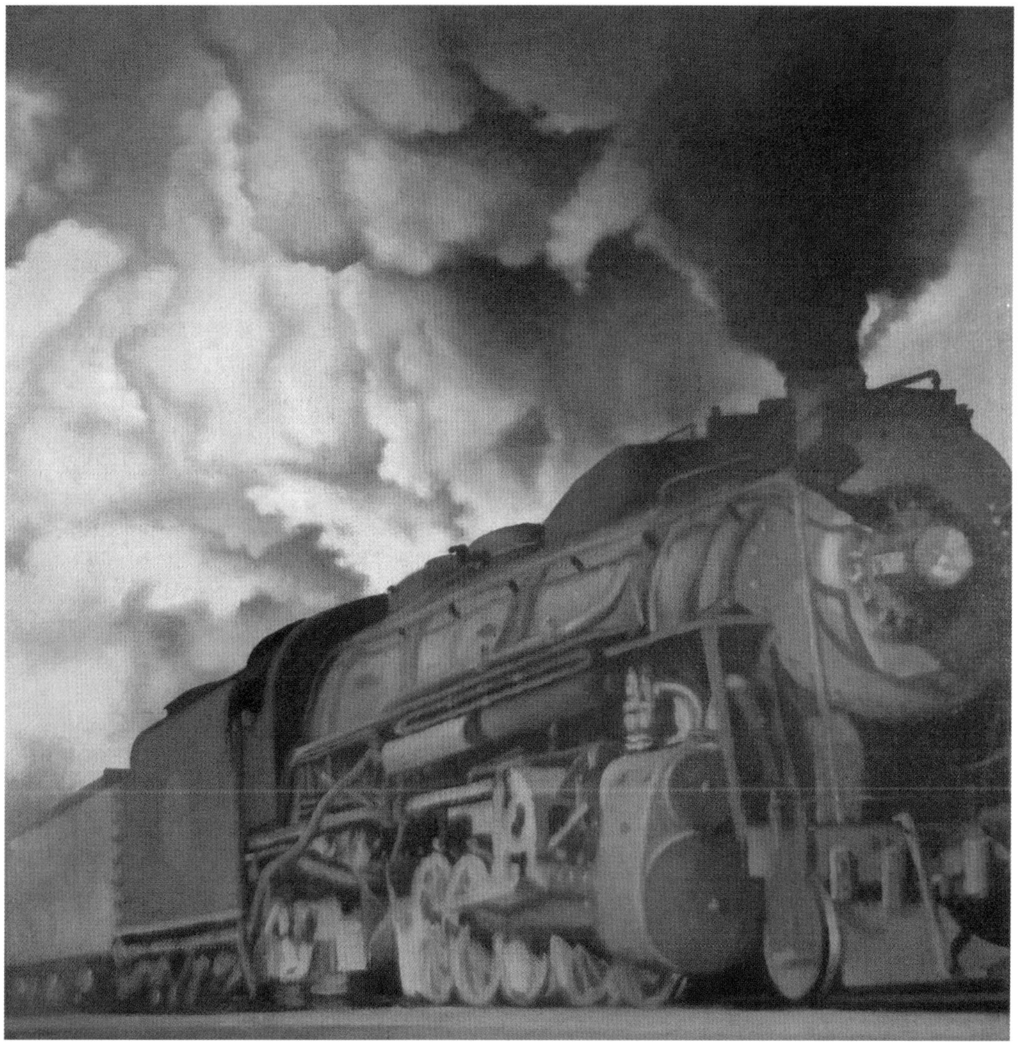

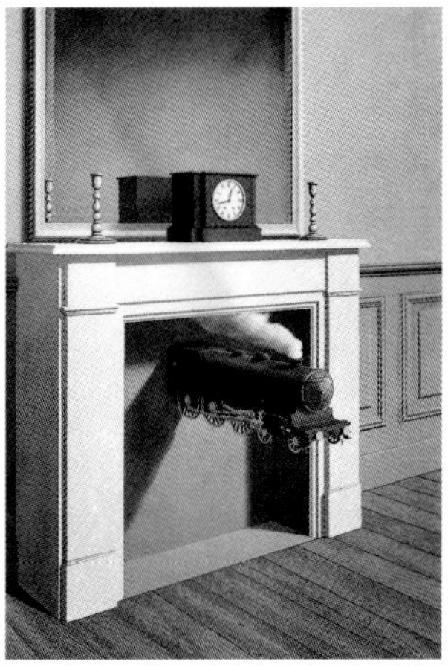

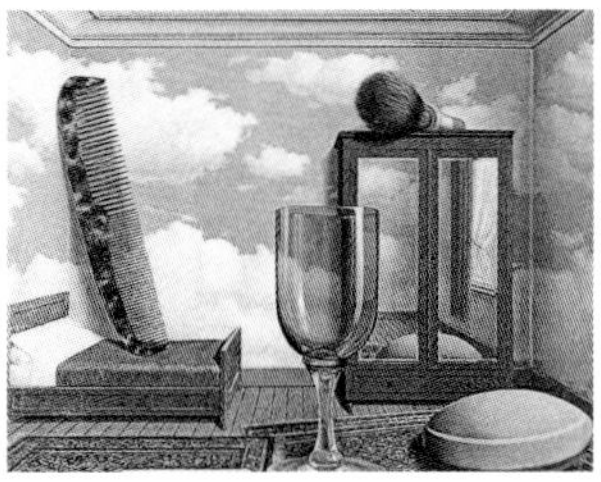

never seen such beauty, such a chalky, glorious blue …

Gober Did you see art as a teenager?

Celmins **No, not really. But I was always drawing. Were you?**

Gober Yeah, I was always drawing.

Celmins **I was always drawing. But I was very, very jealous about showing. I never wanted anybody to see it. I'm still like that, which makes it very difficult to have people come in the studio, you know.**

Gober I hate having visitors in my studio.

Celmins **Oh, I get so … I go into another personality.**

Gober I spend the day hiding things, so I don't have to show them to people.

Celmins **Now, why do you think we have that?**

Gober Well, it makes life easier, for one thing.

Celmins **I get so anxious, and then I go into this other personality, which tries to explain things, then I'm always very remorseful afterwards. That's my**

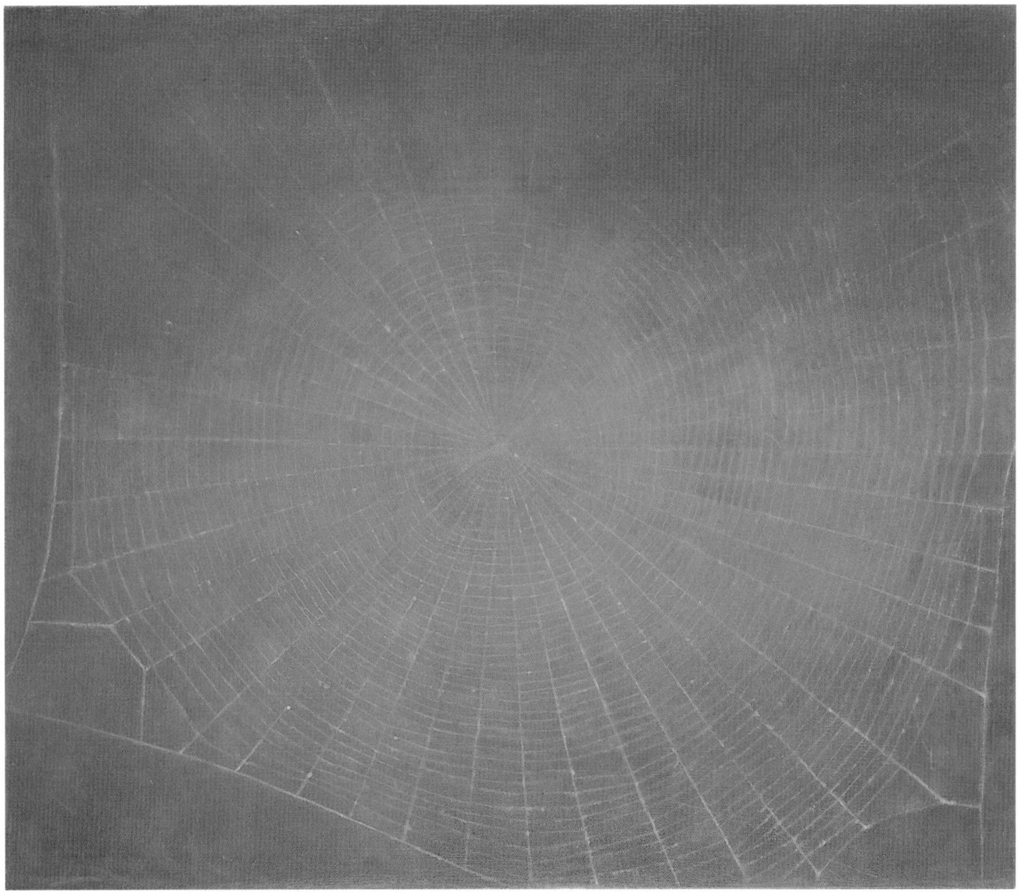

left, **Web**
1992
Oil on canvas
47.5 × 56.5 cm
18.75 × 22.25 in

opposite, **Web #2**
2000–01
Oil on linen
38 × 45.5 cm
15 × 18 in

least favourite part.

Gober Who comes to your studio? Curators?

Celmins **Well, hardly anybody now. I mean, some dealers I let come, because I make a living from my work. You have to show it. And then when I get over the initial anxiety of showing it, I'm able to accept it, and let go of it pretty much, and see it in a different light. Well, not always. I like to … I hate to stop working on something. I have this thing – do you have trouble letting go of the work, or not?**

Gober Not so much, no. Sometimes – but I think this is different – I'll finish a piece, but I won't release it into the world. I won't let go of it that way. But I don't have that much trouble knowing when to stop working on a particular piece; those are two different things.

Celmins **Yeah. I'm always trying to make this form that's very tight, that's very, very complete, and I always think, well, a few more spoonfuls of paint in this will make it more, you know, will make the pie better. So I hate to let it go.**

Gober On a very different note, do you enjoy your success in the world as a deeply admired and accomplished painter?

Celmins **Mmm … I don't know whether I think of myself as that.**

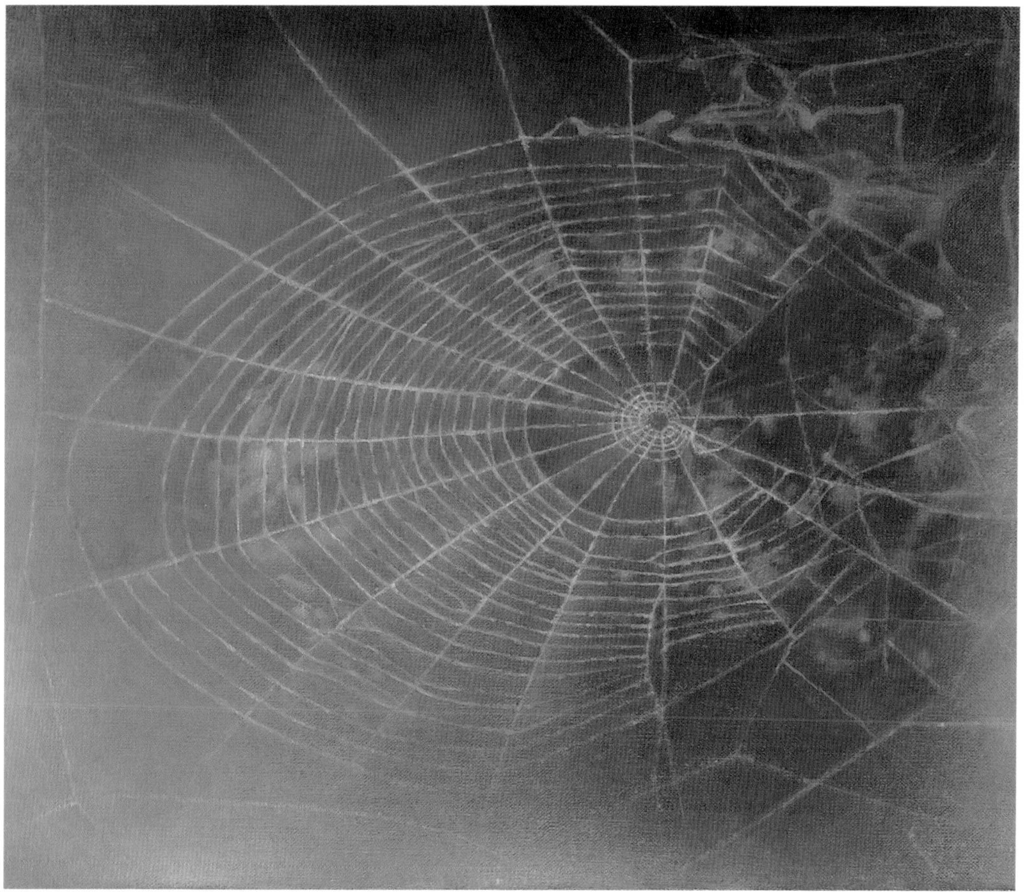

Gober You must, sometimes.

Celmins **I think, yeah, I think I felt a little, I mean, I've been trying to enjoy it. I keep thinking that if I build a studio, and I have another twenty years, maybe I can do some work that seems right to me.**

Gober It's a dumb question.

Celmins **Yeah, why'd you ask it?**

Gober Oh, because it interests me, it interests me in myself. It's a hard thing to talk about, among people, and among friends, and I don't even know you that well. Sometimes I'm just so surprised that I, the person who I am, and who I live with every day, is that other person out in the world.

Celmins **Well, I tell you what surprises me is that so many people can sort of see some of the things that you've done in a totally kind of digging-into-the-self way. It's sort of hopeful about human beings, I think. You know, I don't really think of it much, but I've had some people say that the work has really moved them. They think they understand some things. And I'm thinking, 'Wow, I didn't even understand it'.**

Gober Do you get letters from people you don't know?

Web #3
2000–02
Oil on linen
38 × 45.5 cm
15 × 18 in

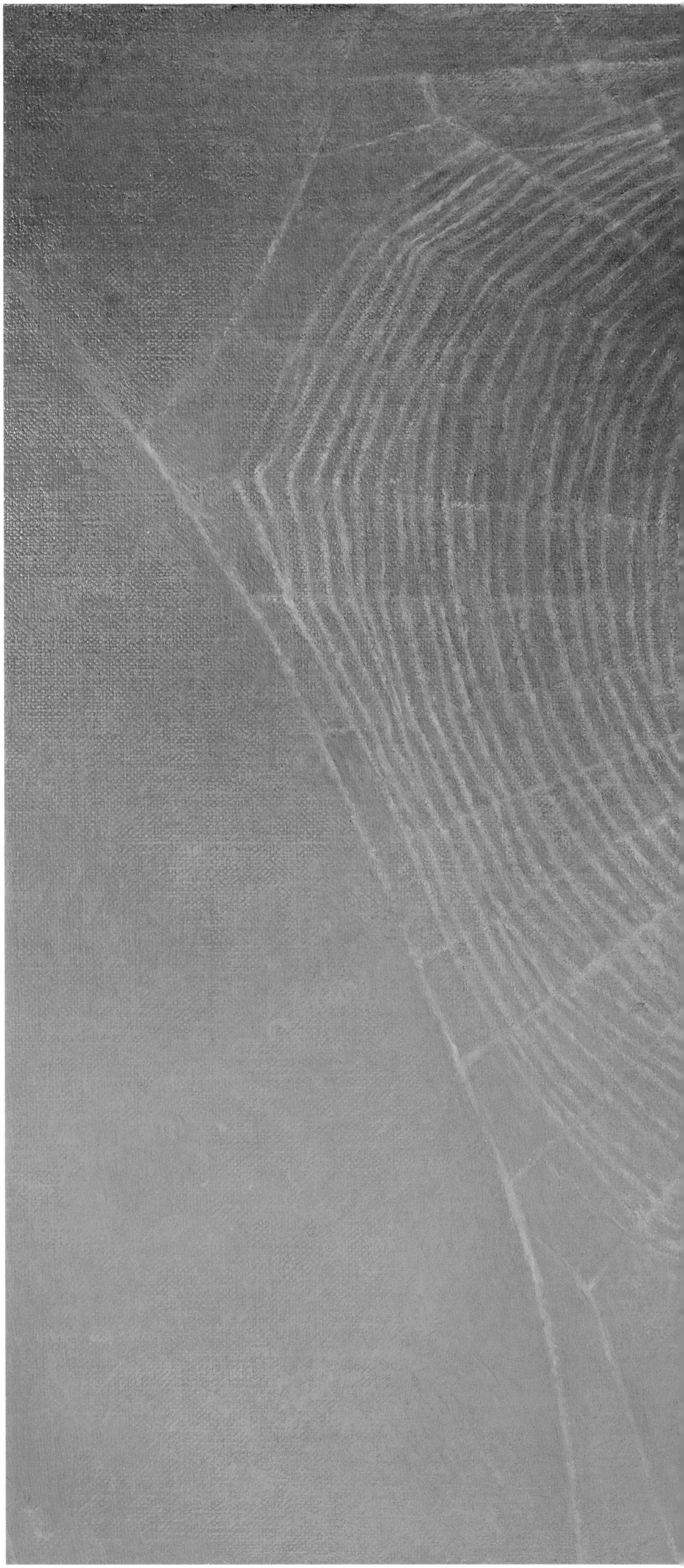

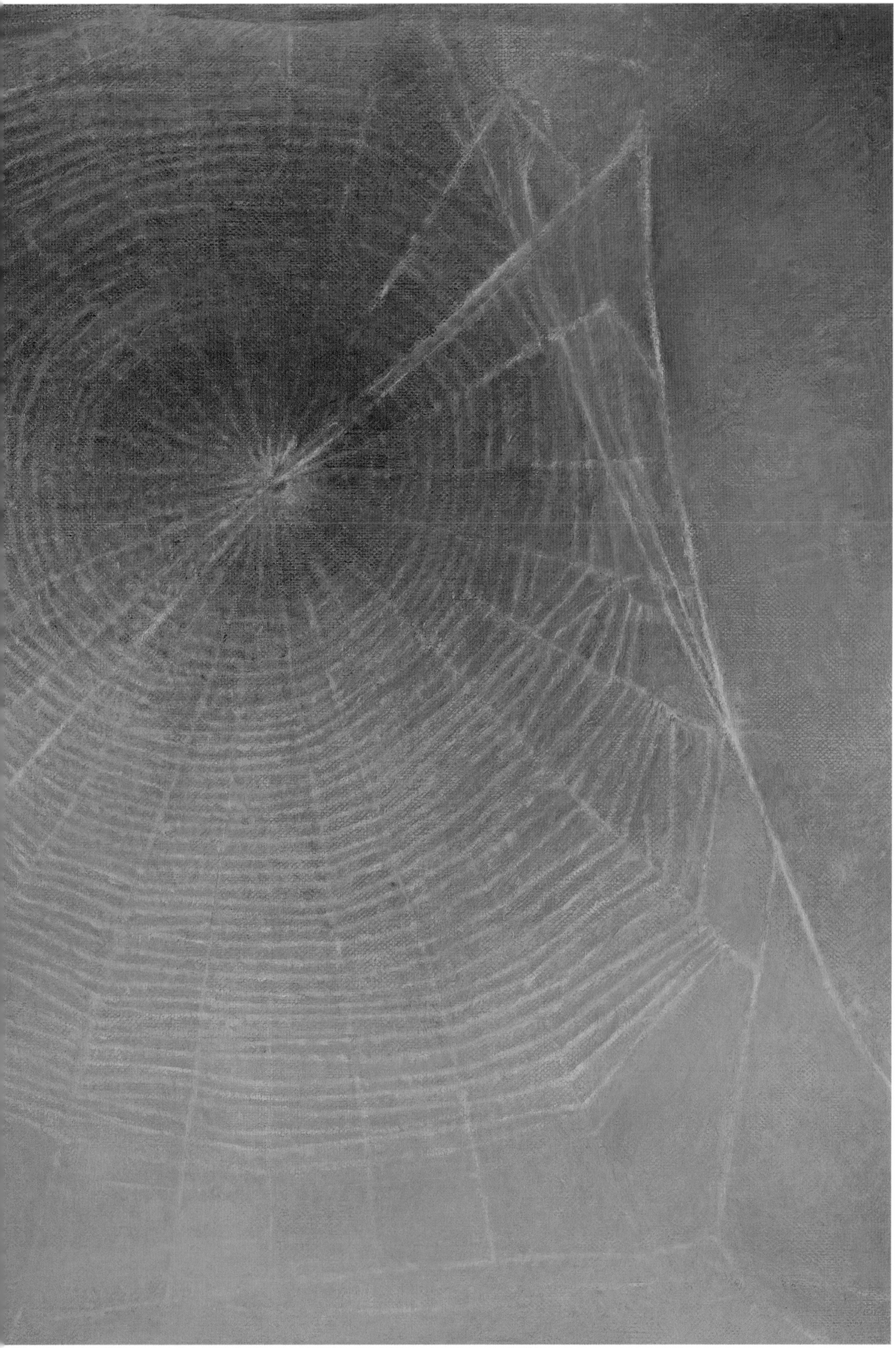

Night Sky #17
2000–01
Oil on linen mounted on wood
78.5 × 96.5 cm
31 × 38 in
Collection Modern Art Museum of Fort Worth, Texas

Celmins **Yes, I do. I get letters.**

Gober It's wonderful, isn't it? When they're not hateful crank letters.

Celmins **It scares me a little to get letters from people about all of this. I think that I was always thinking that I was on the outside because I was so foreign. I was a foreigner in Germany. I was a foreigner here in the US. I was sort of a foreigner in California. Because my whole vision ... my colour tones were too grey, maybe, for California, or the work was too severe. Maybe this is just clichés, but I had that sort of feeling like I didn't quite belong there, even though I loved the gardens and ... I was always fighting. And I was thinking even if nobody gets it, I had a feeling that I could go and I could work. I don't know, it's like building a self through the work. And then the work sort of reflects some aspects of yourself. And I don't mean the brain. I mean like, some aspects of your body and your emotions – and your brain.**

Gober How long can you work in a stretch on painting?

Celmins **Oh, I don't know. I can't ... I don't work in stretches. I work, I jump up, you know, I eat cherries, I pace the studio ... I work again.**

Gober Do you listen to music?

Celmins **I listen to talk radio. To music, to various things. Sometimes I like silence. Sometimes I like jazz. I tend to listen more to classical music. And**

then sometimes I get revved up with the public station that I listen to. How about you?

Gober I go in phases. I tend to work either in complete silence, or I'll find a piece of music that inspires me and I'll just listen to it obsessively while I'm making one work. I'll just replay it and replay it.

Celmins **See, I am able to focus; I have a feeling you're able to focus too. I'm able to focus down and really concentrate. But now that I'm feeling older I'm trying to back away from it, because I don't think that I'm going to have the physical stamina to keep concentrating on the work that much. And I'm trying to figure out ... you know, recently I've picked up this spider web image, which is an image that's very, very fragile, and implies something maybe more broken, more old, more tenuous. I was trying to photograph the spider webs out here in the garden, and finding it impossible. You can't find them. I found them in science images and I was drawn to them. I carried it around in my head, like a memory, for maybe about a year or two, and then, one day I made a painting. That was about ten years ago. Probably because I tend to pick images that sort of describe a two-dimensional space. And it's a collection of small things that somehow engage me, almost force me to be engaged in making this very complicated image ... it sounds a little depressing, doesn't it? Working on it so long and so tediously, as if hoping that something would be transferred. But I'm not really sure what. Because I tend to want to keep the work kind of mindless in a funny way. Mindless, but mindful building. I think we have some similar things. I mean, the building of it, for me ... see I think of it like building, like you build a house.**

Gober My dad built the house I grew up in.

Celmins **Yeah, my dad built the house, too. My dad was a builder.**

Gober I vacuumed the spiders and spider webs out of my house today. And when I was doing it I thought, 'Am I doing this because I am going to see Vija?'

Celmins **Yes, you are, you were. But I've been letting the cobwebs grow and am very delighted that, somehow, from the pictures in books they've come out in the real world. And the fragility of that web ... I've always been interested in very impossible images. Things blowing up, things disappearing in a breath. Things like the sky, which doesn't even exist. There is no thing like the sky. It's like a totally ... who knows what it is.**

Gober Unfathomable.

Celmins **Right. And then trying to invent it on another surface.**

Gober And impossible things, like the duplication of rocks.

Celmins **Right. And there's no way to talk about that piece either (*To Fix the Image in Memory*, 1977–82). I was thinking of it in various ways. When I first was trying to name it, I mean, look at this pretentious name I gave it. To Fix the Image in Memory. I was reading this story by Borges about Funes the**

Memorious. Do you ever read Borges?

Gober I did about a year ago.

Celmins **It's this guy who remembers everything he sees, and his head gets so filled up that he can't function. Because he remembers everything. When I was looking at the rock and painting the bronze, I had to remember what it is I saw even though it was only five inches away. And it was like building a sort of memory. Then I was thinking, well, it's a sort of a criticism of realistic art, you know? Like a kind of a 'fuck you'. You point out that art is always invented, and that there's nothing real about it the way nature is real.**

Gober I came across a quote recently, I can't remember who said it. And I guess because I knew I was going to be interviewing you, I remembered it. It said, 'Art is the thing that makes life more interesting than art'.

Celmins **Who said that?**

Gober I can't recall. I'd have to go back and look it up.

Celmins **Well, I was just talking about that, wasn't I? I never paid any attention to cobwebs and now I'm trying to grow them in my studio and in the corners and everywhere.**

Gober How big is your studio in New York?

Celmins **Well, the studio's about 2,000 square feet, but I live in it. So the painting room is only 21 by 26 ft. Then I have a drawing room that's 21 by maybe 13. In between there's tucked some storage, and the bathroom, and then I live in a ... you know, it's small. I'm longing to have more space. And I'm now also fed up with the tediousness of my work, and I'm thinking maybe I could do something three-dimensional, which always seems to me like a liberation. I never was a sculptor, you know, I always painted all my sculpture – well, you do, too.**

Gober Yeah, the paint is very important. But I think it's different than the way you painted your sculptures. Like your sculpture with the images of the house painted on the house. If I made a house, I would paint it white because the house was painted white.

Celmins **Right. Going back to *To Fix the Image in Memory*, it was a piece I made when I was very sad. I would go driving around in the New Mexico desert consoling myself by mindlessly picking up rocks and throwing them in my car. Later, unloading them in my studio, I had this moment of inspiration. They seemed so beautiful, I wanted to make them myself. I wanted to see how close I could come; that's how the piece started. There was never any symbolism or any real idea. I just went back to looking, which I guess is a theme that runs through my work. Looking at stuff and sort of regenerating something in me that keeps wanting to live – something that sustains me that I'd forgotten about. Going back to looking in such a thorough way reaffirmed something about the business of 'making'. *To Fix the Image in***

opposite, **To Fix the Image in Memory I-XI**
1977–82
11 stones and 11 painted bronzes
Dimensions variable

below, Installation view, 'Vija Celmins', David McKee Gallery, New York, 1983

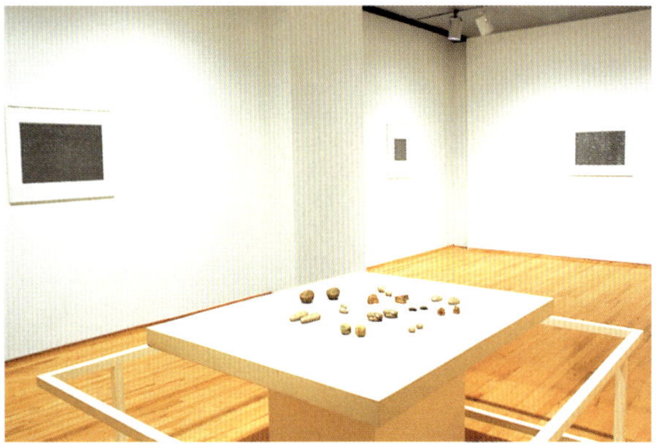

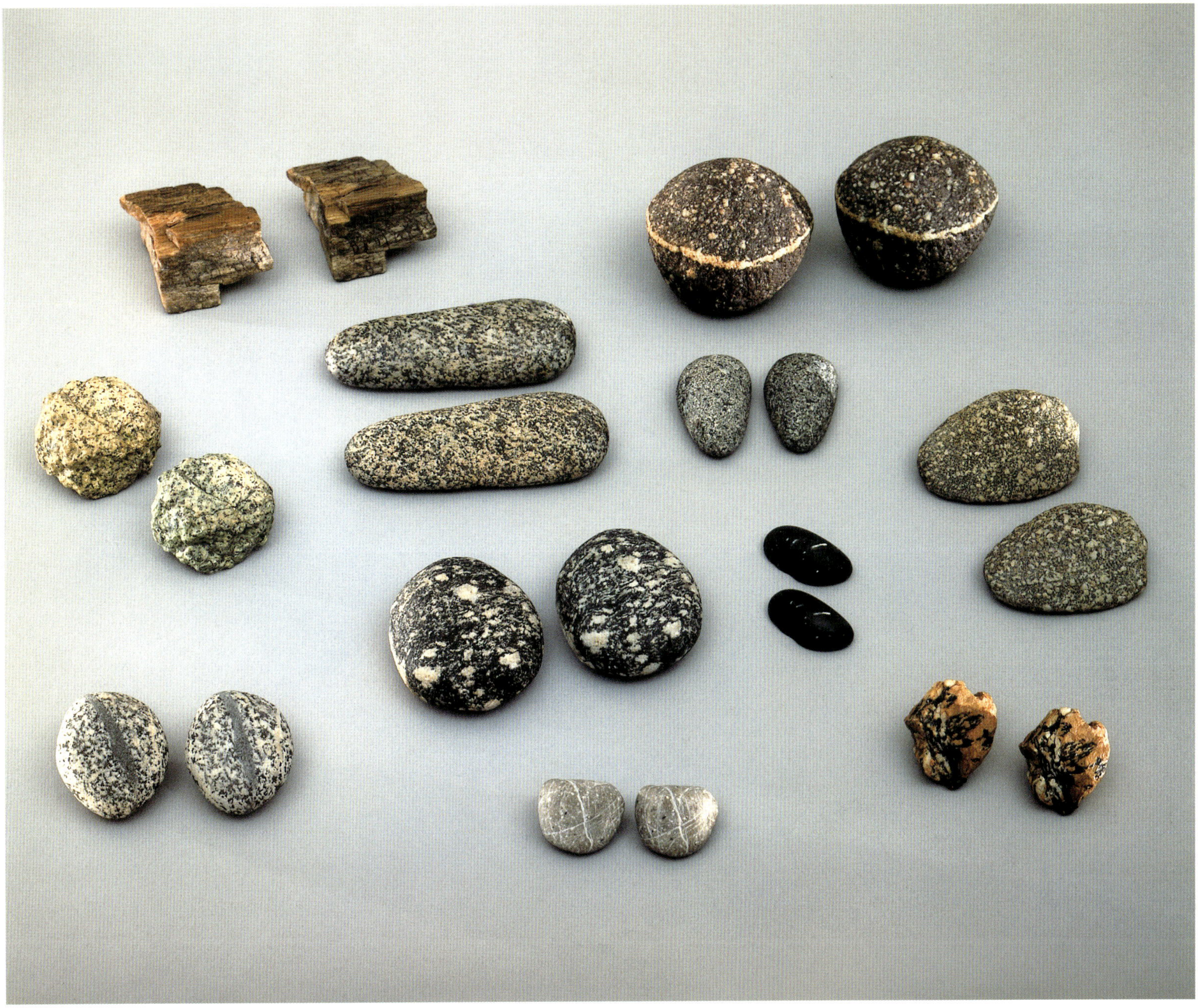

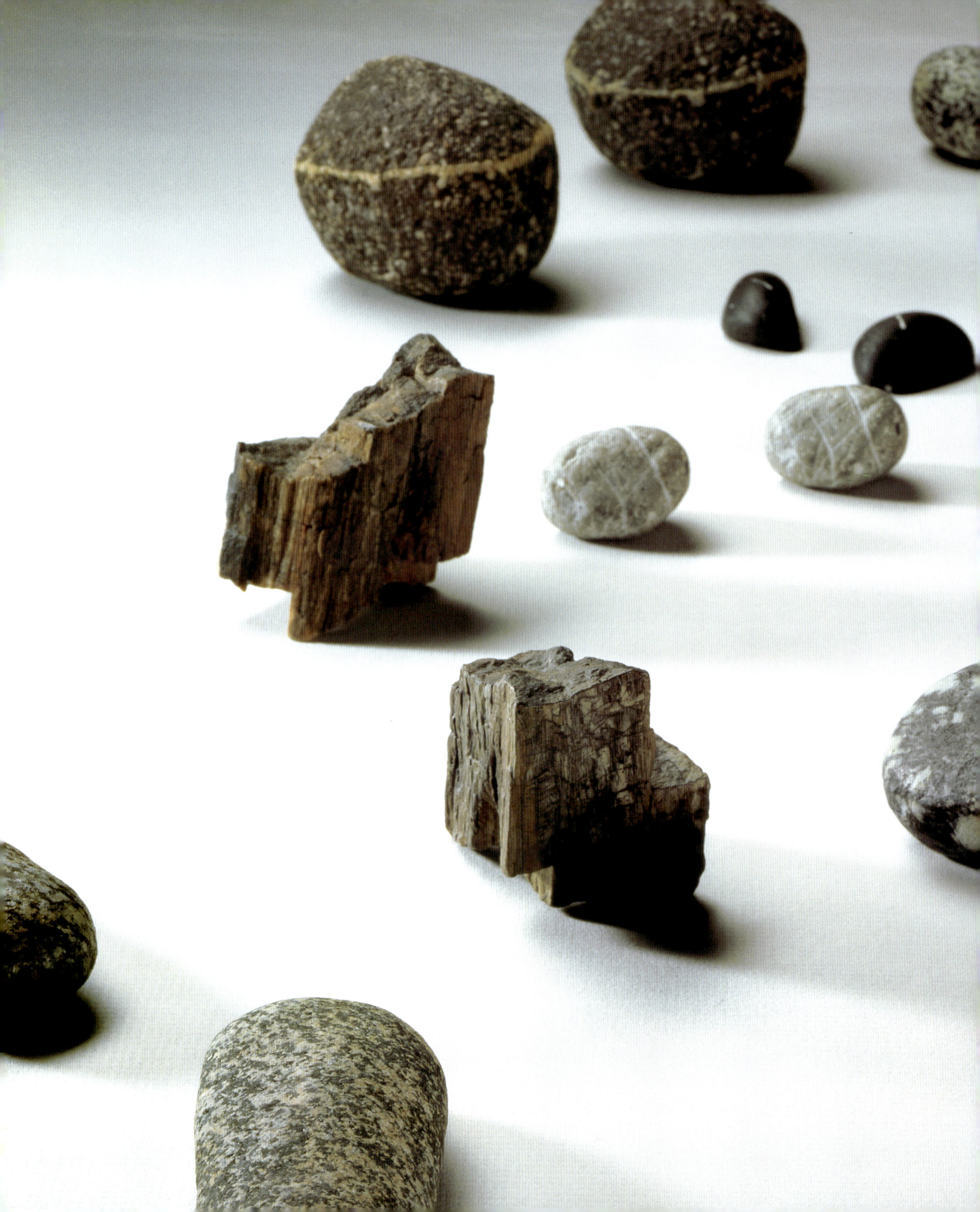

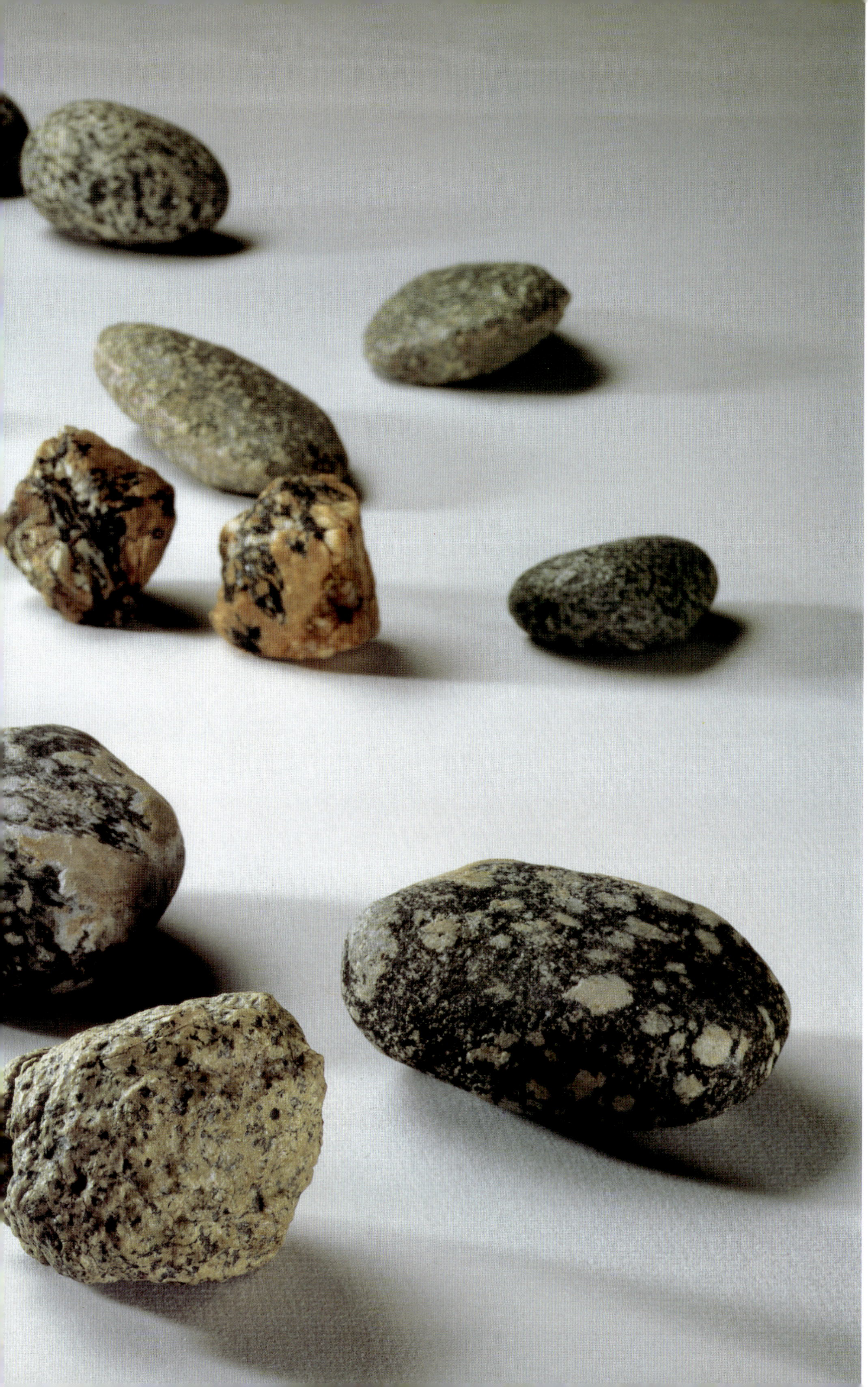

To Fix the Image in Memory I-XI
(detail)
1977–82
11 stones and 11 painted bronzes
Dimensions variable

Memory **was built over five years, mark by mark, in a pointillist sort of way. I could never do that again. I wouldn't want to.**

Gober When you say that you were sad during that time, I can immediately see it in the work, but I never thought it before. I remember when I first saw those rocks I thought they were very funny.

Celmins **Yes, I think other people thought they were funny too. And people said things like, 'How'd you find two rocks the same?'**

Gober Well, part of the humour, I think, is the unexpectedness of it. Because you don't know what they are at first.

Celmins **See, one of the things it points out is that I don't think about how things spin in the art world. I did that piece out of my own head – but I guess that's how you do it too, isn't it, most of the time? Thinking about it later and trying to talk about it becomes impossible.**

Gober What are things that you would want to talk about that don't get mentioned?

Celmins **You mean things that we've never talked about? Or that I have never talked about?**

below, **Untitled (Ocean)**
1969
Graphite on acrylic ground on paper
35 × 47 cm
13.75 × 18.5 in
Collection Philadelphia Museum of Art, Pennsylvania

opposite, **Galaxy # 1 (Coma Bernices)**
1973
Graphite on acrylic ground on paper
31 × 38.5 cm
12.25 × 15.25 in

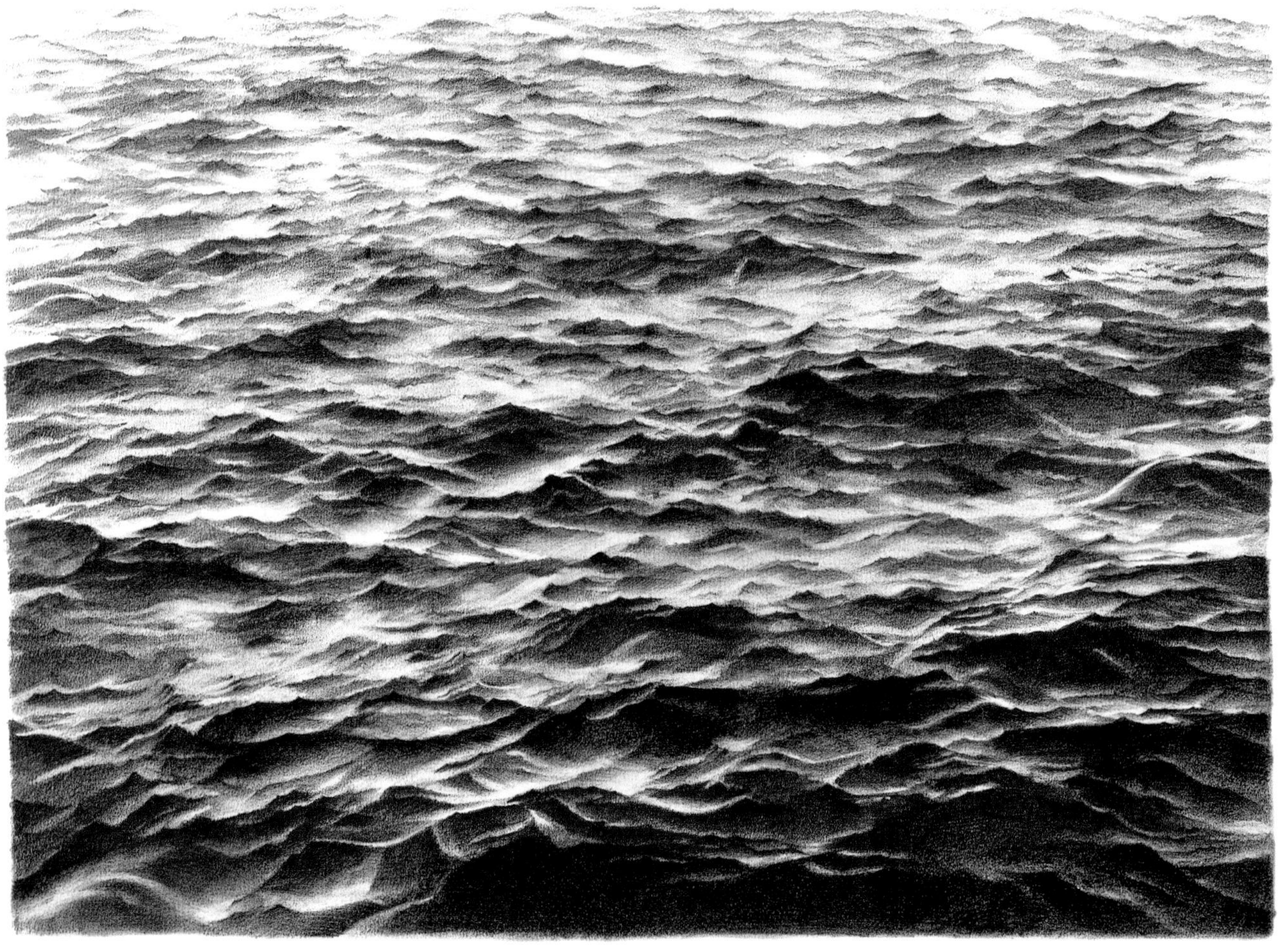

Gober Not just those; perhaps also things that are underemphasized in your work, or things people never notice that you feel are consequential.

Celmins **That's a hard question to answer. What don't they notice? See, I hardly ever read anything anybody writes about me.**

Gober You never read it?

Celmins **No.**

Gober Don't they ask you to vet it or proofread it?

Celmins **Well, I mean, I sort of skim it, and then I start feeling my heart fluttering, and then when they say something that seems kind of great, I get flutters. And then when I see something that is totally wrong, which is often the case, then I get the flutters again, and who wants that much fluttering? (*laughter*) I mean, do you? Do you read the things ... ?**

Gober I do. I went through a brief but not lasting period when I thought, 'I'm never going to read anything again', but it passed.

Celmins **I can understand that, yeah. I don't really mind criticism. I'm so self-critical myself that I don't mind. One time somebody said to me that they thought my work was too careful. And I thought that was not too bad. I hold an image in my head for like two or three years. I'm sure that none of this is**

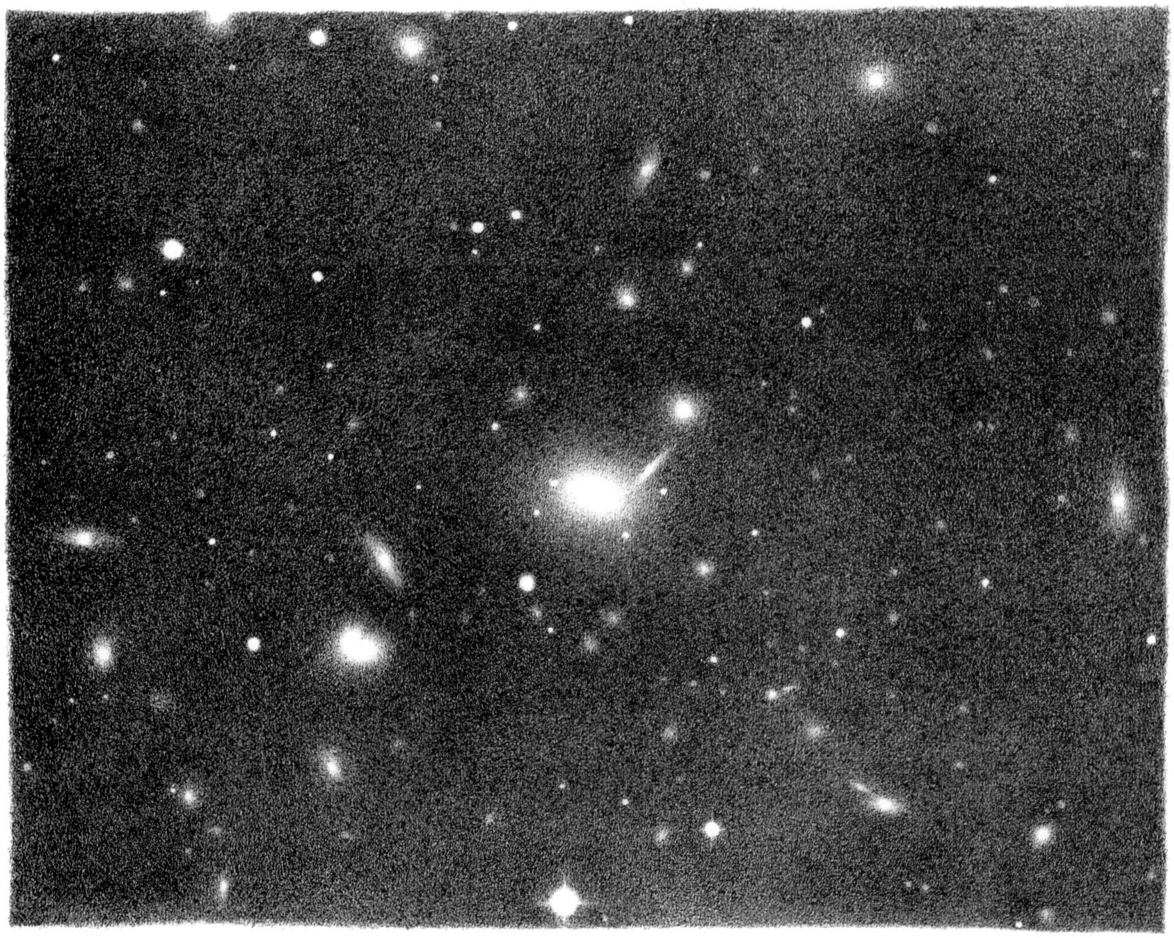

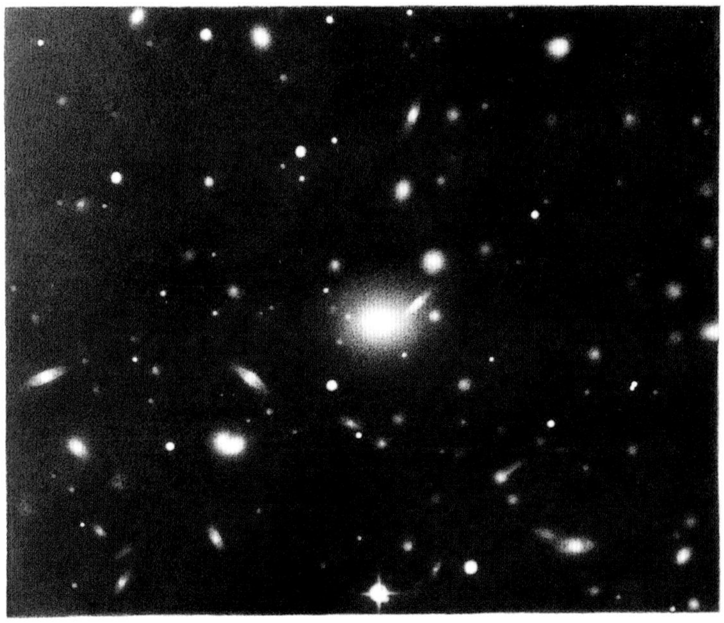

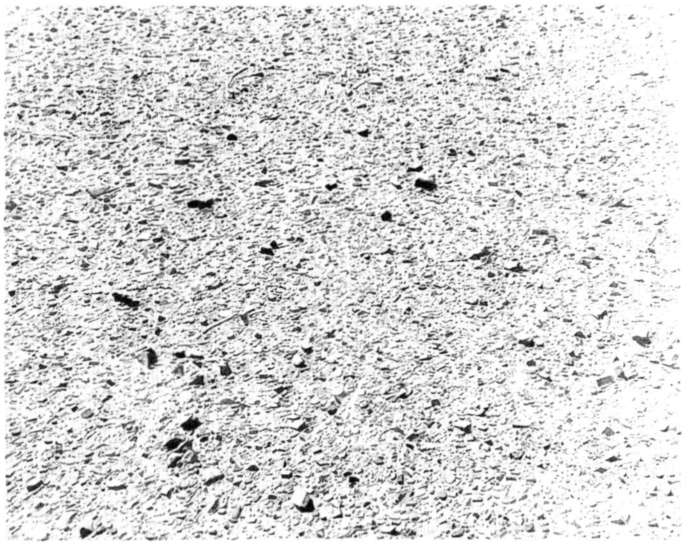

too unusual among artists, or maybe it is. I don't really know. But, I mean, maybe that's part of not finishing the work, not letting anybody really near it, or making it very difficult, then, to take the work apart. Maybe that makes it too careful, I don't know. But that's a good question: what do I think that people don't get about my work? Well I hate it when they keep the drawings in the drawers. I meant for the drawings to be out with the paintings, but I realize that people don't want to ruin the paper.

Gober Right, but you want the drawing to be given the same importance as the painting.

Celmins **Right. Then I also want to have people think more about the space that the work projects and find their relationship to it. A lot of my drawings really project very far into space, especially the early ones of the ocean and desert. You know, they were concentrated, but they sort of came out like this (*wide gestures with her arms*). You know, they came out on a beam.**

Gober Those woodblocks of the ocean are amazing, technically. Were they hard to do?

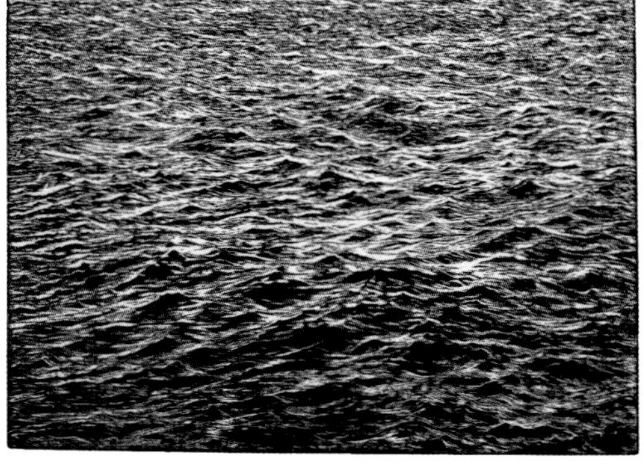

Celmins **OK now hold on, it just occurred to me that maybe the later work, like the work in the last maybe fifteen years, has not projected out, but sort of invited you to come close. And why is that? There's like a shift, and I think it came about because I was doing black things, the night skies. The black projected the proportion, but the image no longer projected, and you had to physically come up and find it, and then find your relationship to it. Before the work sort of projected out; now you have to get way up to it. Maybe that has**

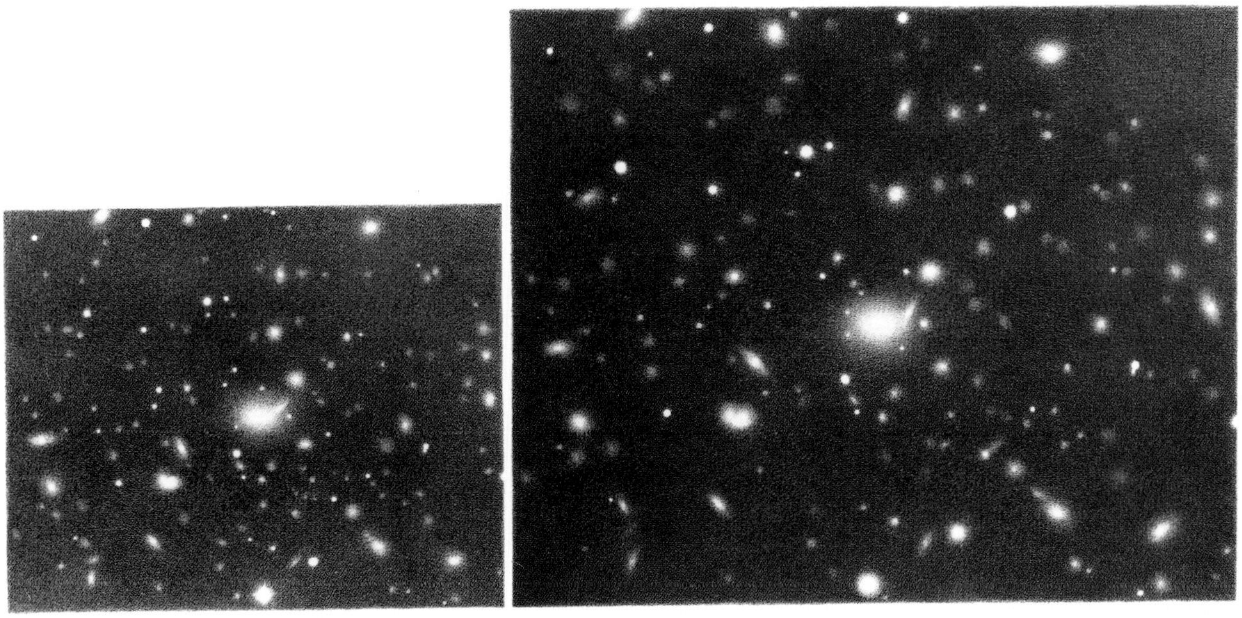

opposite, top, **Untitled (Desert-Galaxy)**
1974
Graphite on acrylic ground on paper
44.5 × 96.5 cm
17.5 × 38 in

left, **Double Galaxy (Coma Bernices)**
1974
Graphite on acrylic ground on paper
32 × 61 cm
12.5 × 24 in

opposite, below, **Ocean Surface Woodcut 1992**
1992
Woodcut on Whatman 1953 paper
49.5 × 39.5 cm
19.5 × 15.5 in
Edition of 50

to do with the image getting smaller and finer, and that was one of the things that happened in the woodblock.

To answer you question, I loved doing it. I mean, my work has always been so involved in the 'physical' that cutting into the wood with this little knife was very satisfying! I lived for months with my face inches away from that block, cutting this way and that. I never really had a technique … just trying to build a solid piece that could hold still and move at the same time. When you come very close to the print I think you feel the touch of the knife.

Gober I wouldn't know how you could direct someone to make your work.

Celmins **Well, I haven't been able to direct them to make the work, damnit! I tend to stay very close to an image right beside me.**

What do you think you might want to know about my work that hasn't been written about?

Gober Well, the thing that's missing to me is the future. Because I see it in an arc or a continuum. So I wonder what the next group of works will be, and how it will illuminate the past.

Celmins **But, you see, I have to tell you, the future's missing for me too.**

Gober (*laughing*) I know that!

Celmins **And, I mean, I think it only comes with the making. I have all kinds of ideas. Certainly I'm not going to tell you my ideas, am I?**

Night Sky #2
1991
Oil on canvas on aluminum panel
45.5 × 54.5 cm
18 × 21.5 in
Collection The Art Institute of Chicago

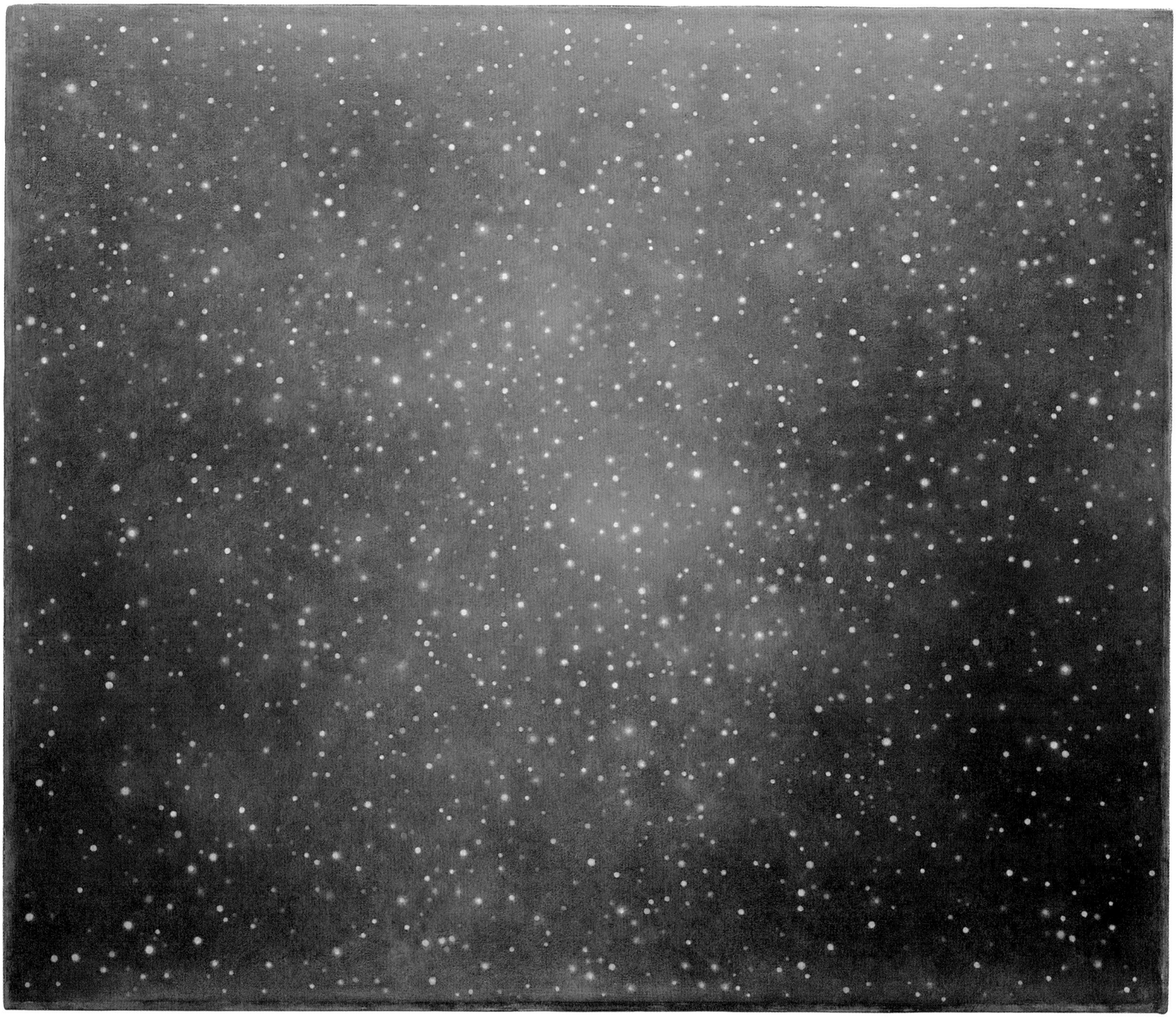

Untitled #2
1994
Charcoal on paper
45.5 × 61 cm
18 × 24 in

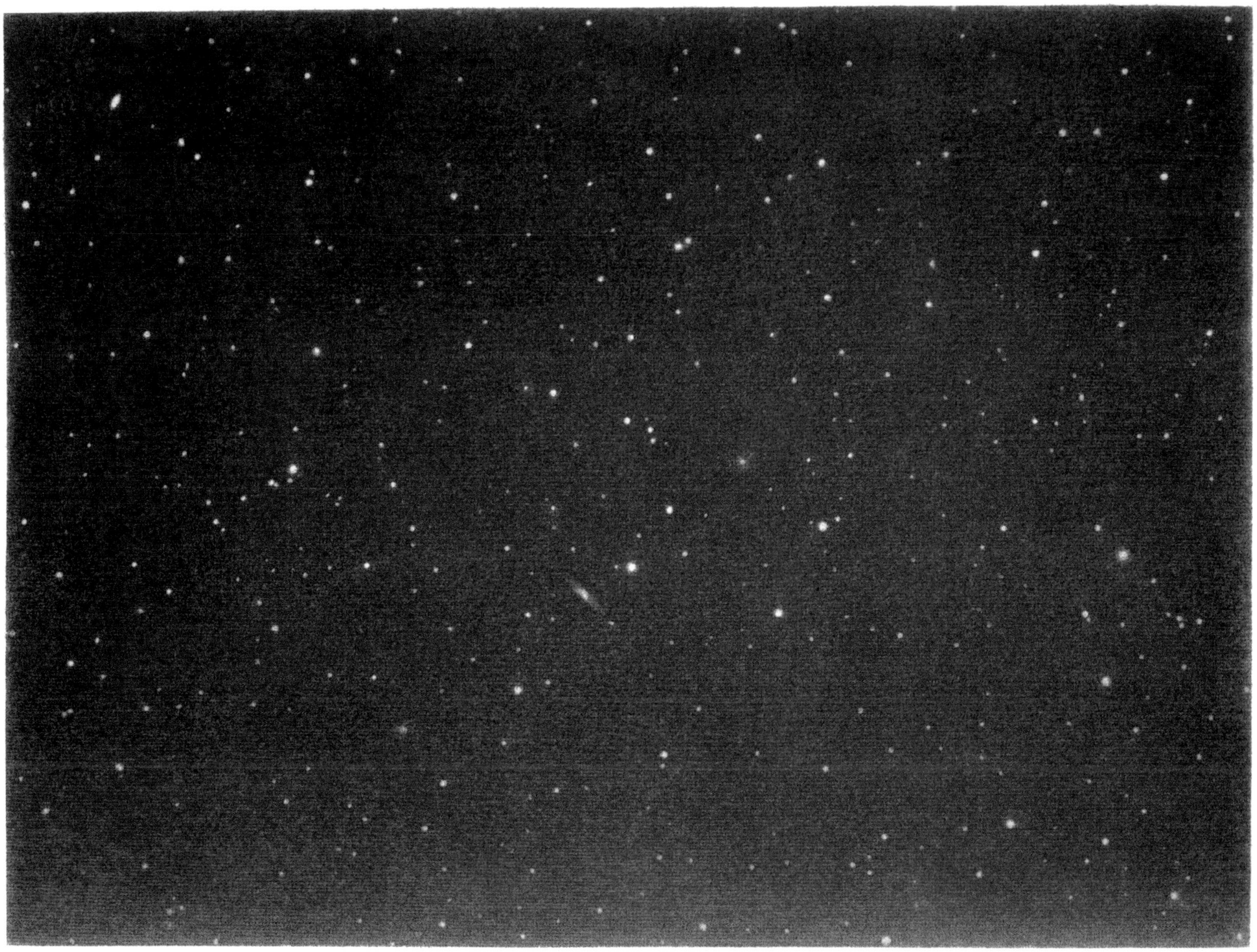

Night Sky #5
1992
Oil on canvas mounted on wood panel
78.5 × 95.5 cm
31 × 37.5 in

Gober No.

Celmins **No. The way I work is that at first I have all kinds of ideas, but then I tend to reject them one by one and sort of end up in a more intuitive, animal state from which I then begin. And then through the work, some things become evident ... but not too evident ...**

Gober Do you still like living in New York?

Celmins **I like living in New York, but having a little house with a garden outside the city has opened up ... you know how hard it is to get nature in your work! I think art and nature are very separate ... and now I seem to have developed a real friendship with nature – we, I've always had it, I guess, but I used to drive around looking at it from a distance. Now I'm in it, and it's been a pleasure ... almost to the point where it is too much – help! (*laughing*) I've been planting things and pulling them up and seeing things close ... and who knows? Maybe some of that will get into the work ... I mean that I tend to keep images in my mind for a few months, where they get bent a little before appearing in the art. I try to leave the evidence of both thinking and making ... like a fingerprint of all I know. Expressive, maybe, but hard to define, and who knows what it means. I've been questioning the meaning of everything. Have you gotten to that point yet? Maybe it's because I'm older. You want a little cold cucumber soup?**

Gober Oh, that'd be wonderful. People always ask me, 'What does it mean, that you make the work yourself? Why don't you just go out and buy it?' I used to try to answer, but now the only logical answer to me is to respond, 'How would I ever find this thing in the world?' You have to make it in order to find the thing that you are imagining. Where would I go to buy a plaster sink?

Celmins **That is a great answer. People used to come up to my things and say, 'God, what a great set of photographs'. I mean, talk about blind! I think one of the things that people tend to look too much for in art is meaning. And they tend to project a meaning much faster than I would like them to. If I was a dictator, an art dictator, I would tie them up and say, 'Here, look at this. And look at it again and look at it again.' And then I might beat them too.**

Installation views,
'Vija Celmins: Works 1964–1996',
Institute of Contemporary Arts,
London, 1996

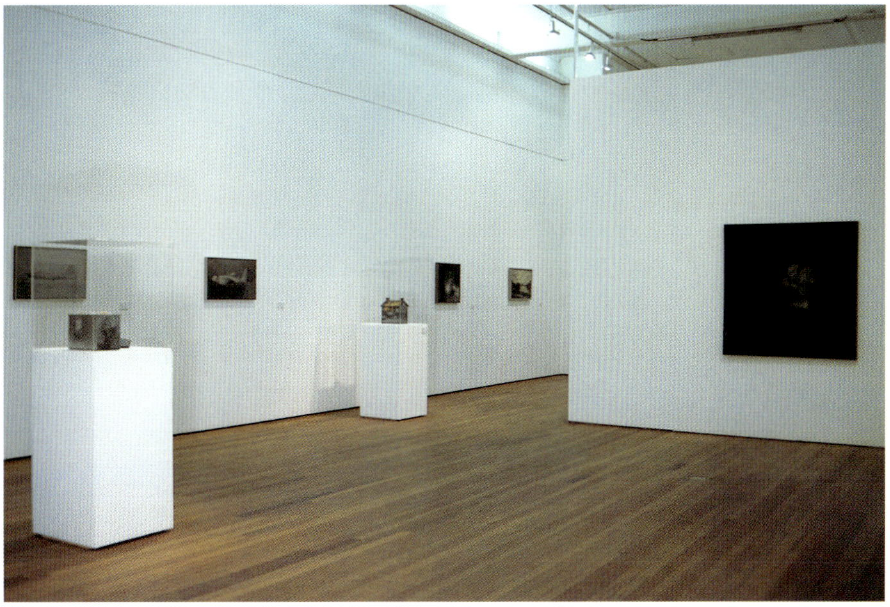

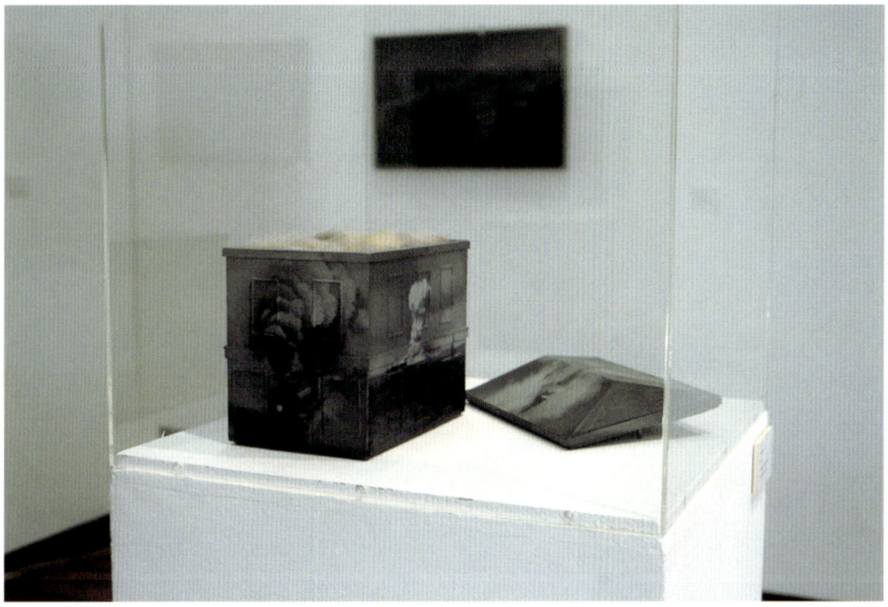

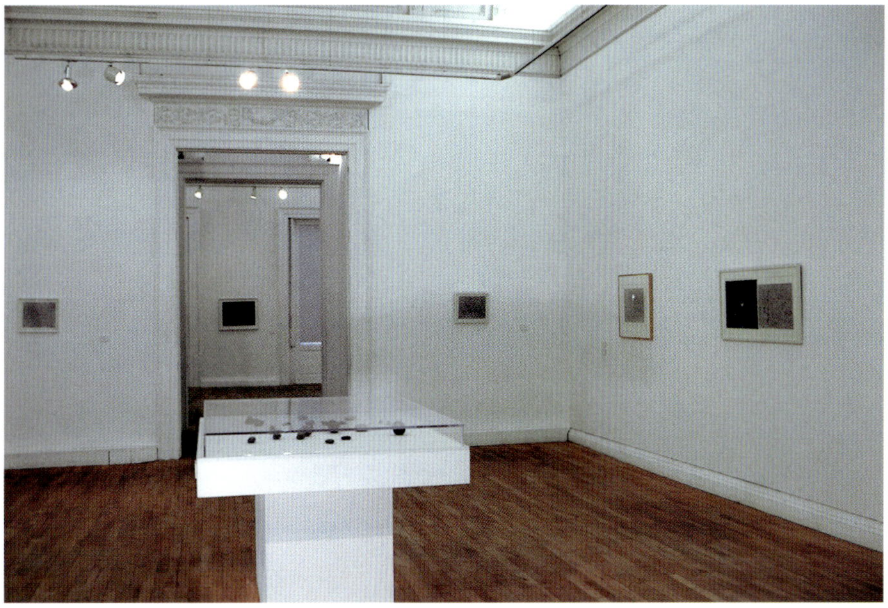

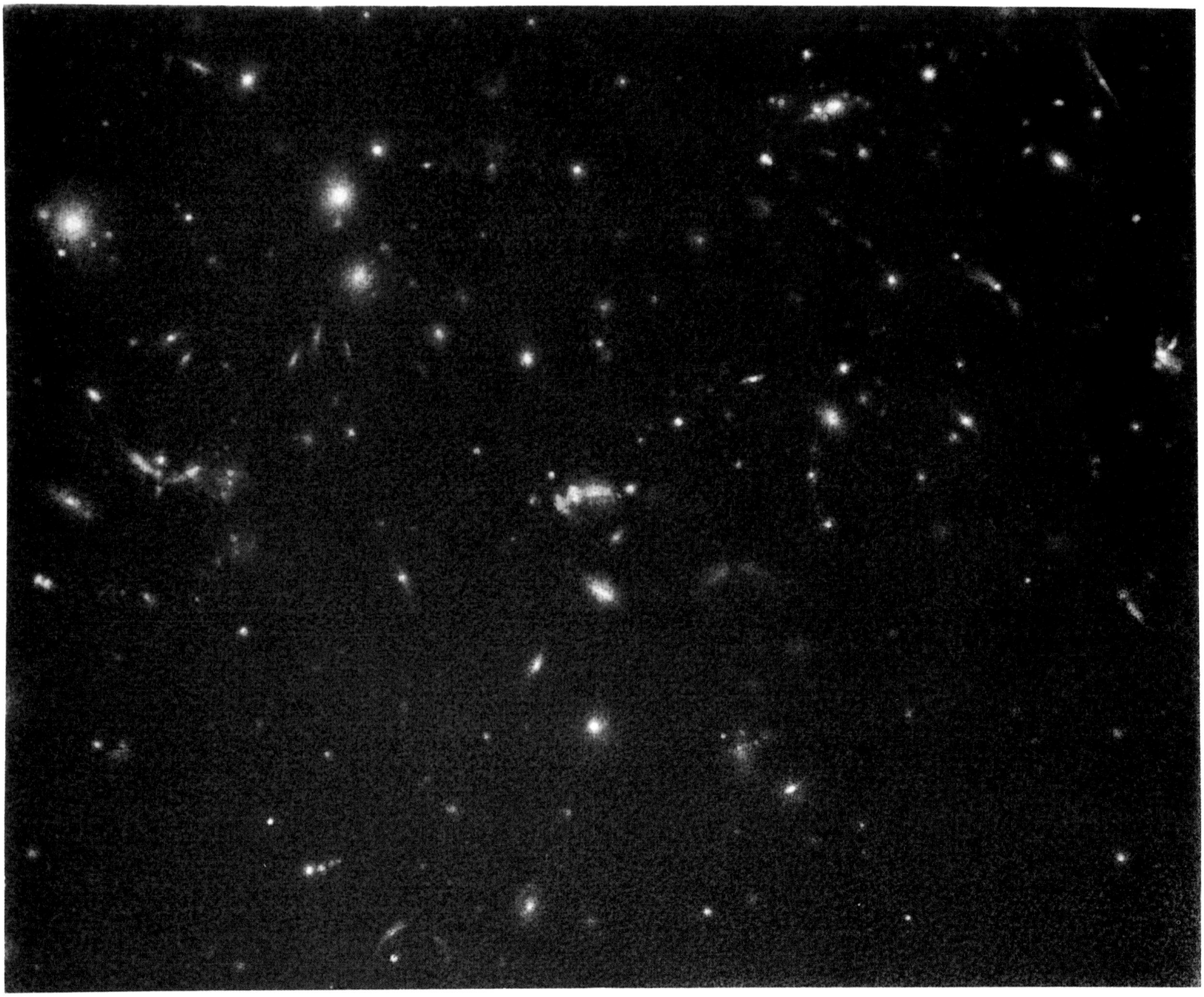

opposite, **Hubble #1**
1998
Charcoal on paper
38 × 44.5 cm
15 × 17.5 in
Collection National Aeronautics and Space Administration (NASA), Washington, D.C.

below, **Hubble #2**
1998
Charcoal on paper
38 × 44.5 cm
15 × 17.5 in

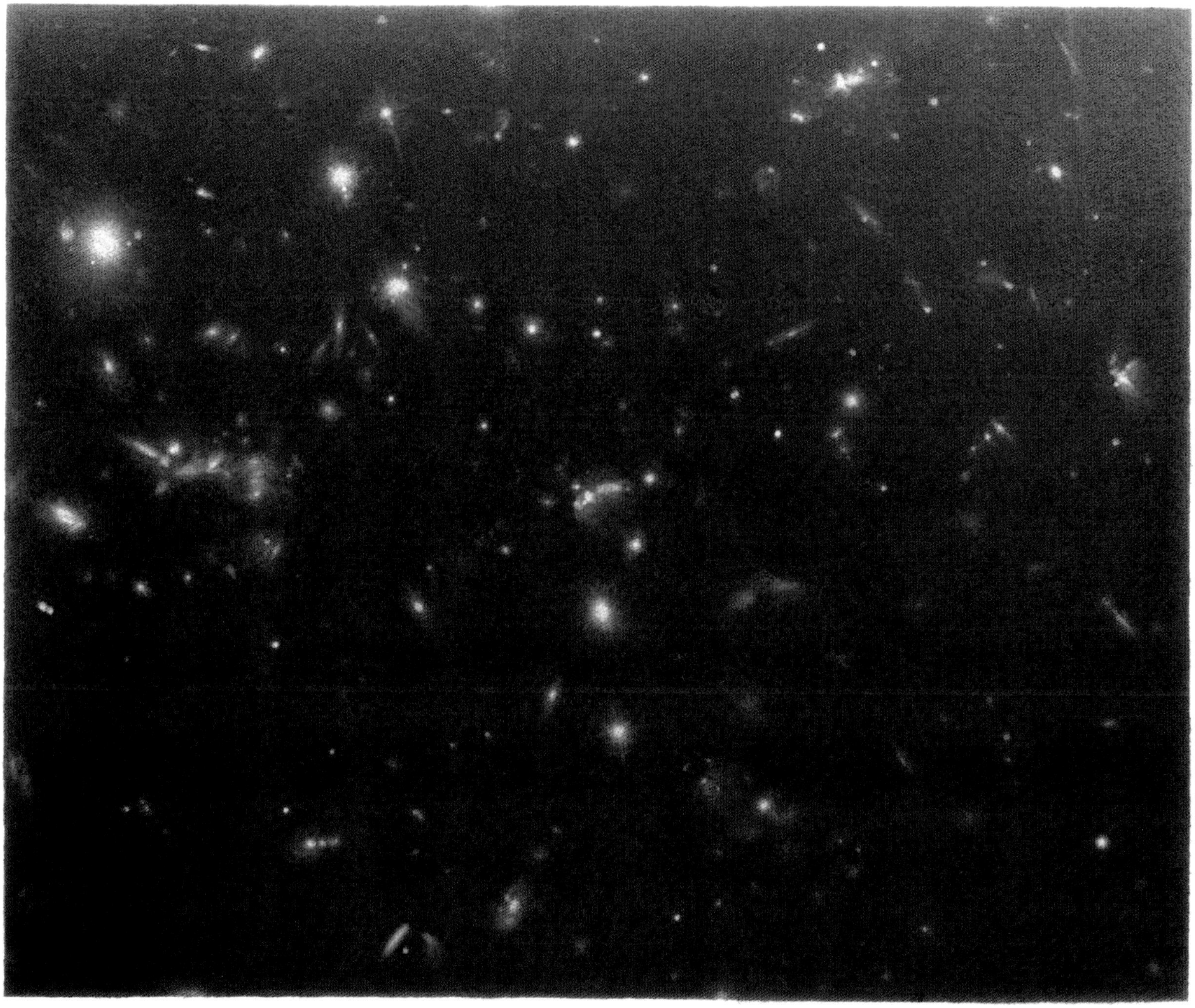

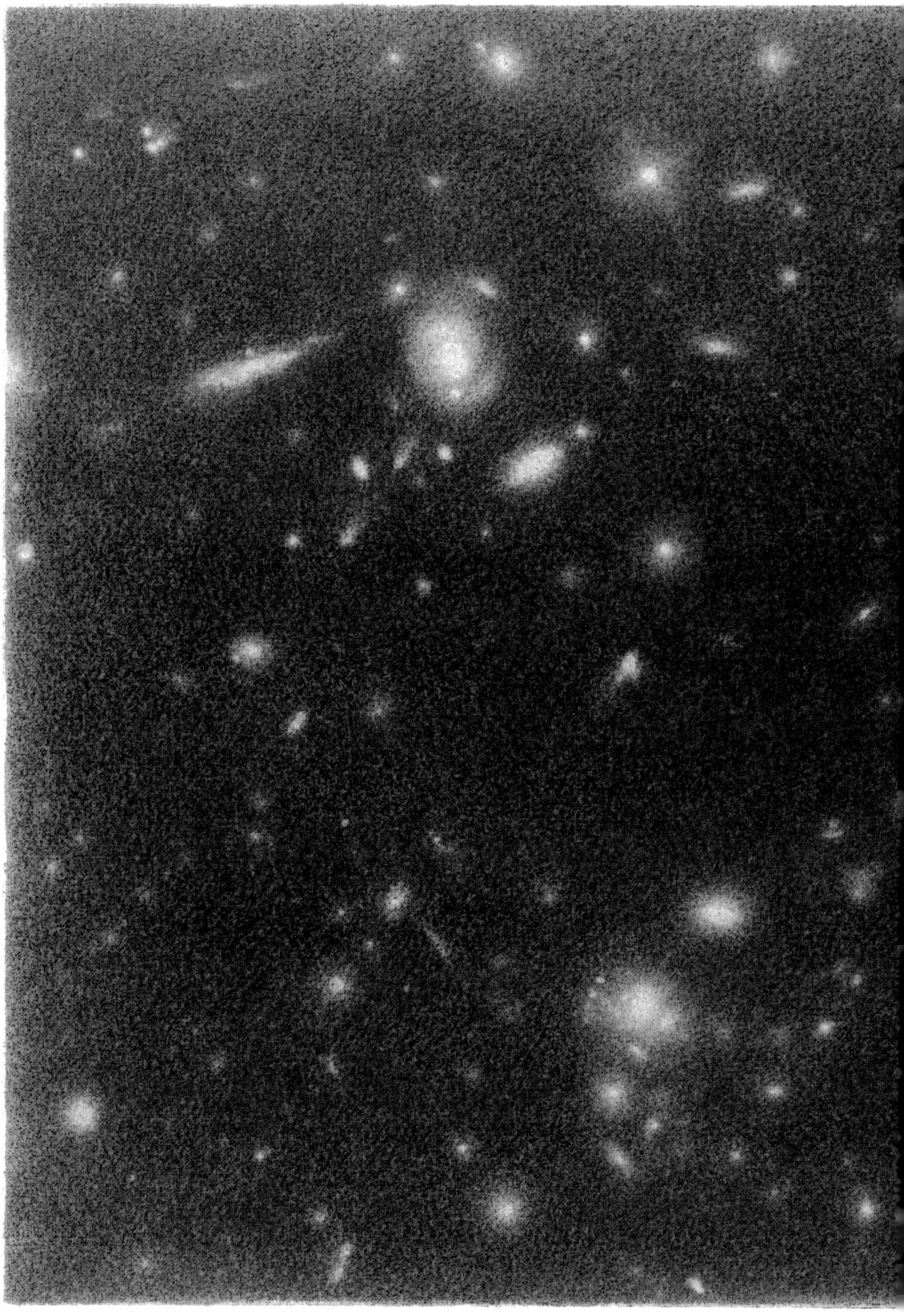

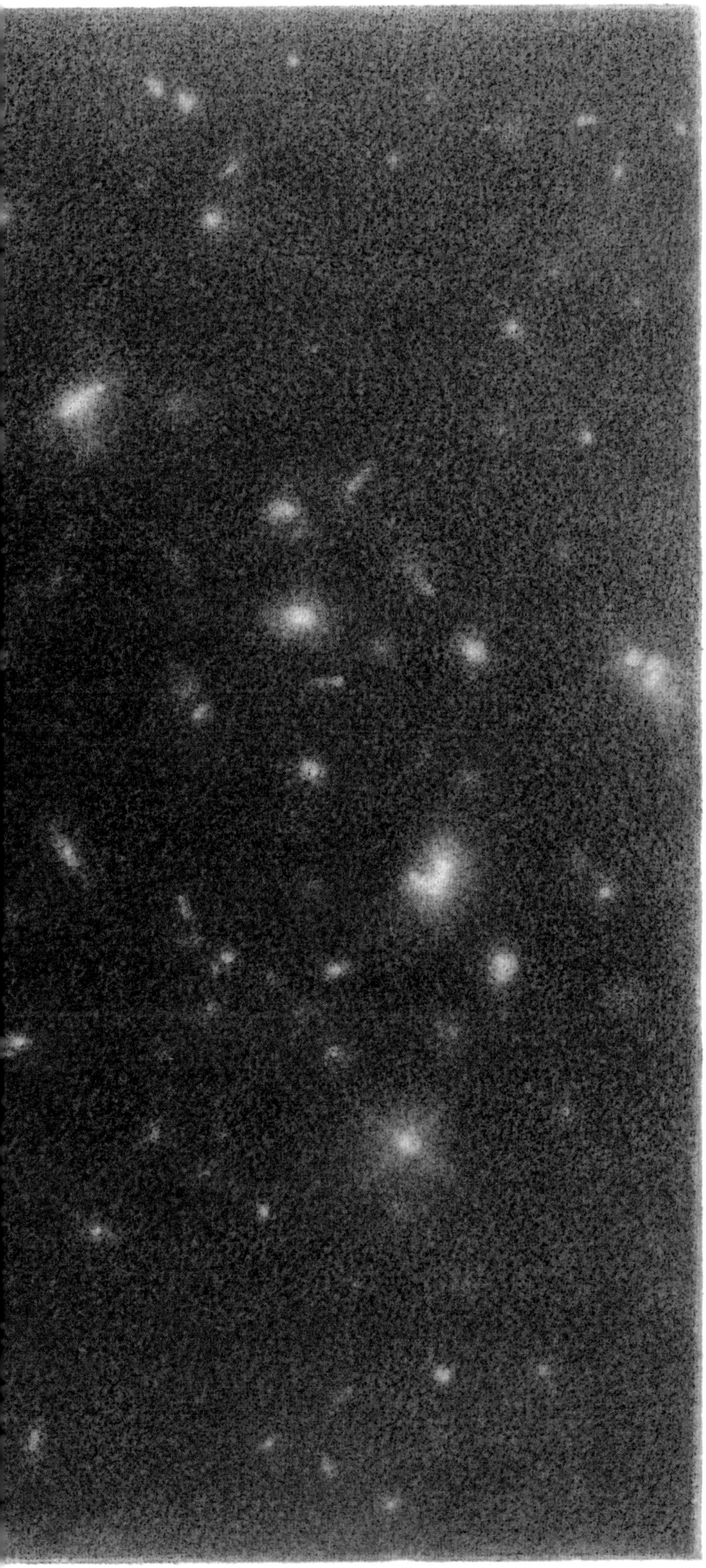

Hubble #3
1998
Charcoal on paper
38 × 44.5 cm
15 × 17.5 in

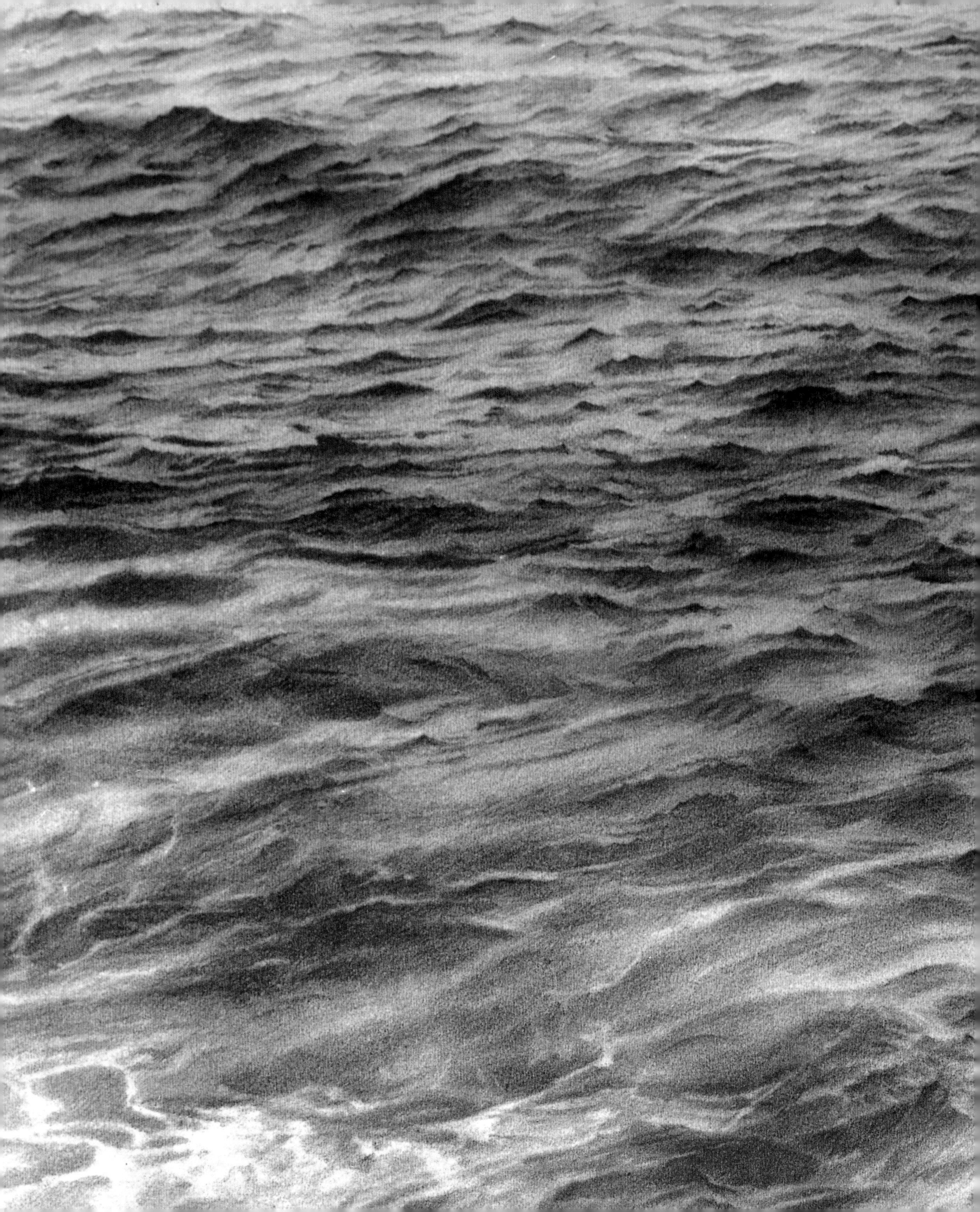

Interview **Robert Gober** in conversation with **Vija Celmins**, page 6.

Survey **Lane Relyea**

Vija Celmins' Twilight Zone, **page 44.**

Focus **Briony Fer** *Night Sky #19*, 1998, **page 100.**

Artist's Choice **Jorge Luis Borges** Funes the Memorious (extracts), 1941, **page 108.**

Artist's Writings **Vija Celmins** Interview with Chuck Close (extracts), 1991, **page 116.**

Chronology **page 144** & Bibliography, List of Illustrations, **page 158.**

'It is as though in the beginning (even if utopian) there were a brute photograph (frontal and clear) on which man would lay out, with the aid of various techniques, the signs drawn from a cultural code.'
– Roland Barthes, 1964[1]

While touring Vija Celmins' 1992 retrospective at the Philadelphia Institute of Contemporary Art, the critic Brooke Adams noticed that the works he found most intriguing had been lent by the artist herself. 'Celmins has kept the best work', he accused in the course of a feature-length review.[2] The truth is that only five of the seventy-five works gathered in the exhibition were labelled 'collection of the artist'. But they do indeed represent pivotal moments; they include a couple of early still lifes of domestic appliances, a portrait in oil of a World War II bomber, and a majestic *Night Sky* painting from the early 1990s. In just these few glimpses it's possible to outline the long itinerary travelled by Celmins in her remarkable career.

One of those keepers is *Lamp #1*, an oil painting from 1964 that can still be found lurking in Celmins' studio. It seems at first to be stupefyingly straightforward, understood at a glance. As its title promises, it's a picture of a standard-issue desk lamp, modern yet sensible in its design, its two light bulbs each sunk into a bell-shaped metal shade suspended from a flexible gooseneck stem that rises up from a squarish base; a lamp and its electric cord, which swan-dives off the bottom edge of the canvas – nothing else. The set-up is aggressively declarative, the lamp displayed frontally in a vice-like composition. Wedged into the picture plane, its bulbs seem to press against a looming blank wall into which its base backs. Calling the background a wall, though, seems wrong; it looks more like a painting, a flat grey monochrome wherein the materiality of stroked-on oils is relieved of the task of serving representation and shown to be just itself. And yet all that painterly grey is only permitted ever so closely to approximate the work's actual surface, not to coincide with it. Instead, it's pushed back a step in deference to the illusionistic depth needed by the foregrounded lamp, which hesitates to claim that foreground, looking idle, moribund, turned off.

In structure and mood, *Lamp #1* bears a close family resemblance to what was often called 'common-object painting' in the early 1960s – canvases like fellow Los Angeles resident Joe Goode's tableau constructions from just two years earlier, in each of which a large pastel monochrome is outfitted with a thin shelf that runs the length of its bottom edge and supports a lone milk bottle poised at its centre. Also called to mind are Jasper Johns' early grey fields that likewise cross declarative frontality with tongue-tied reticence. 'All of Johns' pictures convey a sense of desolate waiting', the critic Leo Steinberg observed in 1960. 'Even those plaster casts have the look of things temporarily shelved for some purpose. And yet, as you look at these objects, you know with absolute certainty that their time has passed, that nothing will happen.'[3] *Lamp #1* seems similarly haunted by premonition and abandonment. The scene is dramatically lit at an angle from the upper left, which creates deep

Lamp #1
1964
Oil on canvas
62 × 89 cm
24.5 × 35 in

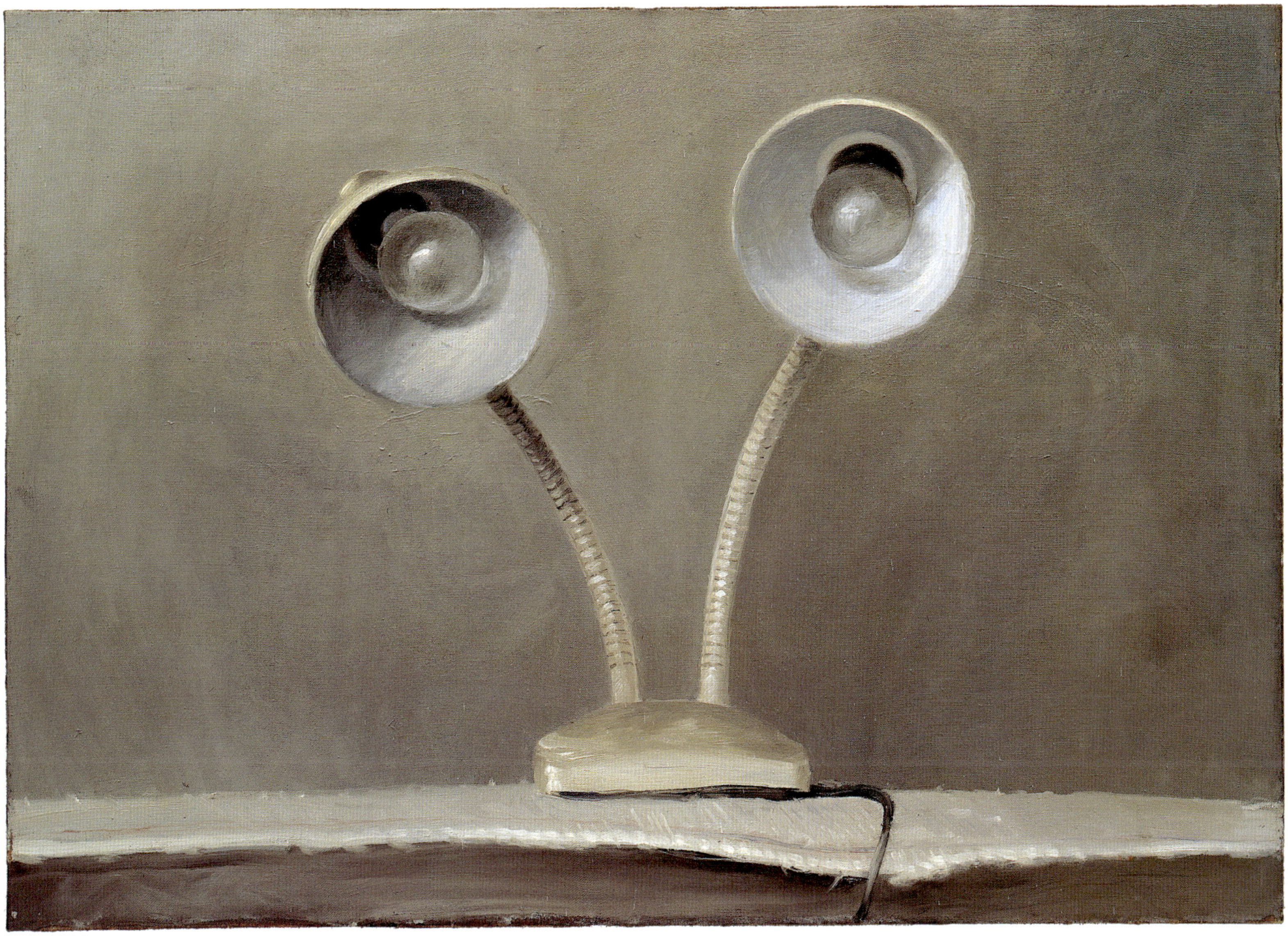

shadows in the lamp's metal shades, a darkness from which the bulbs half-emerge, peering. A sense of anticipation suffuses the picture, as if it were teetering on a threshold; the lamp is thrust on to centre stage but, not yet switched on, hasn't started its act. But it's an act both awaited and feared, since staring this close up into bright lights would no doubt inflict real pain. But why the drama at all? Why stare at such an ordinary appliance? Shouldn't the lamp be illuminating some more appropriate object of vision, rather than being that object itself? Awarding this much attention to it is like focusing only on the theatre usher over the course of an entire play. What should be an aid and accessory in the effort to comprehend through eyesight is turned upon by vision and made its very target.

But the longer one stands in front of *Lamp #1*, the less certain one feels about the precise identity of what is being targeted. Isolated out from the typical still-life throng, the lamp is offered as the one and only focal point; but immediately that focus is split, divided between the two most prominent of the lamp's components, the light bulbs, which are disturbingly set at differing angles, the left one tilting slightly to the right, the right one listing off to the left. In addition, each bulb possesses a dual role – both solid and not-solid, illuminated thing and source of illumination. The painting calls simultaneously for proximate and distant viewing, asking the beholder to zoom in on a graspable object and zoom out in anticipation of a blast of dispersed light (an anticipation goaded by the overly aggressive presence of that electric cord, which increasingly resembles a bomb's lighted fuse). If the light bulbs lead the viewer into the pictured space, they also ricochet his or her sightlines away from the centre of the painting towards its opposite upper corners. But not all is scattered and divided: the two lights seem to lead out of the picture as well, to possess sightlines of their own. And, like accusing fingers, the bulbs point at one common suspect: 'the lines, like rushing streams, converge towards the foreground', writes Meyer Schapiro about a similarly paranoid perspectival inversion in Van Gogh's late landscapes such as *Wheatfield with Crows* (1890), 'as if space had suddenly lost its focus and all things turned aggressively upon the beholder'.[4] Celmins' lamp succeeds where its viewer fails: it is able to focus its beams, to centre its gaze, on a single, stable vantage point. Its two bulbs point at us, have us cornered. As Schapiro puts it, 'The spectator has become the object.'

It would be nearly a decade before Celmins finally granted herself permission to turn on the lights. And when she did, the foreground bulbs would at last merge with the airless monochrome backdrop, thus reconciling the former separation between object and field and uniting the work from edge to edge. This all happens in her first picture of a star-filled night sky, the 1973 drawing *Galaxy*. Now the two lights have dispersed into millions of tiny incandescent stars, and they sit embedded – but only provisionally – in the thick graphite residue of the work's surface, twinkling at the viewer as they threaten to fall away, far, far away, light-years upon light-years away.

Celmins was born in Riga, the seaside capital

T.V.
1964
Oil on canvas
66.5 × 91.5 cm
26.25 × 36 in

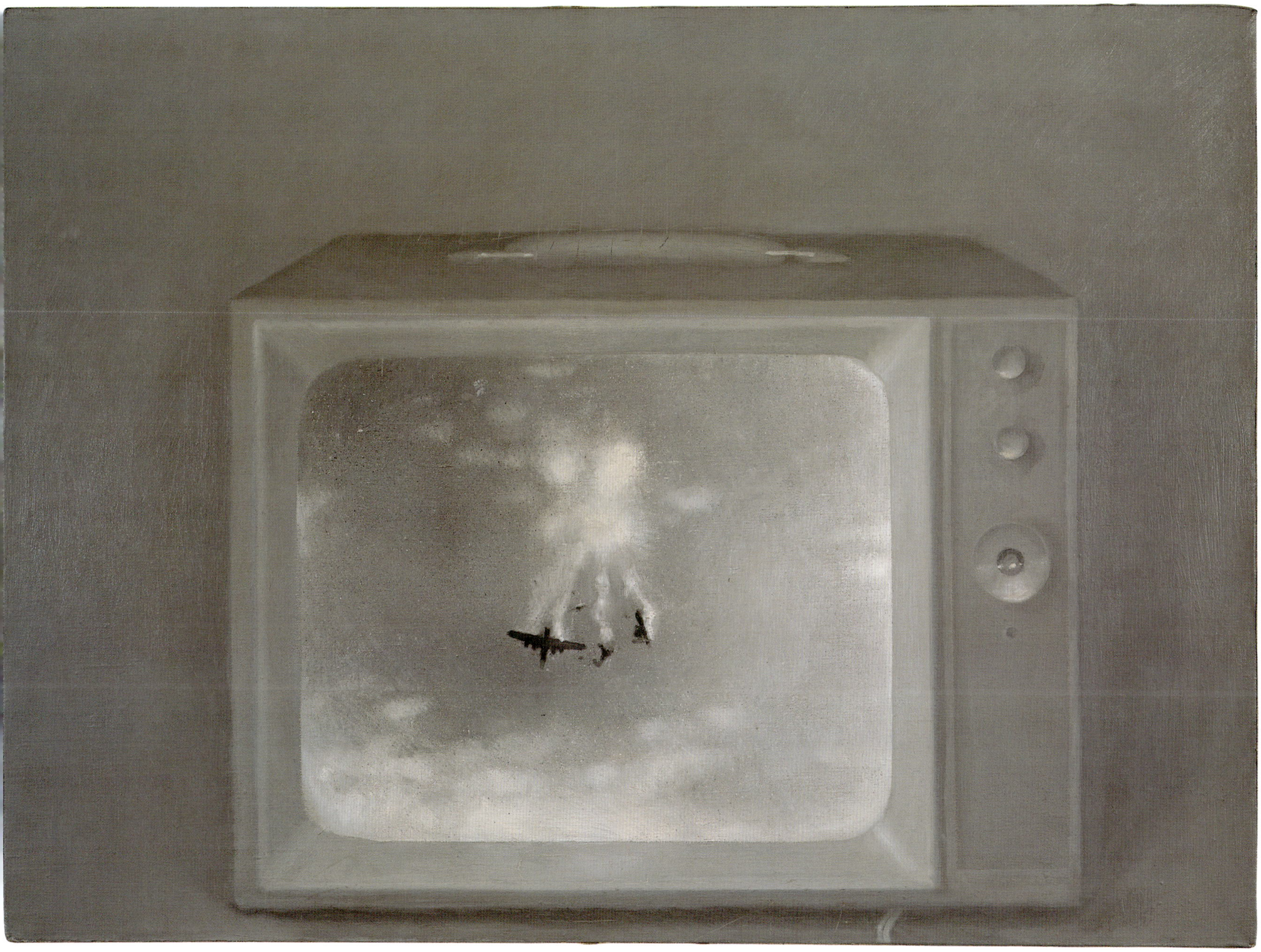

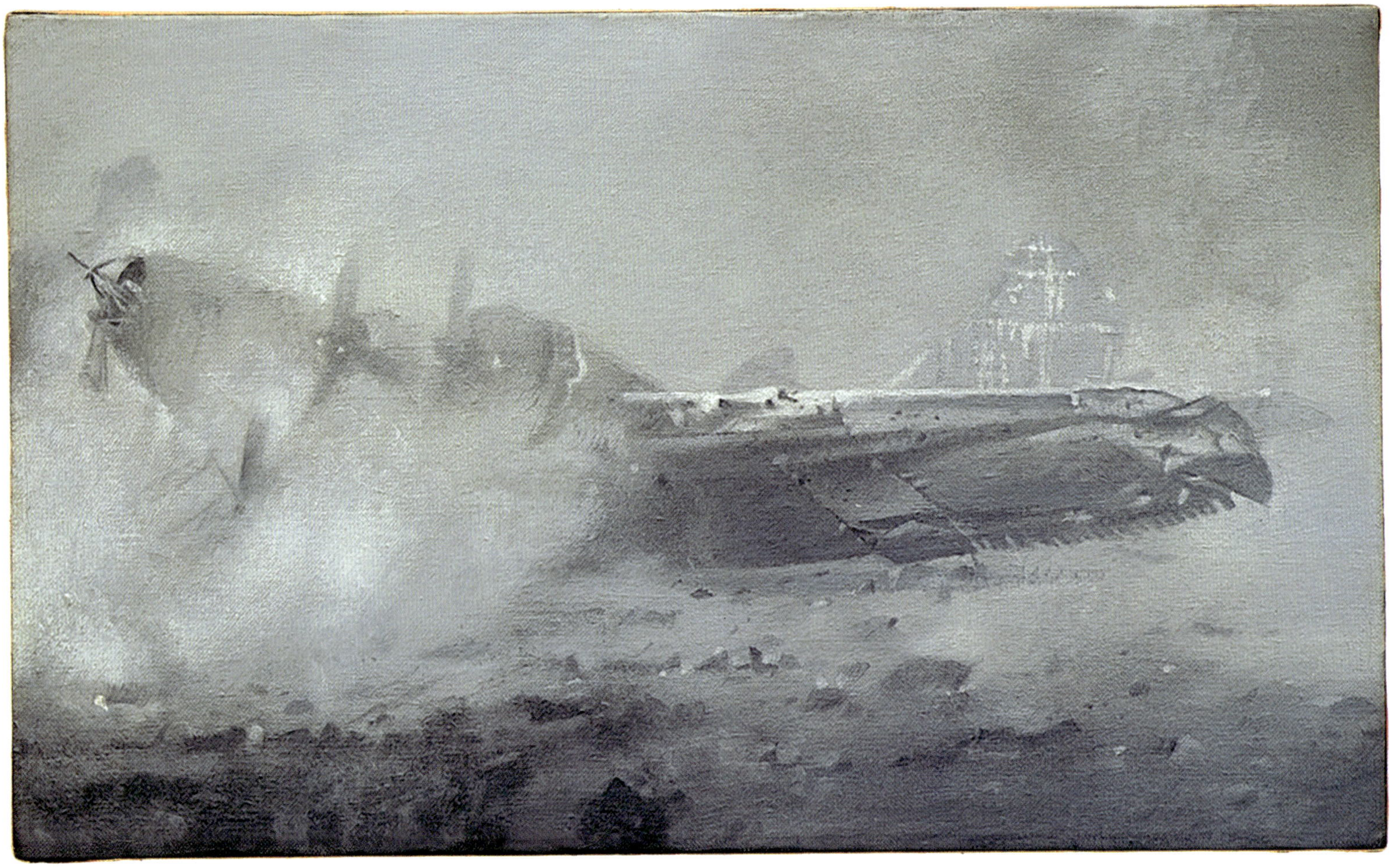

Burning Plane
1965
Oil on canvas
37 × 61 cm
14.5 × 24 in

of Latvia, in 1938, around the time Michael Fried, Judy Chicago and Larry Bell were born. Their generation would come to inherit a world very different from the one populated by their elders. 1939 was also the year when Clement Greenberg wrote 'Avant-Garde and Kitsch', and the Museum of Non-Objective Painting (later christened the Solomon R. Guggenheim Museum) opened in lower Manhattan. Greenberg, like most avant-garde artists and critics in the US and Europe at the time, was a socialist, which meant juggling optimism concerning the movement's cresting popularity (in 1939 membership of the American Communist Party peaked at 100,000, up from only 12,000 just a decade before) and revulsion over the recent Moscow Trials and other signs of unbridled Stalinist despotism. In August, a week before the World War II broke out, Nazi Germany and the USSR signed the German-Soviet Non-aggression Pact, a treaty outlining the Soviet annexation of Latvia and other Baltic states within a year's time. Views of the world – political, artistic and otherwise – soon disintegrated as the world itself was set on fire. Many European artists migrated to the US, where disgusted avant-gardists quit the Communist Party and its various satellite organizations *en masse*, cutting themselves politically adrift.

In 1940 the Red Army invaded Latvia, only to be forced out a year later when the Nazis launched their own invasion. Celmins' family fled in advance of the Soviet re-invasion in 1944 and settled with other Latvian refugees in the German town of Esslingen before migrating to the US in 1948. The family quickly found a home in Indianapolis, known as the 'Crossroads of America' after all the interstate highways that knot together there. At the age of sixteen Celmins started attending art classes and reading art magazines, and with other students would pilgrimage to New York to witness de Kooning-style painting first-hand. By the time she graduated from Indianapolis' John Heron Art Institute, she too was making large-scale gestural abstractions.

It's not hard to imagine why Celmins was attracted to what the critic Harold Rosenberg called 'Action Painting'. Its innovation – he wrote in a 1957 issue of *ARTnews* that Celmins specifically remembers reading – was that 'the action on the canvas became its own representation ... An action ... by its nature is a sign – it is the trace of a movement whose beginning and character it does not in itself ever altogether reveal.'[5] For Rosenberg Action Painting was an art without origin or sanction, a defiant cry of individual agency that floated free of any social endorsements, that took itself as the only trustworthy reality and spurned the rest. 'Everything had to be in the tubes, in the painter's muscles and in the cream-coloured sea into which he dives', Rosenberg wrote in 'The American Action Painters' (1952), his defining essay on such painting.[6] Rosenberg imagined this art's practitioners like loose debris hurled from a former exploded reality, and yet without any new reality in which to land. 'Many of the painters were "Marxists" ... they had been trying to paint Society. Others had been trying to paint Art ... it amounts to the same thing. The big moment came when it was decided to paint ... just TO PAINT.' Action painting was, in other words, an art suited

Flying Fortress
1966
Oil on canvas
40.5 × 66 cm
16 × 26 in

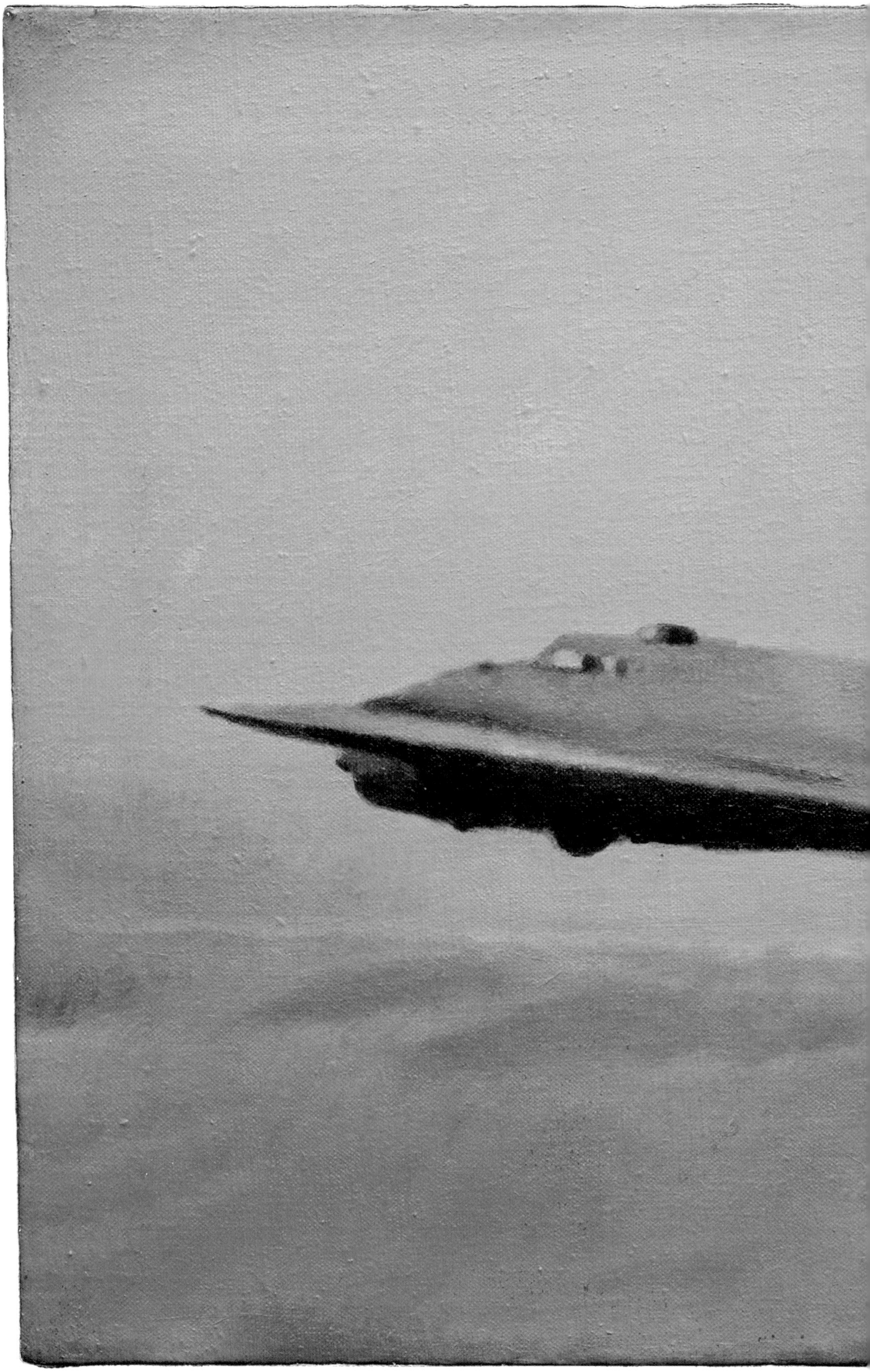

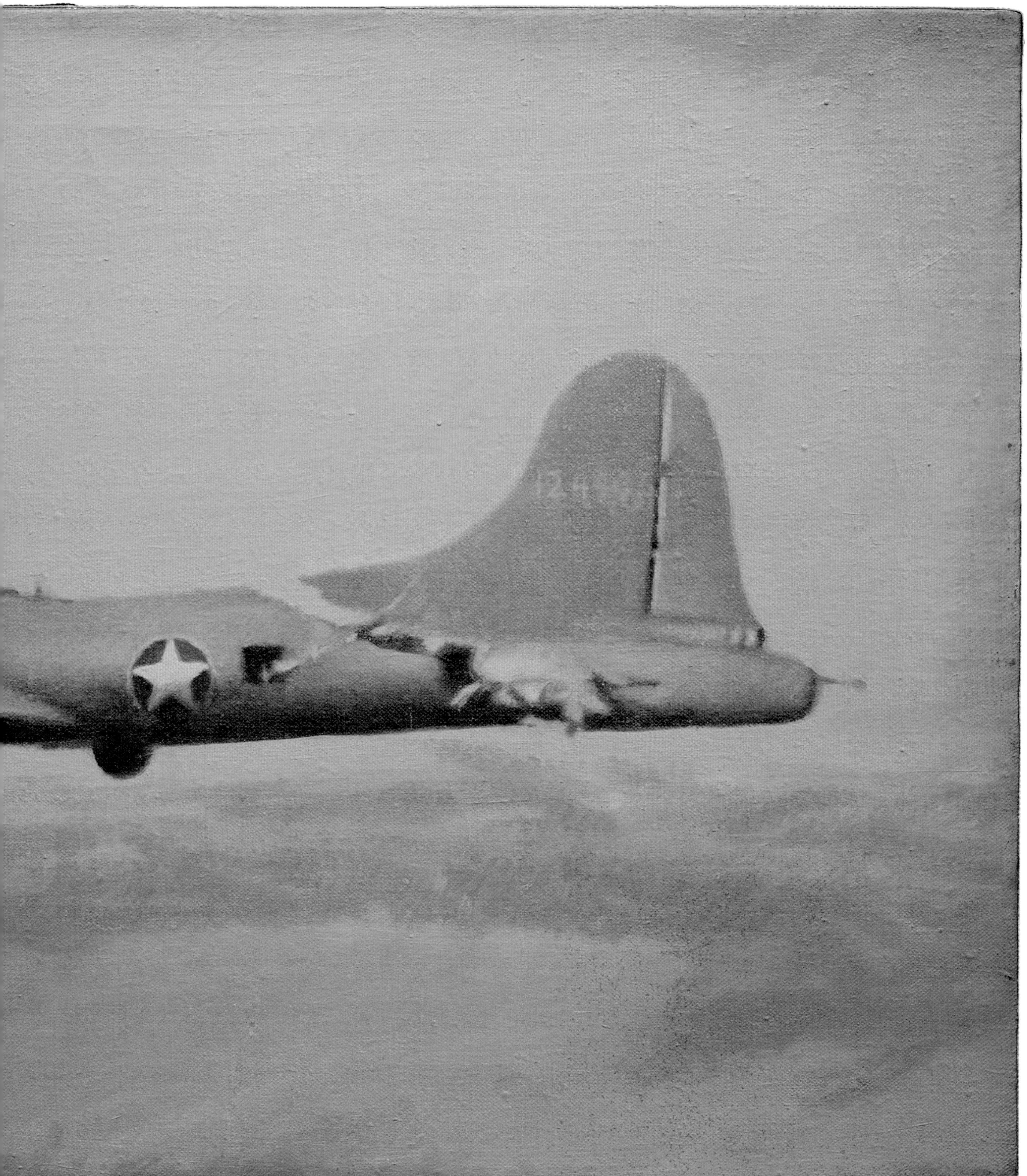

to cultural and political exiles, a refugee's art. 'Most of the artists of this vanguard found their way to their present work by being cut in two', the critic observed. 'Their type is not a young painter but a reborn one. The man may be over forty, the painter around seven. The diagonal of a grand crisis separates him from his personal and artistic past.'

How Celmins' nomadic, bomb-dodging childhood might have predisposed her to an early infatuation with Abstract Expressionism is important, but it shouldn't be over-stressed. As Rosenberg was the first to admit, by the late 1950s young artists, no matter what their upbringing, were making big gestural painting as much a fad as bootstring ties and leather jackets. All the same, it's a significant correlation, albeit adamantly denied by nearly every critic who's chronicled Celmins' career. Too often her early biography is said to exempt her from any participation in the main currents of postwar art history. It's as if her art were a thoroughly private affair, shaped only by personal determinants, not culturally shared ones. The trope was established early on: in a 1970 round-up of promising Los Angeles artists, Jane Livingston wrote that Celmins 'has consciously avoided identification with any regional style or coterie ... she is an entirely self-sustained and stylistically independent artist'.[7] More recently, Dave Hickey explained in the catalogue that accompanied the 1992 retrospective that Celmins' work 'has always made a virtue of displacement and has never found a comfortable niche within the art world's sedentary fiefdoms of style and territory ... It always seems to have just arrived from someplace else ... having a kind of stateless foreign accent.'[8] Of course, avoidance of 'sedentary fiefdoms of style and territory' was precisely what Rosenberg had counselled (don't 'paint Art', he'd scolded), and the fact that such avoidance eventually calcified into a rigid formula of its own is precisely why Celmins, like most of her generation, dumped the approach during her first year in graduate school. Displacement was a pervasive condition of the art world into which Celmins emerged, and her art is as exemplary in its response to that historical condition as anybody's. To say that displacement came naturally to her, like her accent, is overly to privatize her stylistic independence, to cocoon her art and unnecessarily cut it off from that history.

The problem is all too familiar. In terms of her reception, Celmins has at least three strikes against her. First, by the time she mounted her debut solo show in 1966, the art world had shed all semblance of coherence, as discourses, critical criteria and historical narratives lost the capacity to wrench any sense out of the fast-changing course of events. This was the year in which modernism was galloping off in full retreat, with critics like Michael Fried cursing bitterly that 'no more than an infinitesimal fraction of the art produced in our time matters at all', while Lucy Lippard pronounced that even Minimalism had become 'a new cliché'.[9] Rosenberg himself threw up his hands:

'Compared with even three years ago the current scene is virtually unrecognizable. Then, neo-dadaist and Pop art were crowding Abstract Expressionism and it seemed pertinent to discuss

which was really newer and might have greater staying power. Today, both Pop and Action Painting, as well as two or three subsequent "vanguards", have passed into the swelling reservoir of modernist modes and no discussion seems pertinent.'[10] Over ten years would pass before a self-styled postmodernist criticism would attempt to resurrect an authoritative set of evaluative categories and criteria in the visual arts. Celmins belongs to a group of painters (Mary Heilman, Neil Jenney, Malcolm Morley and David Reed are just a few others) who came of age during the intervening years, and whose work never benefited from being swept up in and magnified by the arguments of modernism, neo-avant-gardism or postmodernism. To compound matters, Celmins spent her formative years as an artist in Los Angeles, and thus suffered the dominant New York chauvinism that dismisses everything outside its zip-codes as ahistorical, idiosyncratic, provincial and finally without consequence. Third, she bore the taint of being a woman artist, and so her work, like that of Lee Bontecou, Anne Truitt, Eva Hesse, Lynda Benglis and too many others, was accordingly described not as a decisive contributor to public debates and cultural advances but as a private, inward-turned expression of timeless feminine sensibility.

To a large degree, the reason why Celmins appears bracketed from the historical record is precisely due to the way in which she and her art have been recorded. For example: during 1964–68 she inventoried a shocking array of violent imagery in her art – guns, riots, bullet-ridden cars, bombs exploding, warplanes patrolling or being blasted out of the sky, houses and people on fire. She's offered a simple explanation for this: 'The Vietnam War was going on, which I was totally crazed about.'[11] Indeed, Celmins participated – along with Donald Judd, Eva Hesse, James Rosenquist, Roy Lichtenstein and hundreds of others – in the earliest mass demonstration by artists against the Vietnam War, the 'Artists Tower of Protest' erected along La Cienega Boulevard in Los Angeles in February 1966. 'War was a major issue', Celmins' contemporary Brice Marden agrees. 'It was like the call of death. Your country is making death. There is going to be a reflection of that in the art.'[12] Marden's comments are contextualized alongside those of twelve other painters in a special feature on 1960s abstract art run by *Art in America* in 1983. Celmins', however, appear outside such a public forum, without the crowd of historical actors all proclaiming on momentous events. Instead, she was speaking as if privately to old friend Chuck Close while reminiscing in her studio, their conversation devoted to – and transcribed in a catalogue about – her uncategorizable art. The effects she so vividly produces in her work are all too often projected back on to her very person, read as part of her innate disposition: she, along with her art, is described as isolated, alone, staring off into the distance, lost in her own world.

The point is not to regard Celmins' work as devoid of any and all personal inflection. (It's particularly impossible to appreciate the grisaille, war-themed children's toys that she made in the mid-1960s – especially the ones with numerous small, intricately shaped puzzle pieces, such as *WWII Puzzle Toy* (1965) – without thinking about

Explosion at Sea
1966
Oil on canvas
34.5 × 59.5 cm
13.5 × 23.5 in
Collection The Art Institute of Chicago

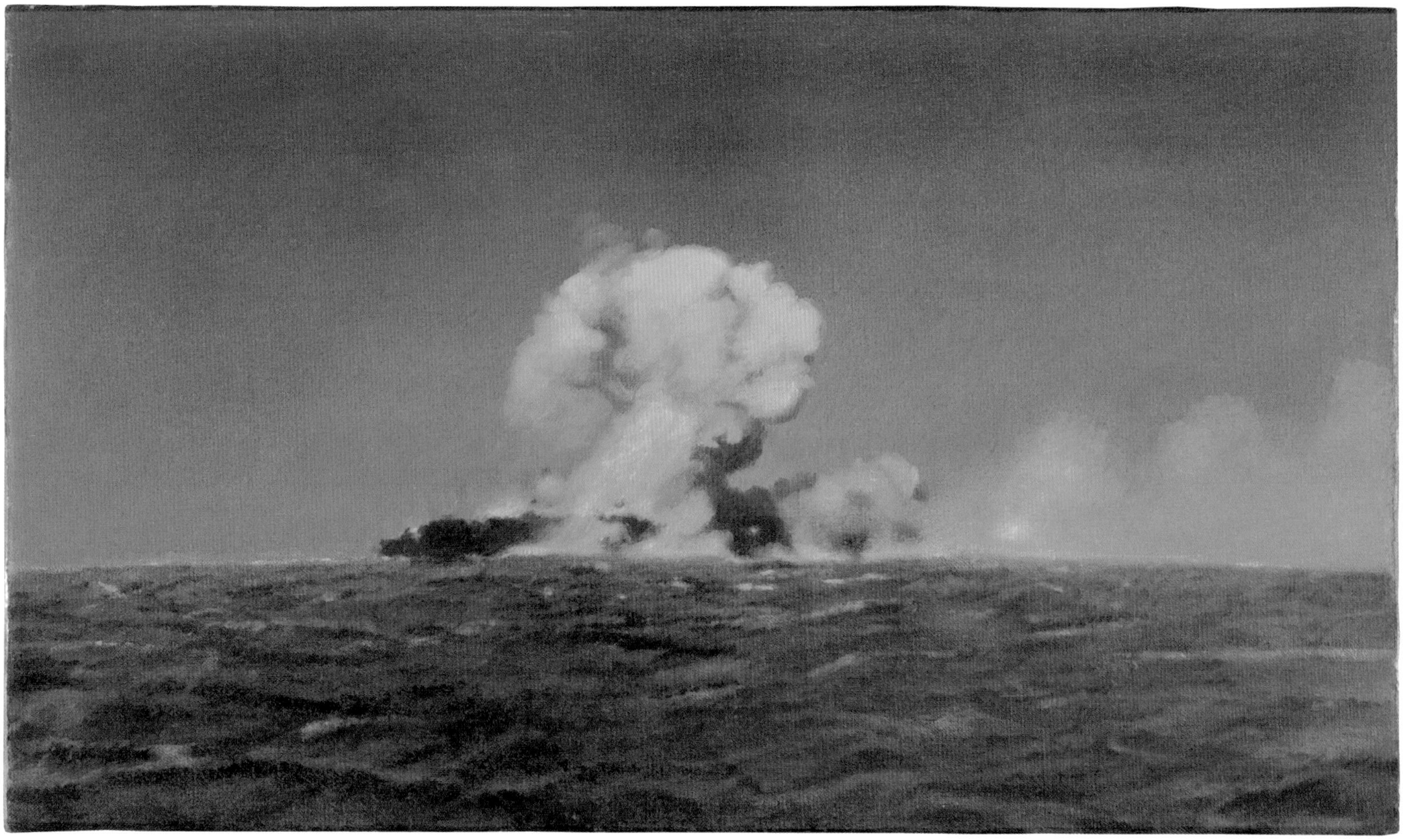

Suspended Plane
1966
Oil on canvas
40.5 × 68.5 cm
16 × 27 in

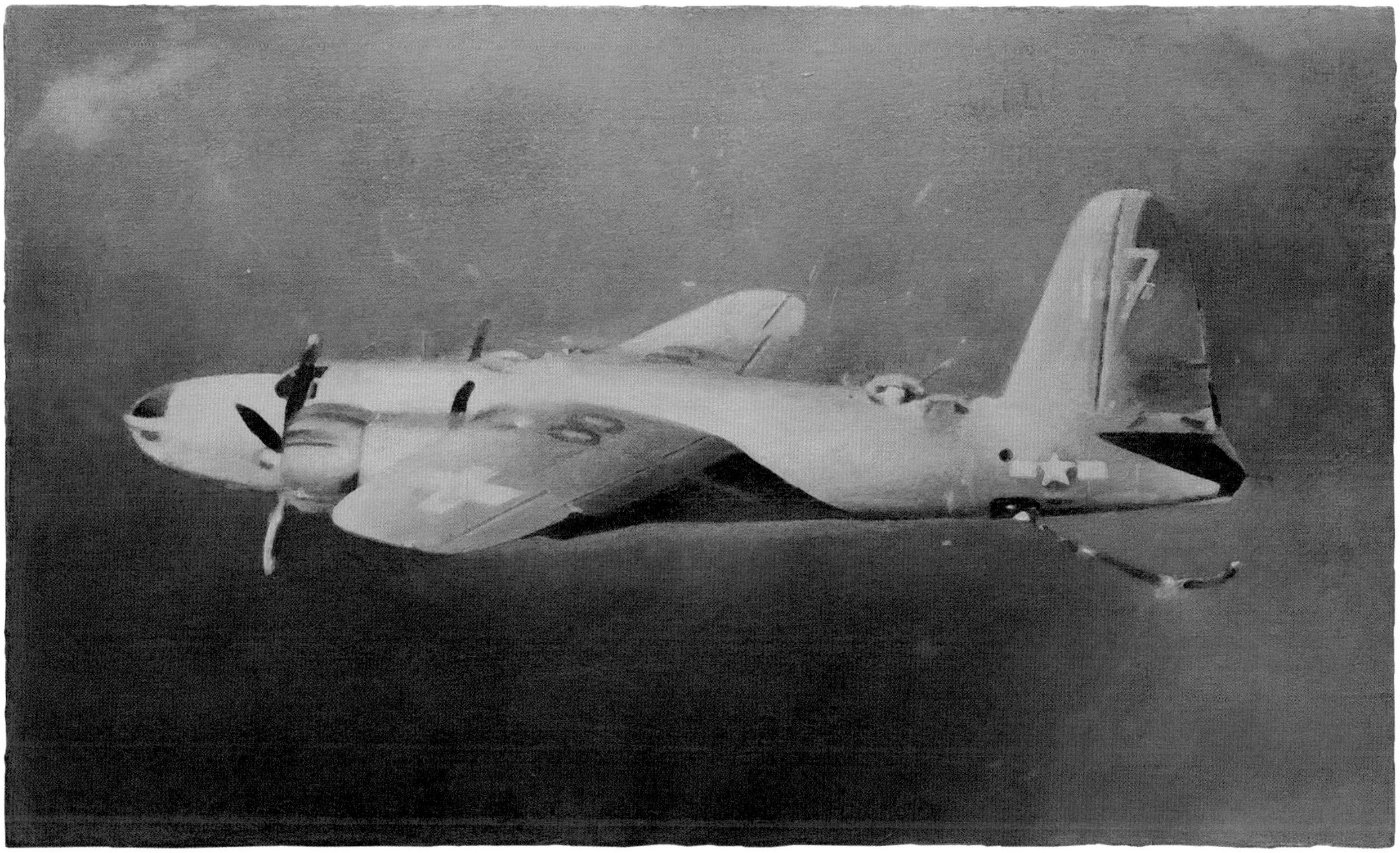

below, **Puzzle**
1965–66
Oil on wood
5 × 30.5 × 25.5 cm
2 × 12 × 10 in

opposite, **WWII Puzzle Toy**
1965
Plastic, wood and oil on canvas
h. 11.5 cm, ∅ 20.5 cm
h. 4.5 in, ∅ 8 in

her accounts of eagerly sifting through rubble and debris as a child in bombed-out Germany.) On the contrary, it's the rich universe of experience she brings to bear that gives her manipulations of style and medium their profound resonance, while her insistence on style and medium is what in turn focuses and concentrates as well as expands and generalizes all that experience. The same could be said of any art, except that in the later half of the 1960s a set style and medium were no longer readily available resources on which artists could draw; instead they had to be improvised as if on the spot. Celmins makes evident in her work her allegiance to a modernist conception of the medium and its efficacy, and to a kind of post-Cubist, all-over field as the grand style best given to organizing modernist pictures. And yet she ends up picturing the medium a little too figuratively and metaphorically, distending and dispersing its self-referentiality a little too much to flatter orthodox modernist tastes. According to these tastes, her works don't disclose themselves quickly and definitively enough, and in their melancholic reserve and fugitive ghostliness they in turn foreshadow a more Postmodern sensibility, pointing the way towards the self-conscious and self-othering structure of Postmodernism. Celmins' art is by no means the first to have to contrive a home for itself out of the terms of its own displacement; it just doesn't mistake that home for Modernism's boastful autonomy. Nor does it surrender itself to displacement as anxiously as Postmodernism's precious floating signifiers. Her work is not at all displaced from history; it participates in a long line of modern art elaborated around the theme of displacement. But it must fend for itself as that history momentarily sputters and unravels, loses itself, and in losing itself seems to pull the rug right out from under her entire generation.

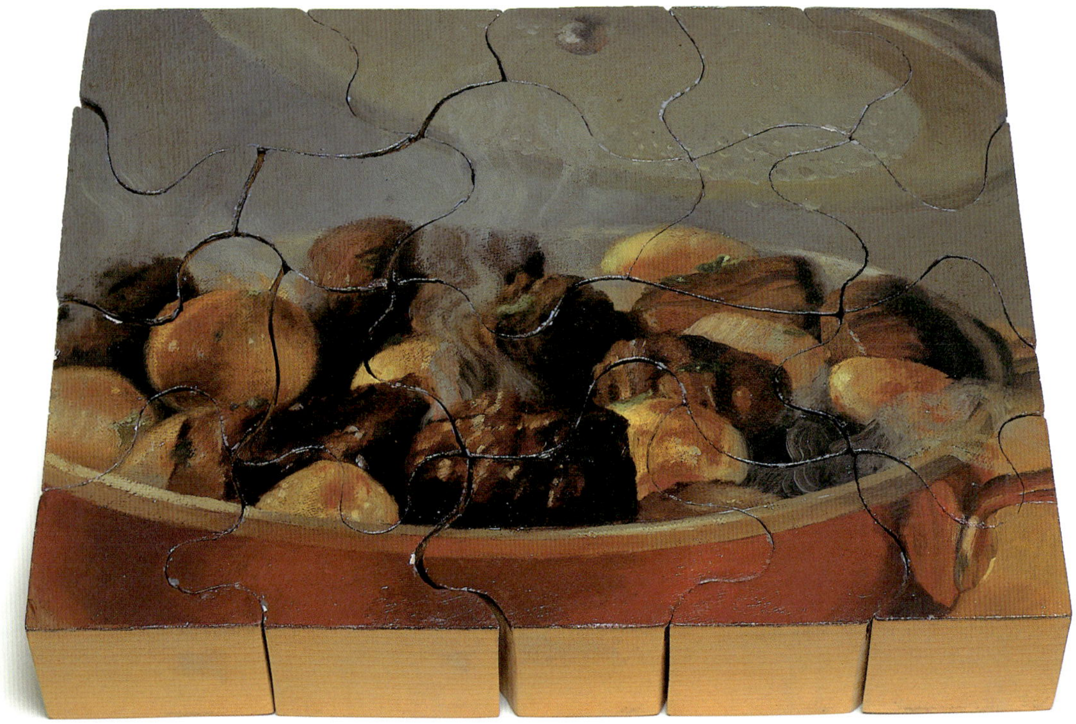

Celmins befriended Brice Marden and Chuck Close when the three attended the Yale Summer School in 1961. The previous two years had witnessed the emergence of a variety of artistic approaches – happenings, assemblage, colour-field, neo-dada, hard-edge abstractionism – that brought to a sudden close the dominance of action painting. The common issue now facing young artists was how to navigate a path beyond the gestural abstraction still being force-fed them in art school. Celmins recalls her initial loss of faith in the impetuous and charged surfaces of Abstract Expressionism. 'I couldn't resolve the stroke-making with the essential stillness of the

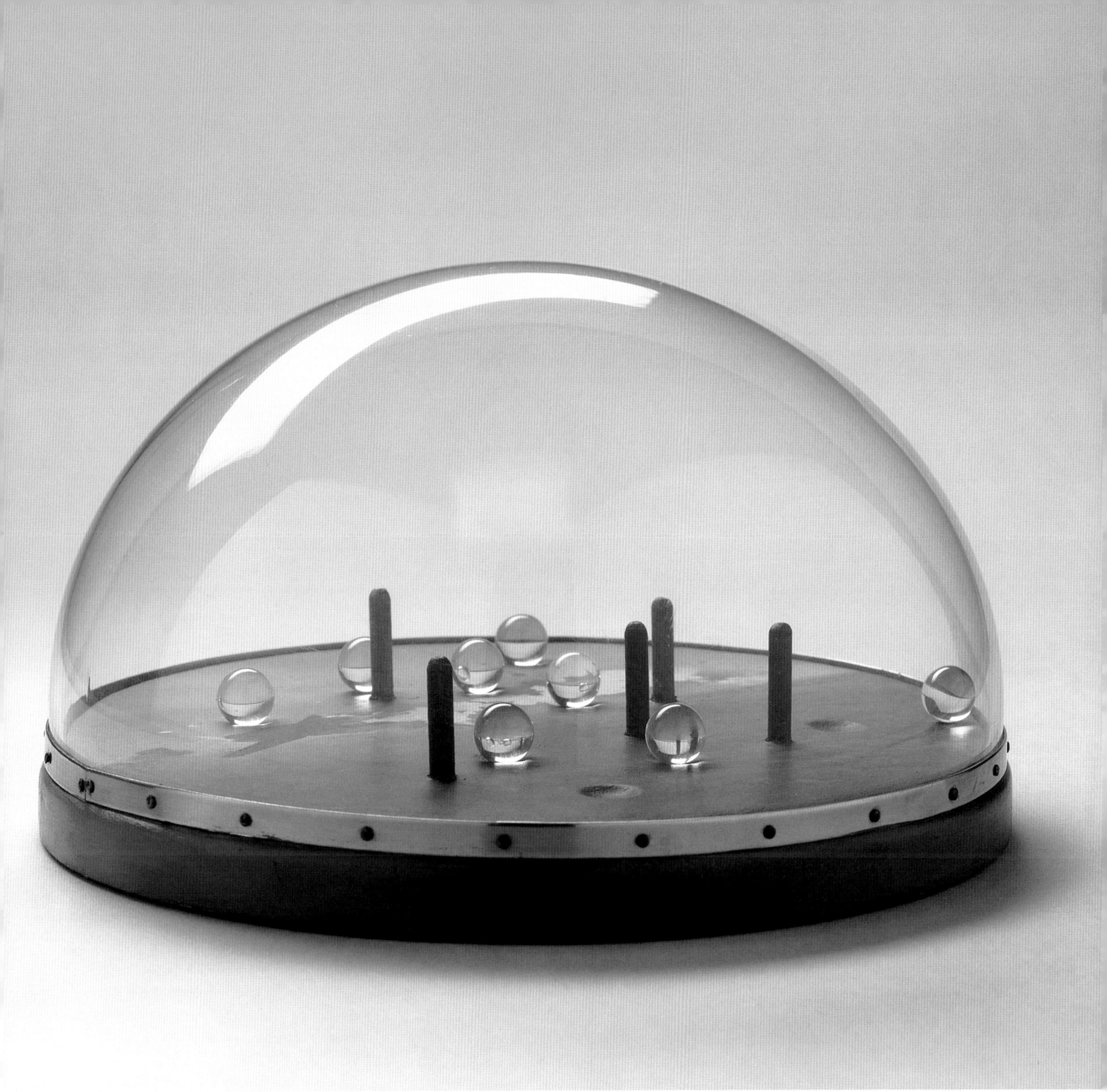

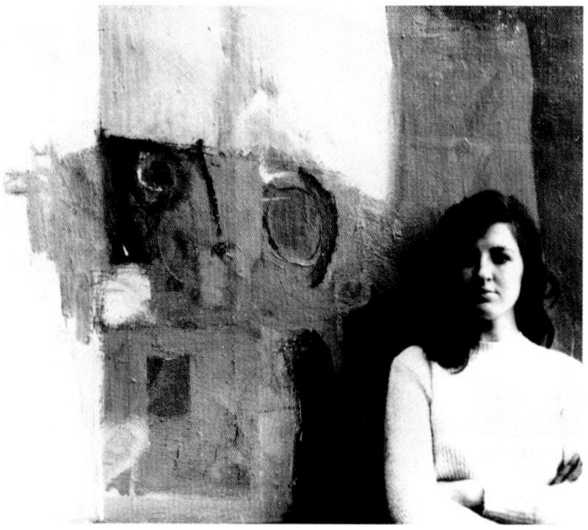

The artist with one of her abstract paintings
No title
1961
Oil on canvas
Approx. 106.5 × 165 cm
42 × 65 in

painting.'[13] The first step towards a solution can be seen in a couple of roughly six-foot-square canvases from 1962 (which today survive only in the background of some old photographs), as well as several smaller prints from that year such as *View of the Quarry*. Here Celmins still hatches and scrubs the picture vigorously, but the resulting marks combine less to effect an immediate surface presence than to describe a pulled-back view of a dramatically receding landscape. Representation is re-introduced, albeit in the form of a soaring withdrawal from the viewer. This was a solution that didn't satisfy Celmins for long; after little more than a year she would again alter her approach so radically that it made any link to previous work nearly unrecognizable. But a link remains. Towards the end of the decade, with her first drawings of oceans and lunar surfaces, Celmins would again return to an image of a vast, remote 'landscape', using once more a horizon line placed just shy of or well beyond the top edge of the picture. From 1962 on, she would never stray far from a kind of image that at once declares the integrity of its surface while threatening to suck that surface into a deep oblivion.

'Art is still and dead.'[14] This is how Celmins later phrased the realization that came to her at that time – a realization that what she wanted was for her work to take up residence in an experiential here and now as well as always already residing elsewhere, and that to achieve this she would need to insist on both the material reality of her art and, being art, that reality's dislocation. Of course, it had been the original aim of Action Painting to create such an elsewhere, to posit the canvas as an 'arena' beyond the known and codified, where fresh encounters would be possible. The model that Rosenberg had in mind was dialectics, in which subject and object, painter and painting, square off in an exchange that ends with a profound alteration in the nature of both. By the time Celmins came to it, though, Action Painting's dialectics had petered out: now canvas and paint offered not resistance but passive accommodation to the gesturing subject's celebration of itself. When the backlash against such painting erupted, one form that it took was a straightforward demotion of heroic subjectivity in favour of plain, humble, unadulterated objects. As Celmins remembers, '*I decided to go back to something outside of myself. I was also going back to what I thought was this basic, stupid painting. You know: there's the surface, there's me, there's my hand, there's my eye, I paint.*'[15] She reduced her means: the size of her canvases and brushes abruptly shrank, and her physical labour likewise grew more confined, involving little of her arm beyond the wrist and knuckles. Celmins no longer engaged painting as a dramatic struggle, but instead used it like a forensic tool, cautiously and patiently rendering objects as if she were dusting them for fingerprints. But her art grew as a result.

She wasn't the only one to be thinking along these lines. In 1962, when Celmins arrived in Los Angeles to attend graduate school at UCLA, 'common-object painting' was seemingly everywhere. A couple of months before the start of her first semester, the Ferus Gallery debuted Andy Warhol's complete set of thirty Campbell's Soup Can paintings. In late September the Pasadena

Museum followed with the compendium 'The New Painting of Common Objects', which gathered works by Warhol, Roy Lichtenstein, Jim Dine, Ed Ruscha and Joe Goode among others (the fledgling *Artforum* responded by featuring one of Goode's monochrome-and-milk-bottle tableau on its November cover). Two months later the Dwan Gallery mounted 'My Country 'Tis of Thee', which included a lounging Oldenburg hamburger sculpture, as well as works by Robert Indiana, Lichtenstein, Ed Kienholz, Marisol, Robert Rauschenberg, Larry Rivers, James Rosenquist, Warhol and Tom Wesselman. All this by winter, when the Janis Gallery in New York opened 'The New Realist' show and supposedly 'launched' Pop art.

During this time, young artists in Southern California – Celmins among them – were given the opportunity to become immersed in works by Jasper Johns, who was not only included in all the above group shows but was also awarded a 'retrospective' at LA's Everett Ellin Gallery in late 1962. Johns's impact was decisive: Ed Ruscha has described it as 'the atomic bomb of my education',[16] and Celmins acknowledges the debt as well. The Ellin show included ten paintings, among them *Drawer* (1957), *White Numbers* (1958), Device (1961–62), *Fool's House* (1962) and *In Memory of My Feelings* (1962), as well as numerous drawings and lithographs. No doubt it was the sense of detachment in Johns' work to which many responded, a kind of objectivity that could spotlight without modification such everyday items as a broom, a towel, a fork and spoon, a ruler. As if to underscore the point, Johns often literally spelled out the names of the objects affixed to the canvas – writing, say, the word 'brush' with an arrow pointing to an actual paintbrush, or 'cup' next to an actual cup – 'stupid painting', as Celmins called it. 'The only way you could get away from style and "art" was to paint things as they really looked', remembers West Coast painter Robert Bechtle, who finished his first photo-realist canvas two years later (at roughly the same moment when, on the other end of the continent, Richard Artschwager began to paint grisaille versions of photographs on celotex, and Malcolm Morley dropped abstraction to inaugurate his own photo-realist phase).[17] With the action painter's subjectivity enthroned as 'art', now it was objectivity to which artists turned for fresh possibilities, for a chance to produce paintings that, as Gerhard Richter would say about his own photo-based work from the mid-1960s, 'had nothing to do with art'.[18]

Celmins cites a number of painters (Giorgio Morandi, Agnes Martin) who also caught her attention at that time, but besides Johns, perhaps the strongest influence on her work was not an artist but a writer, the Frenchman Alain Robbe-Grillet, proponent of the *Nouveau roman*. During her residency at UCLA, Celmins became absorbed in Robbe-Grillet's fiction, especially 'the way he repeats passages many times over to build a very concrete image'.[19] Linda Nochlin has gone so far as to cite the author's 1953 novel *Les Gommes*, translated into English as *The Erasers* in 1964, as the inspiration for Celmins' *Pink Pearl Eraser* sculptures from two years later.[20] 'To describe things, as a matter of fact, is deliberately to place

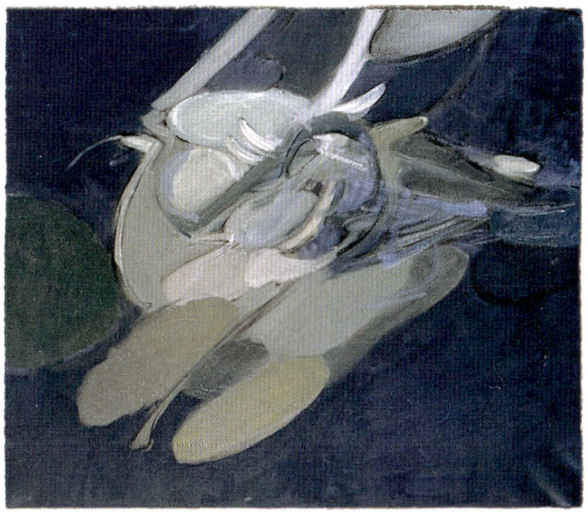

No title
1961
Oil on canvas
Dimensions unknown
Painting produced while at
Indiana Art School

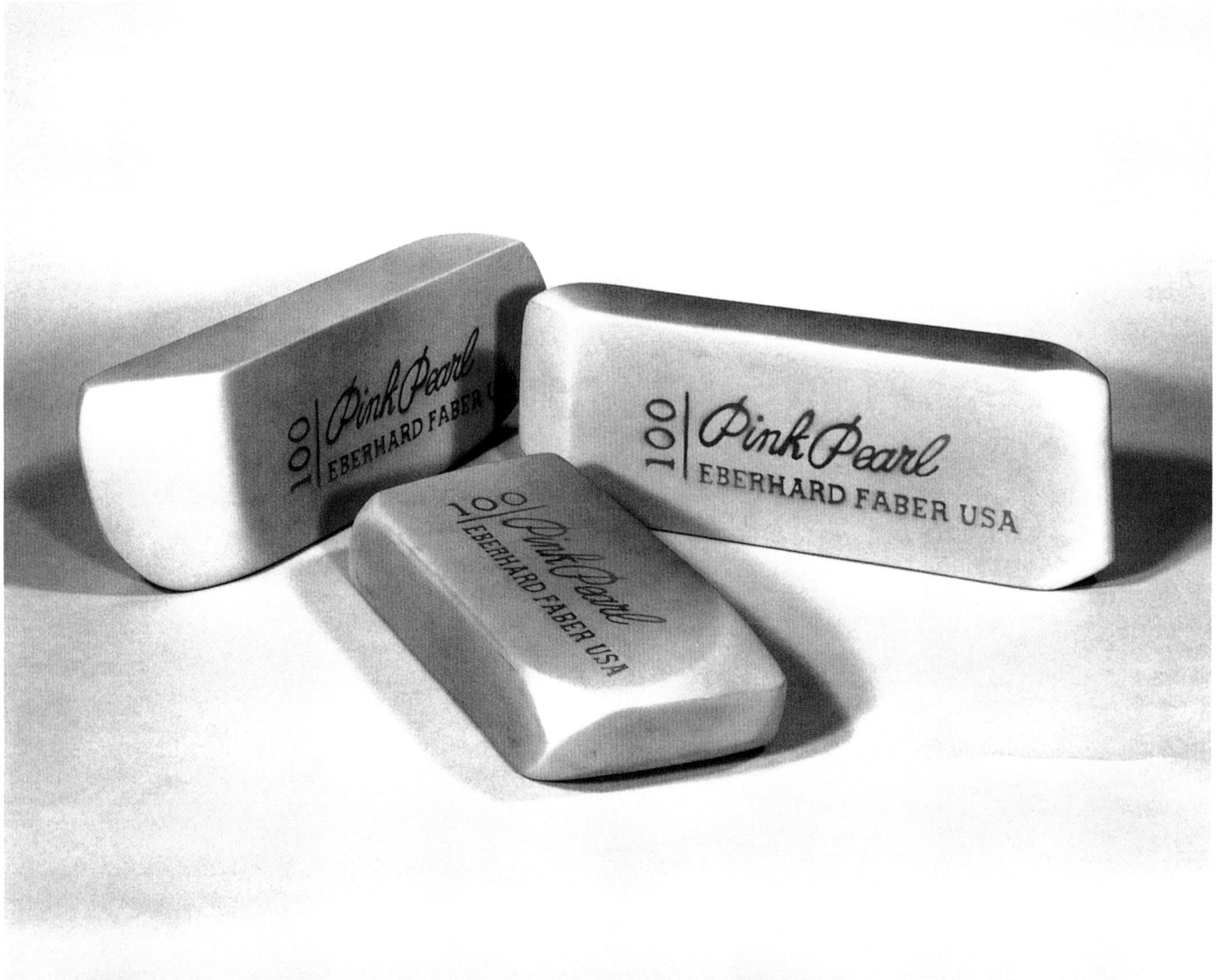
100
Pink Pearl
EBERHARD FABER USA
100
Pink Pearl
EBERHARD FABER USA

oneself outside them, confronting them', Robbe-Grillet announced, articulating what could have been the rallying cry for much art of the 1960s and its varied attempts to restart dialectics from the object's side. 'It is no longer a matter of appropriating them to oneself, of projecting anything on to them. Posited, from the start, as *not being man* they remain constantly out of reach.'[21] In the small catalogue accompanying 'The New Realists' exhibit at Janis, the poet-critic John Ashbery credited Robbe-Grillet as well as filmmakers Alain Resnais and Michelangelo Antonioni as predecessors of what would soon be called Pop art. Irving Sandler also blamed Robbe-Grillet when writing a condemnation of the Janis show: 'These artists describe only the surface of the world around them, impervious to any system of meaning', he scowled.[22] Like Johns' influence, Robbe-Grillet's was strong enough to extend across a range of seemingly unrelated disciplines and styles. Mel Bochner, for example, borrowed a quote from the author's 'For a New Novel' to begin a review of the big 1966 Minimalism exhibition 'Primary Structures'. 'There is nothing behind these surfaces', the epigraph goes, 'no inside, no secret, no hidden motive'[23].

Robbe-Grillet often wrote of how much he admired photography and wished to follow its example of objective description. And a number of artists who reached for photographs as subject matter in the 1960s in turn adopted the writer's defiant, polemical tone ('I reject humanist issues in my work', Close would declare in 1973[24]). Celmins, too, has repeatedly dismissed attempts to read romantic content into her pictures, and at times has even been mistaken as a proponent of a purely denotative, zero-degree art. Nochlin, for one, has judged that 'Celmins' extraordinarily muted yet rapier-sharp realist imagery offers, perhaps, the best parallel to Robbe-Grillet's attempt to abolish significance in literature.'[25] No doubt this was largely the motive behind Celmins' 'stupid paintings', whether of appliances or news photographs – to reduce decision-making, to follow obediently the dictates of the object, recording rather than transforming it, almost mechanically, like a camera. 'I dropped scale and composition altogether', she explains, 'and painted the objects one by one, life-sized.'[26] But she also never went so far as to embrace photo-realism's cold, steely optics, its boastful assurance in the certainty of objective visual fact. Instead of the teeming Pop cornucopias typical of photo-realism, Celmins' painted observations fill with detail only to end up seeming vacated and abstract; their visual approach is more zombie-like than mechanical. To borrow a distinction that Roland Barthes makes in *Camera Lucida*, her work concerns as much retention as presentation; rather than parading visual minutiae, she seems to be attempting to hold on to, or hold out for, something rare and elapsing. As in so much of Robbe-Grillet's prose, what she undertakes is detective work: her intensive looking – trying to approximate the source closely, to reconstitute an object or scene exactly, 'life-sized', one-to-one – is always also a look away or look beyond, an anticipation of something yet to arrive or a

opposite, left to right,
Pink Pearl Eraser
1966–67
Acrylic on balsa wood
16.5 × 50 × 8 cm
6.625 × 19.75 × 3.125 in

centre, **Pink Pearl Eraser**
1966–67
Acrylic on balsa wood
16.5 × 45.5 × 8 cm
6.625 × 18 × 3.125 in

right, **Pink Pearl Eraser**
1967
Acrylic on balsa wood
16.5 × 49.5 × 8 cm
6.625 × 19.5 × 3.125 in
Collection Newport Harbor Art Museum, Newport Beach, California

Fan
1964
Oil on canvas
122 × 122 cm
48 × 48 in
Collection The Oakland Museum of Art, California

lingering over the already departed.

This is what Celmins distills from Robbe-Grillet, and from photography as well. And the object paintings already begin to manifest it, namely in the heavy sense of temporal unease that hangs over them. Evacuated from any familiar setting or order of things, each object is shown relegated to a purgatorial no-man's land, something like a waiting room or interrogation cell. But while isolated, the objects are often not self-contained and static – especially not the appliances. The electric cord is emphasized in each painting: it doodles lyrically across the generous width of *Fan*, threatens to poke through the picture plane in *Hot Plate*, and makes an otherwise sturdy shelf buckle under its negligible weight in *Lamp #1*. Moreover, being plugged-in encourages these items to be seen less as objects than as vehicles of some larger force – wind, heat, light. It's these forces that Celmins suspends: she pictures the hotplate with nothing warming atop it, the lamp with no reading material nearby. Each is bracketed out from motive or consequence, from anything that would absorb the brunt of the action. It's as if, like Rosenberg's exhortation 'to paint', Celmins' works were rendering transitive verbs – 'to illuminate', 'to heat' – suddenly intransitive. Instead, to borrow again from Rosenberg's description, 'the action on the canvas is its own representation ... a sign – it is the trace of a movement whose beginning and character it does not in itself ever altogether reveal'.

Here, perhaps, Celmins brings Robbe-Grillet most clearly into contact with Johns – especially if

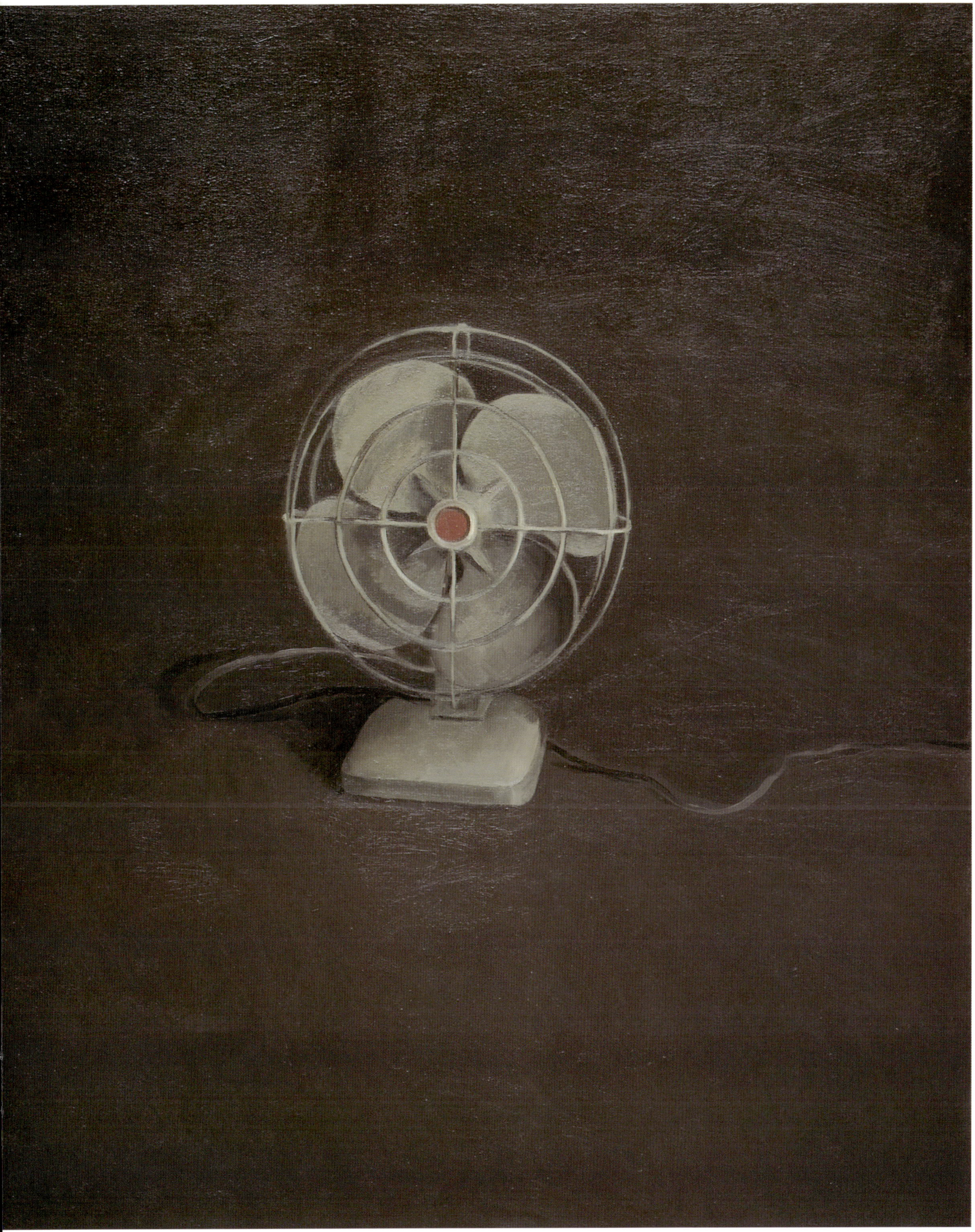

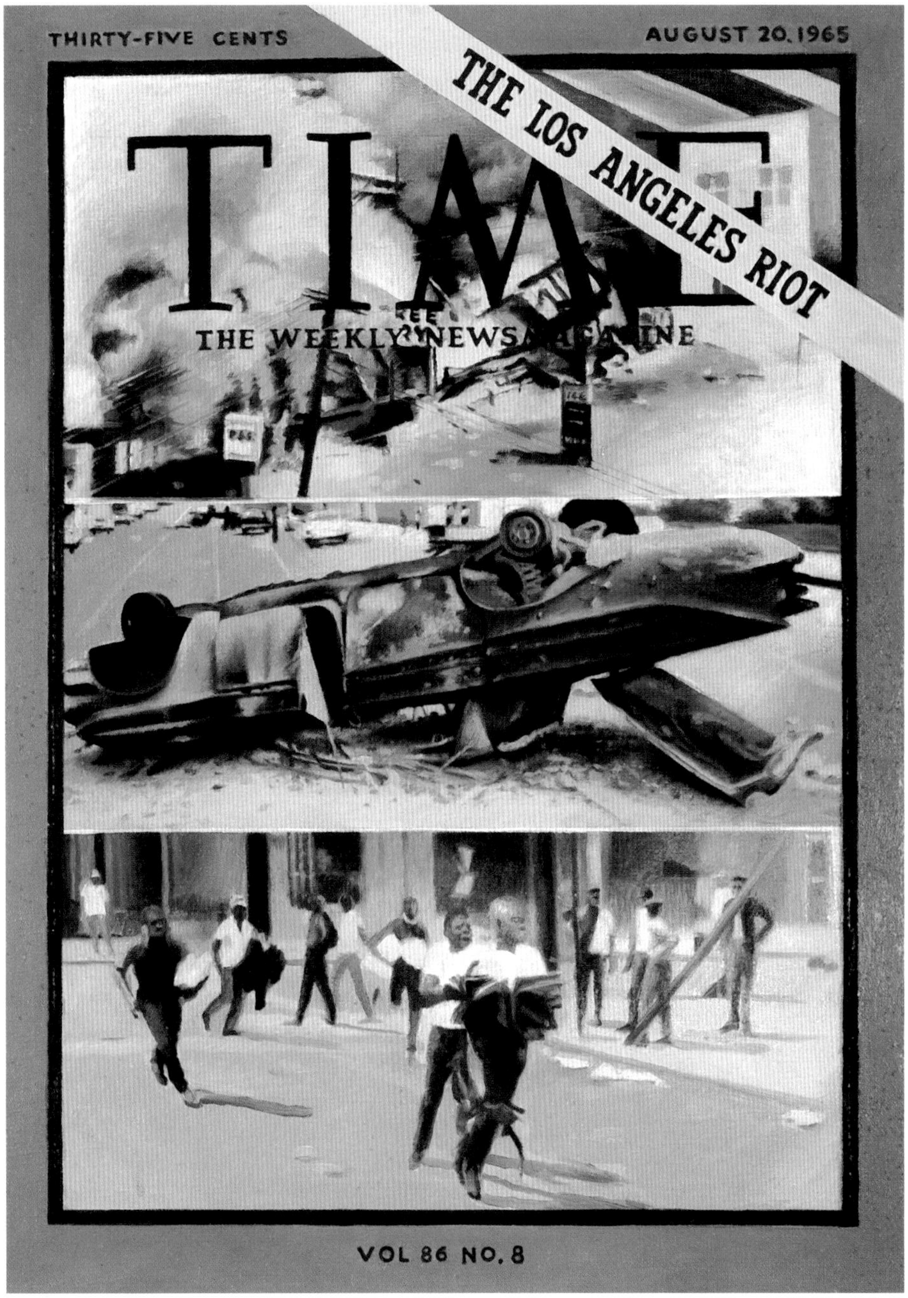
THIRTY-FIVE CENTS
AUGUST 20, 1965
THE LOS ANGELES RIOT
TIME
THE WEEKLY NEWSMAGAZINE
VOL 86 NO. 8

Johns' work is seen as something of a summation, not just the eclipse, of Action Painting. This at least was how Greenberg considered Johns: 'He brings de Kooning's influence to a head', the critic wrote in 1962, 'by suspending it clearly, as it were, between abstraction and representation'.[27] Celmins' art is likewise suspended, on the one hand mercifully delivering common objects into a more timeless, autonomous realm, while on the other hand also treating that realm as incurably haunted by the day-to-day and its temporality, its transience, expectancy and loss. 'Homeless representation' is the label Greenberg used to describe Johns' work, and it applies to Celmins', too. Stuff lying around the house, pictures in some old books: the items in her early paintings all appear so routine and yet uncanny, apprehended with shocking attentiveness even though they seem trapped beneath a layer of dust. The imagery feels buried alive, a breathing corpse. Very much like what Steinberg sensed in Johns' paintings, behind all their poker-faced irony: 'These pictures by Jasper Johns', he shudders, 'come to impress me as a dead city might – but a dead city of terrible familiarity'.[28] And likewise it's what Barthes, the early champion of Robbe-Grillet, found in photography: 'By attesting that the object has been real, the photograph surreptitiously induces belief that it is alive ... but by shifting this reality to the past ("this has been"), the photograph suggests that it is already dead.'[29] This is just the status that Celmins imagined for her art: still and dead.

The photograph makes its official entrance into Celmins' practice without much fanfare, merely to carry out a simple task. A problem needs to be solved. Though plain and straightforward, the artist's paintings of isolated items found in her studio – a fish, hotplate, lemon, radio, paint tube, fan, kettle, heater – reveal a noticeable degree of indecision concerning how exactly to pose the figure within the rectangular field. Some paintings showcase the object in the centre, others nudge it to the side; sometimes it rests against the bottom edge of the canvas, as if it were about to tumble out of the picture space entirely; at other times it's safely nested in a deep shadowy middle-ground. Celmins deposits things on shelves or tabletops set flush against a wall, or she reels in the ground plane like a drawbridge until it stands upright like a wall, against which she pins the object *trompe-l'oeil* style. In at least two instances – with a coffee pot and a banana – Celmins went so far as to cut out the painted object and hang it as a flat, profiled relief. Not only did she paint a portrait of her space heater, she also made a life-size, three-dimensional replica of it, which she then exhibited complete with a faux electric cord plugged into the gallery wall socket. It's as if Celmins were trying to coax the surrounding space out of its passive neutrality, to make the spatial container equal the tension welling in the object, to inflate it with the same mix of precariousness and resignation. And it's in her search for an answer that she discovers a role for photography in her practice following the object paintings. She begins taking snapshots explicitly to aid in certain paintings, and she begins to base works on found photographs she culls from thrift stores and old books.

The photograph ends up solving for Celmins

Time Magazine Cover
1965
Oil on canvas
40.5 × 56 cm
16 × 22 in

Gun with Hand #1
1964
Oil on canvas
62 × 87.5 cm
24.5 × 34.5 in

below, working photograph by the artist
1964

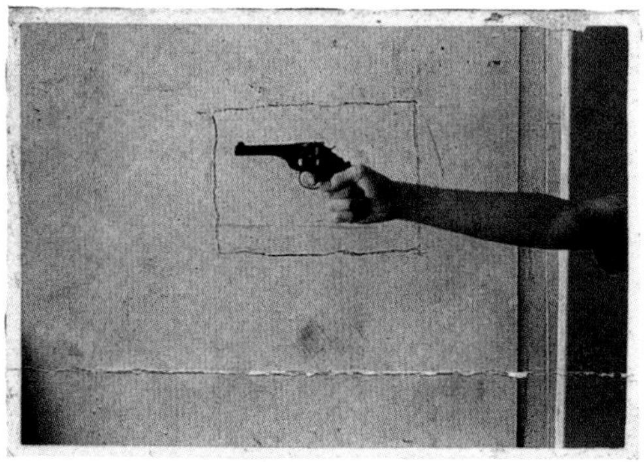

the problem of the field, precisely as it replaces and becomes the object that she renders. Or rather, the photograph offers itself as at once object and field. 'I treat the photograph as an object', she remarks, 'an object to scan'.[30] The two are inextricably bound, as if a seamless continuity exists between the object featured in a photograph and the photograph itself as an object, albeit an object that is nothing but a field: a flat, all-over surface. More importantly, the photograph fuses object and field by suspending both in time, trapping them together in a single, frozen moment. That moment is what makes the photograph an indivisible whole, one homogenous, congealed unit. But thus objectified, the photograph also shows that moment to be itself suspended, orphaned outside the temporal continuum, an artifact broken off from duration, exiled. (Celmins titles one of her early paintings, based on a photograph of a World War II bomber, *Suspended Plane* [1966].) The photograph captures fleeting life and paralyzes it, making it still and dead.

Celmins charts this important transition in her work with a series of canvases from 1964. In each a six-cylinder revolver is steadied in the centre of a blank field by an anonymous forearm reaching in from the right. The paintings – including *Pistol*, *Gun with Hand #1* and the now-destroyed *Six Barrel* – were based on a photograph that Celmins took of a friend levelling the gun as if about to shoot. The paintings all depict the moment when the shot is fired; as the fist tightens, the trigger is squeezed and smoke suddenly empties from the chamber. In many ways the scene is typical of Celmins: the act of firing is rendered oddly intransitive, like a sovereign entity not tethered to any larger story, to a protagonist who takes aim, or an antagonist who's targeted. The only thing that seems uncharacteristic is that Celmins has digressed from her source material, created a fiction by making up parts of the picture. In the photograph the gun never goes off; the smoke pouring from the barrel has been added by the artist after the fact. And yet, what Celmins perhaps captures here is not so much the shooting of a bullet as the event unleashed by the photograph itself – that is, the shooting of a picture. The paintings portray an event that did in fact occur, an event crucial to Celmins' art: the aiming of a camera, a shutter clicking, an exposure being made; all happening in a flash.

In the mid-1960s many painters turned to photographs not just as source material and studio aid but as their primary subject matter. There are the examples already mentioned, like Artschwager, Close, Morely and Richter; there are also neo-dadaists like Rauschenberg, Bruce Conner and George Herms, as well as pop artists like Warhol and Tom Wesselmann. Ed Ruscha began collecting his prosaic snapshots into small books like *Twenty-Six Gasoline Stations* (1962) and *Every Building on the Sunset Strip* (1966). Photographs came to play a pivotal role as documentation of happenings, performances and conceptual art, and even formalist painters drew from the medium of photography, especially as increased emphasis on staining and process meant having to cut out or crop final paintings from larger expanses of marked canvas ('cropping was something new,'

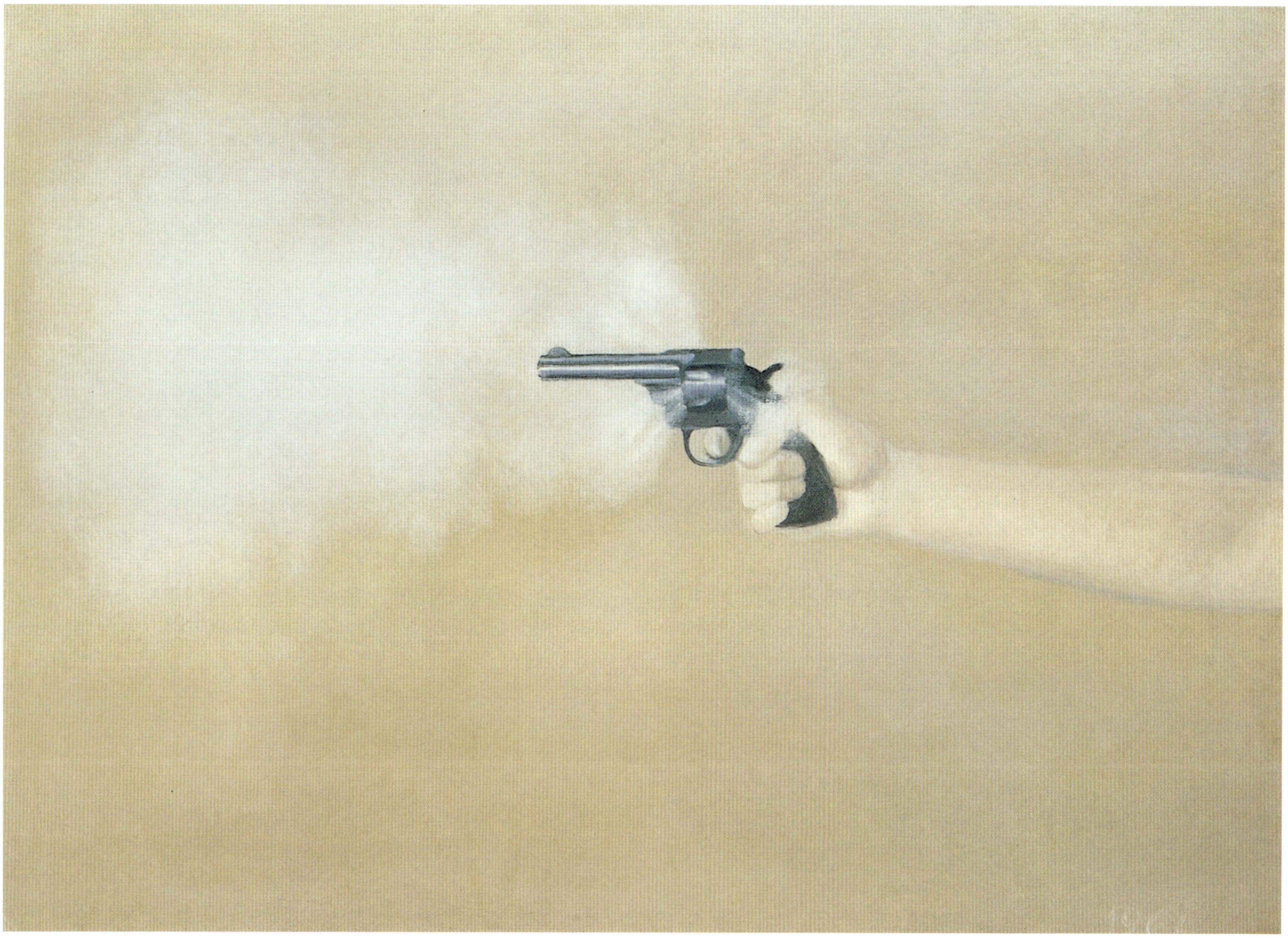

Pistol
1964
Oil on canvas
62 × 87.5 cm
24.5 × 34.5 in

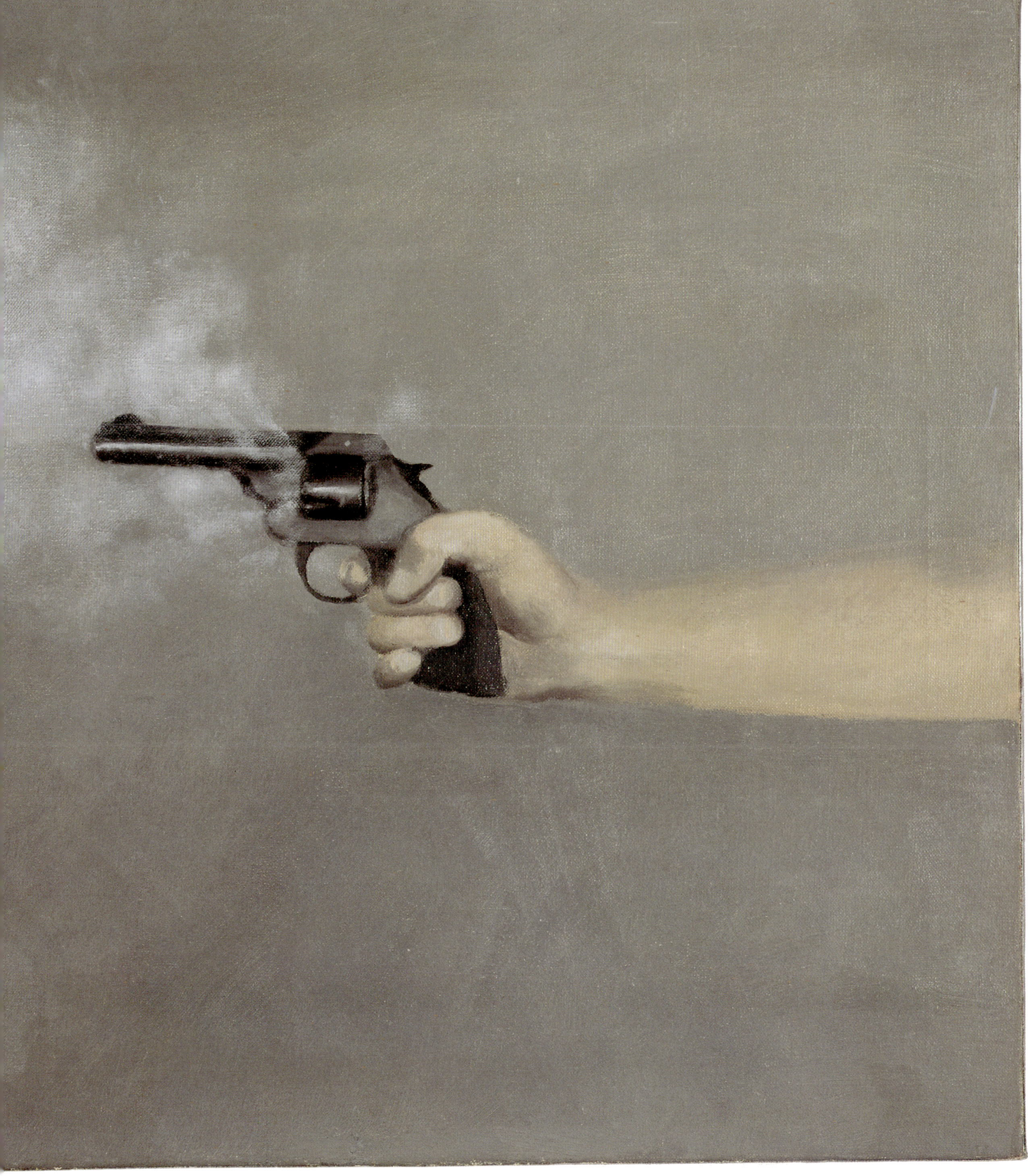

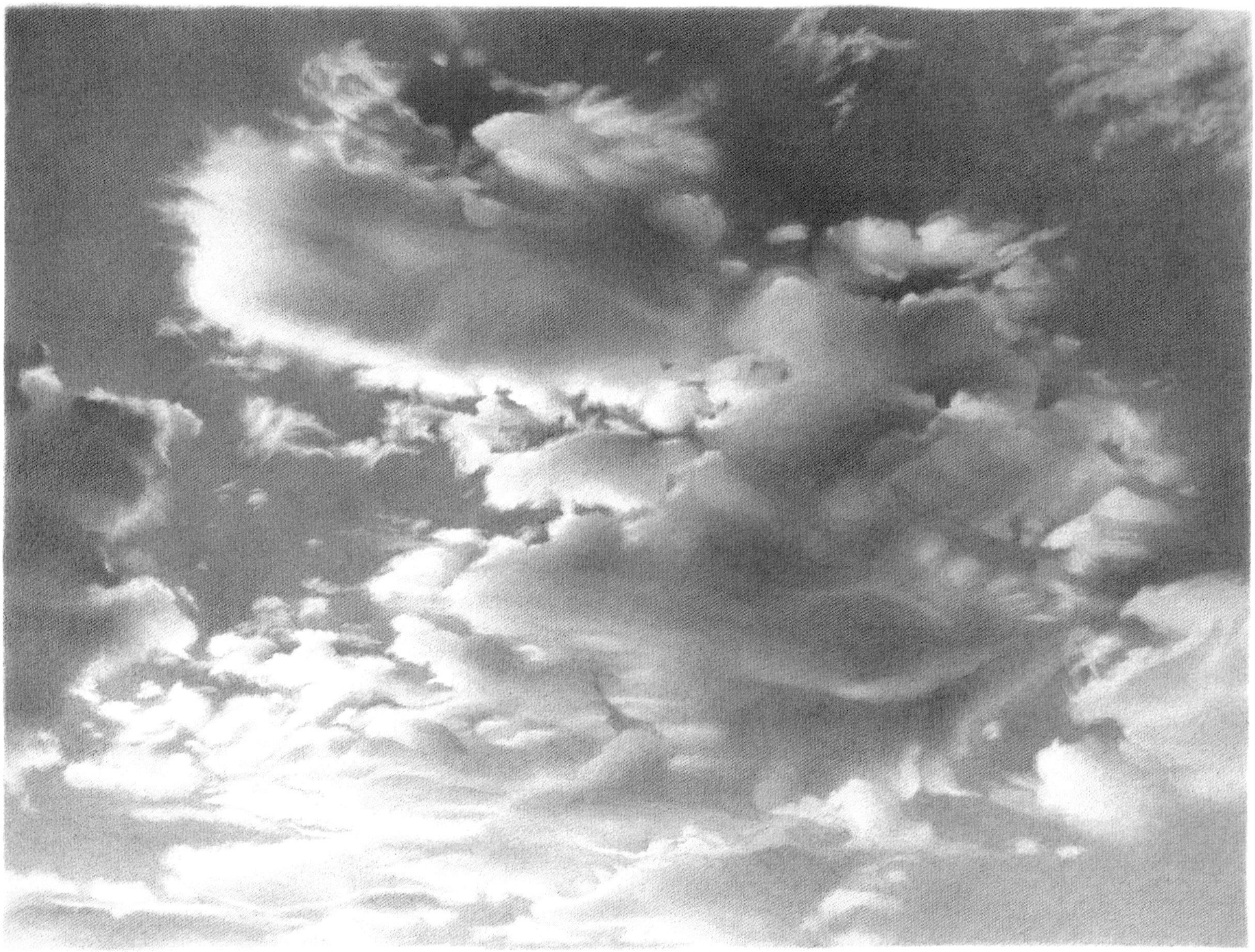

claims Kenneth Noland, and 'it came from photography').[31] Possible reasons for this phenomenon abound, foremost among them being simply the explosion of reproductions and media images that, as everyone noticed at the time, was suddenly inundating the art world. Henry Geldzahler puzzled over 'the new availability of a much wider range of images' in 1965:

'We have ARTnews*, Harry Abrams, Phaidon, André Malraux, and jet travel – instant international communication. Between them nothing is unavailable. This ... multiplies incalculably the amount of visual material that can, and in many cases must, be brought to bear in the intelligent appreciation of contemporary art.'*[32]

Allan Kaprow had put it more bluntly just a few months earlier: 'Picasso competes with Walt Disney who in turn competes with "Mary Worth".'[33] More and more artworks and artists were being reported on by popular media, featured in general-interest magazines, documentary films and television shows, and popular media in turn were

above, **Clouds**
1965–69
Graphite on paper
35 × 47 cm
13.75 × 18.5 in

opposite, artist's source material photograph from Surveyor I

infiltrating the artistic process, with more magazines and TVs crowding into studios, and their imagery and apparatus crowding into actual works of art. Indeed, among the appliances that Celmins painted in 1964 was her TV set (*T.V.*, 1964).

Preoccupation among artists with all things photographic was bestowed official art-world recognition by mid-decade. Bracketing the events of 1966 (the year that Minimalism was canonized in such shows as 'Primary Structures' at the Jewish Museum, New York, and 'Systemic Painting' at the Solomon R. Guggenheim Museum, New York) was the exhibition 'The Photographic Image' – which opened at the Guggenheim in January and included Artschwager and Morley as well as Lynn Foulkes, Suzi Gablik, Joseph Raffaele, Rauschenberg and Warhol – and the publication in *Arts Magazine*'s December issue of Dan Graham's *Homes for America*. As Graham and other Conceptual artists demonstrated, reproductions in magazines and catalogues were considered not only a means of circulating artworks but capable of serving as the very medium of art. In addition to all this, many artists were swept up in the enthusiasm over emerging space-age photographic technologies, especially in Southern California, where the close proximity of NASA's Jet Propulsion Laboratory (JPL) encouraged the establishment of the Los Angeles County Museum's Art and Technology Program between 1966 and 1971. The influence of space-exploration imagery is found, for example, in Bruce Nauman's 1967 *My Name as Though It Were Written on the Surface of the Moon*, as well as in Celmins' 1969 drawings of lunar and Martian surfaces based on JPL photographs.

But there's another reason behind photography's appeal at the time, particularly among painters. The photograph was seen as answering afresh the dictates of modernist painting; that is, with its immediacy and consistency of image detail, the photograph was thought to perpetuate what Lawrence Alloway described, while writing on artists' use of photography in the 1960s, 'abstract painting [and its] many ways of achieving the twentieth-century dream of an instant, unrevised, all-at-once art form'.[34] The critic William Dyckes, too, urged people 'to think of Photo Realism in terms of field painting instead of Pop art'.[35] What Dyckes refers to as 'field painting' reached its apogee in the mid-1960s, with crowning surveys like Clement Greenberg's 'Post-Painterly Abstraction' mounted at the Los Angeles County Museum in 1964, followed a year later by Michael Fried's 'Three American Painters' at Harvard's Fogg Art Museum in Cambridge, Massachusetts. Like Pop and Minimalism, colour-field painting was often praised as an antidote to 1950s gestural abstraction. Fried, for example, appreciated the 'sovereign impersonality' of Morris Louis' canvases, how they appeared to have been made without any subjective interference, as if automatically, much as a camera makes a photograph. Louis's 'best paintings', in Fried's estimation, succeed by 'seeming to have come into existence as if of their own accord ... as if the paint *expressed itself* upon the canvas through the painter, and not at all as if the painter expressed himself through the medium of paint'.[36]

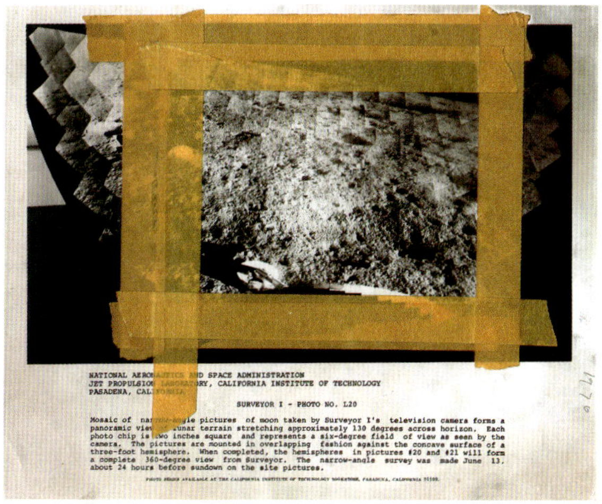

Moon Surface (Luna 9) #1
1969
Graphite on acrylic ground on paper
35 × 47 cm
13.875 × 18.5 in
Collection The Museum of Modern Art, New York

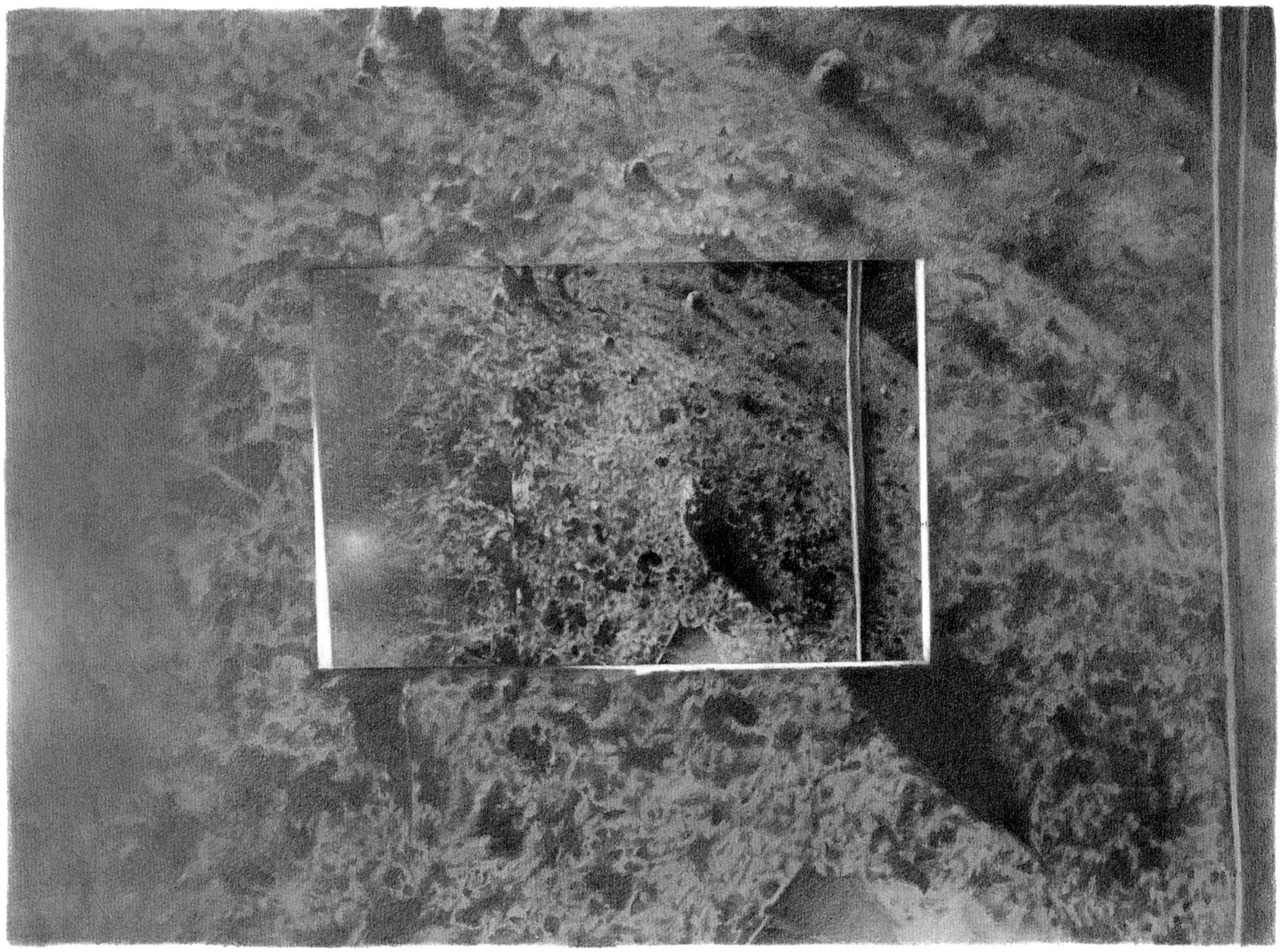

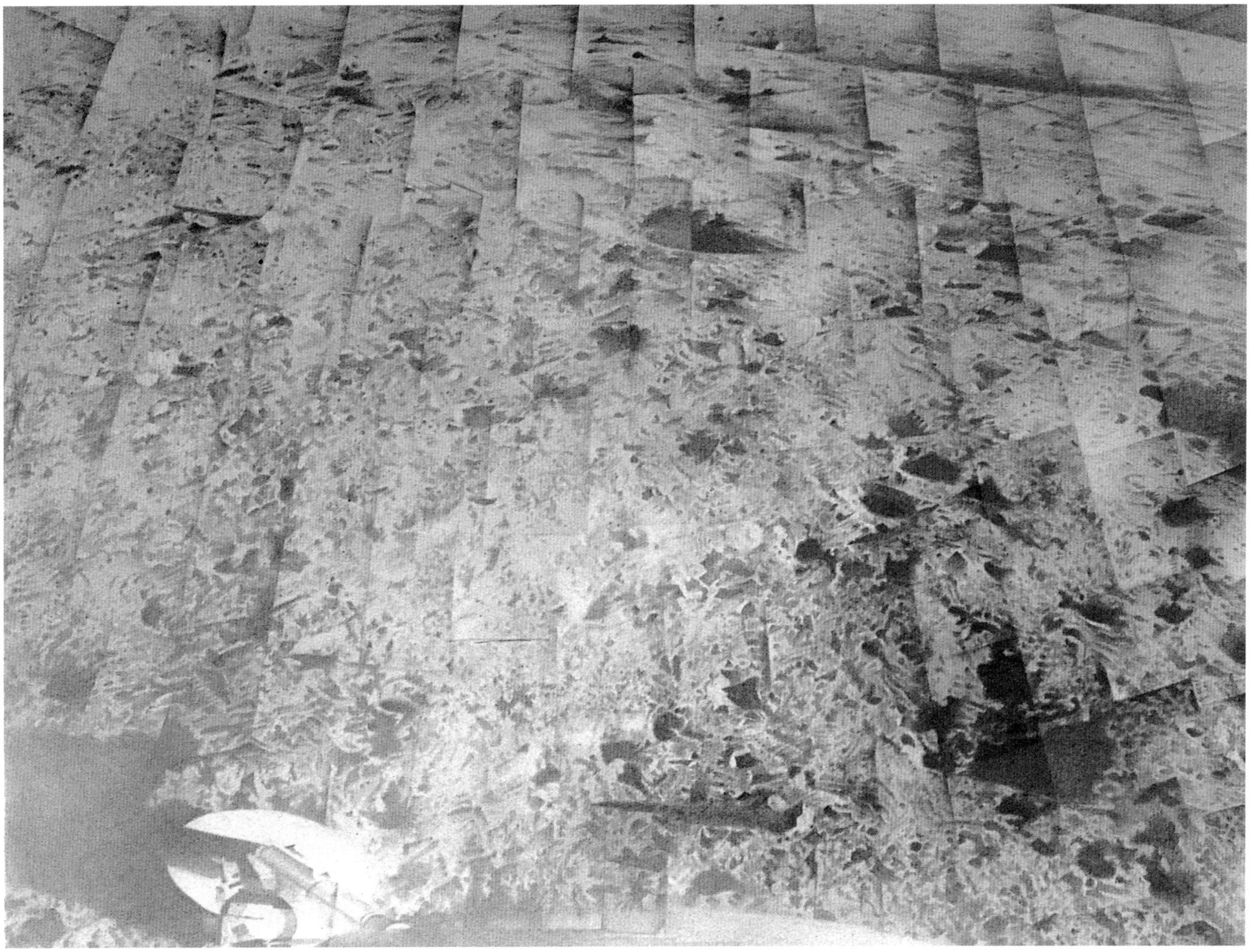

Moon Surface (Surveyor I)
1971–72
Graphite on acrylic ground on paper
35.5 × 47 cm
14 × 18.5 in

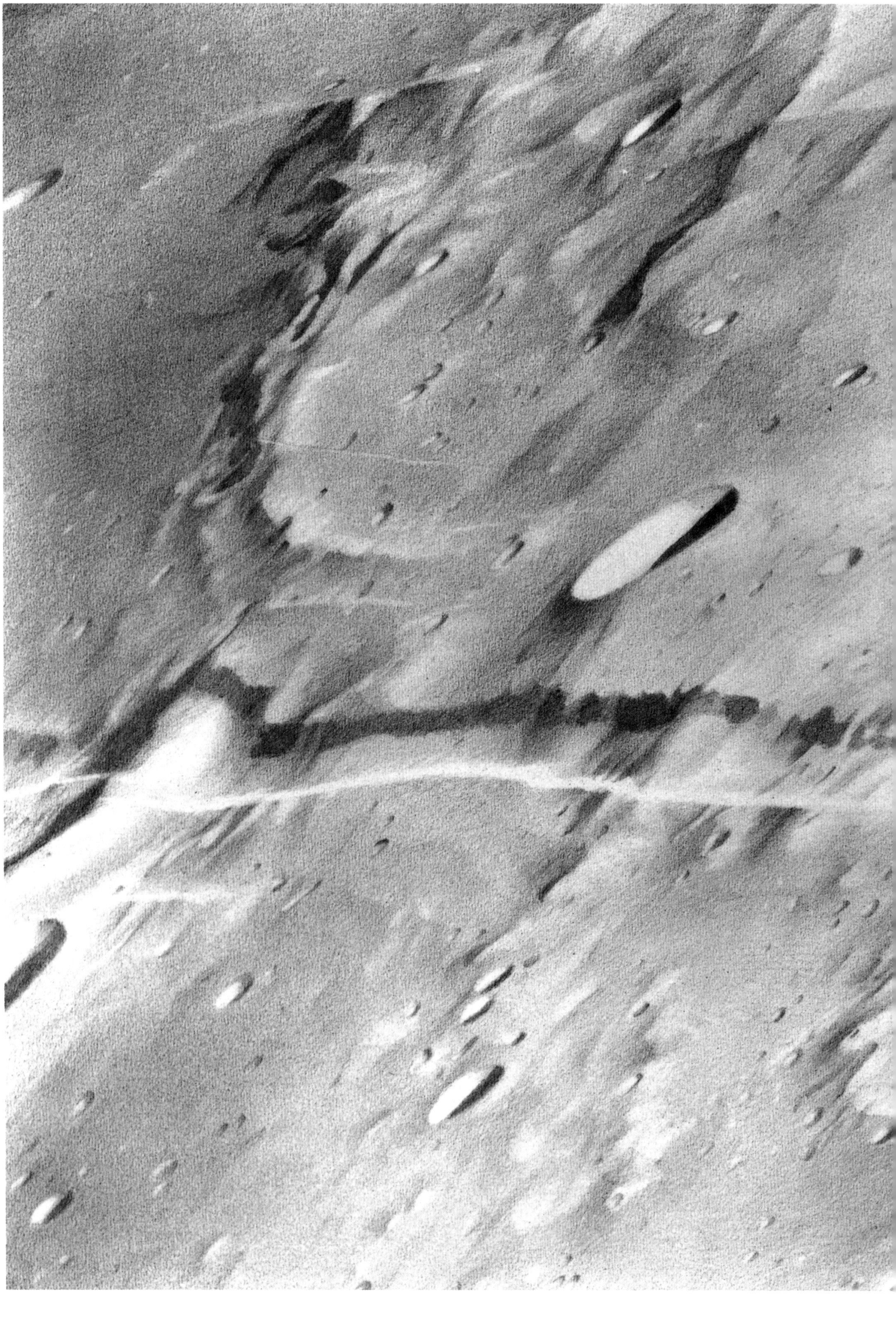

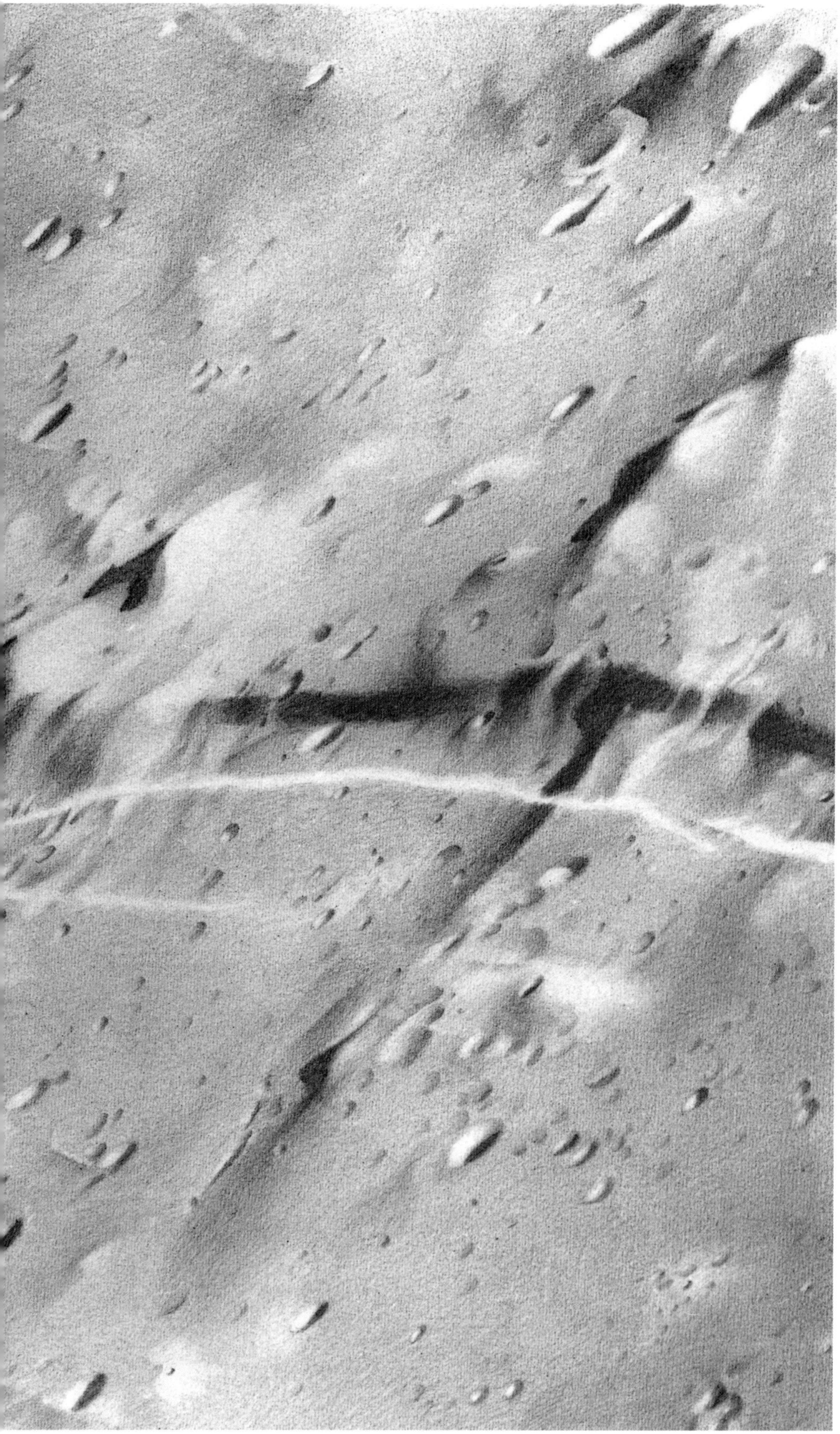

Untitled (Moon Surface #1)
1969
Graphite on acrylic ground on paper
35.5 × 47.5 cm
14 × 18.75 in

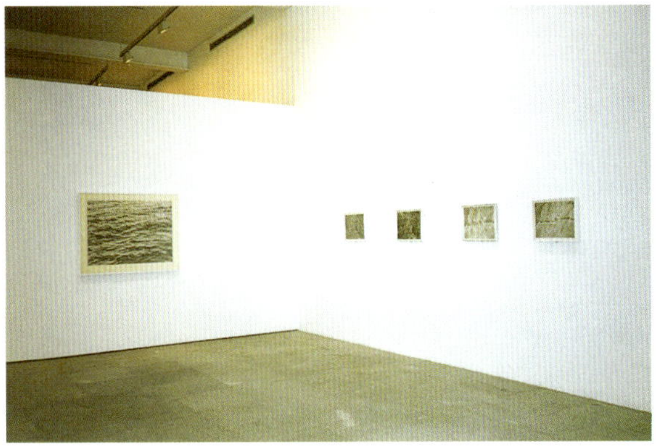

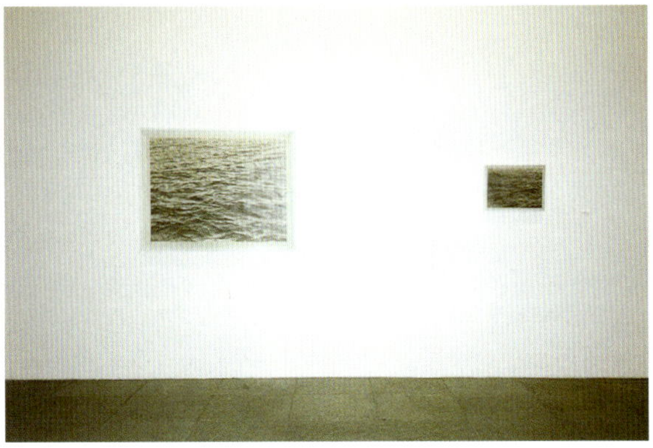

Installation views, 'Vija Celmins Works 1964–1996', Museo Nacional Centro de Arte Reina Sofia, Madrid, 1997

It wasn't long after Celmins adopted photographs as her subject matter that she began rummaging for – and taking her own snapshots of – flat, all-over fields. After 1966 the only objects she allowed herself to render on paper or canvas were flat – a letter, say, or a picture torn from a book. Anything more volumetric ends up as sculpture. (Likewise, with the sculptures there's a new emphasis on evenness: the *Pencil*, *Comb* and *Pink Pearl Erasers* of the late 1960s are all materially and formally one thing through and through, inside out and beginning to end; moreover, together they seem to imply the action required by the newly all-over, two-dimensional work – the depositing and removal, even the raking and combing, of graphite across a flat field.) Increasingly, Celmins' pictures refer to an external world only as that world in turn metaphorically figures her artistic medium. By 1968 her source materials are predominantly photographs of evenly spread surfaces – water as it spreads out into an ocean, land as it spreads out into a desert. She still paints things 'one at a time', eliminating any play of differences: there are no coastlines or trees or landmarks, no framing devices, no composing of distinct elements into hierarchies of attention. Nothing distracts from the even saturation of either the photographic exposure or the finely articulated, recreated flatness of the drawing or painting based on it.

More than the all-over flatness of her seas, deserts and skies, it's the photograph itself that provides Celmins with a way succinctly to answer the demands of 'field painting'. For one thing, photography is 'exact to the point of disarray', as Roger Fry put it, and thus notoriously veers from strict hierarchic compositions. Rather it tends to turn out images in which, as Greenberg wrote of colour-field painting, 'there are no longer centres of interest, highlights, dominating forms, every part ... being equivalent in stress to every other part.'[37] The emulsion's openness to imprinting, its global responsiveness, floods the photograph edge to edge with detail, and the results draw close to the quality that Fried discovered in Pollock's drip paintings, the 'visual fabric' of which 'invites the act of seeing ... and yet gives the eye nowhere to rest once and for all'.[38] But all-overness was not the only requirement of field painting. Indeed, Greenberg frequently worried over 'the danger of monotony that arises from the even, all-over design'. 'Painting of a kind that identifies itself exclusively with its surface', he wrote, 'cannot help developing toward decoration'. All-overness and the unlimited lateral extension it threatened had to be balanced by unity and 'at-onceness'. 'Ideally the whole of a picture should be taken in at a glance', Greenberg continued, 'in an indivisible instant of time ... all there at once, like a sudden revelation'.[39] As with all-overness, the photograph supplies just as promptly, automatically as it were, this 'delimiting of flatness'. Photography imposes at-onceness with the decisiveness of a judge's gavel, stopping spatial extension with its merciless crop, and freezing temporal extension with its sudden shutter click.

Of course, Celmins' work also departs from field painting in crucial respects. Albeit impersonal, the aim of colour-field painting was certainly not to swing dialectical emphasis back to

Untitled (Ocean)
1968
Pencil on paper
37 × 50 cm
14.5 × 19.75 in

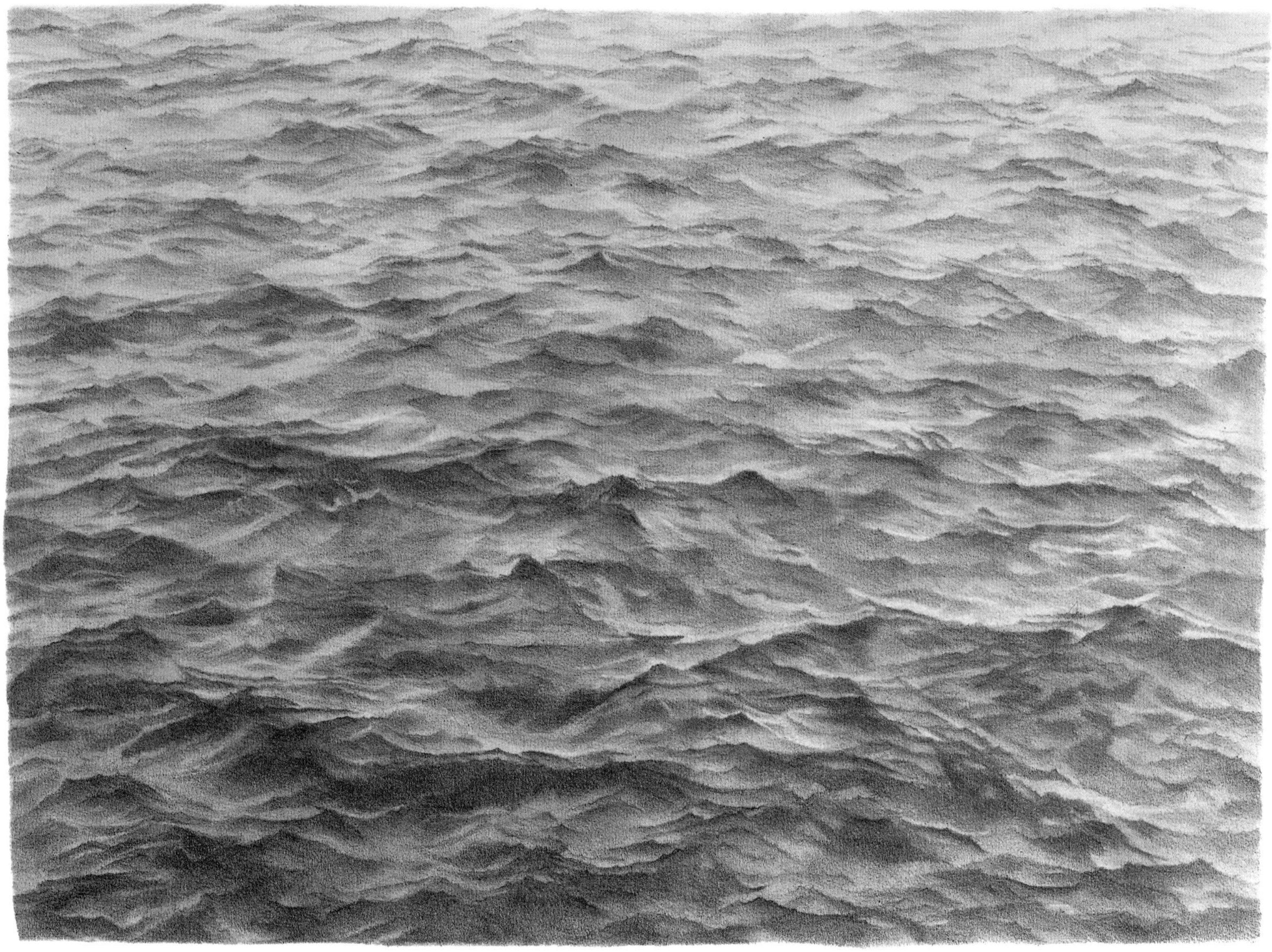

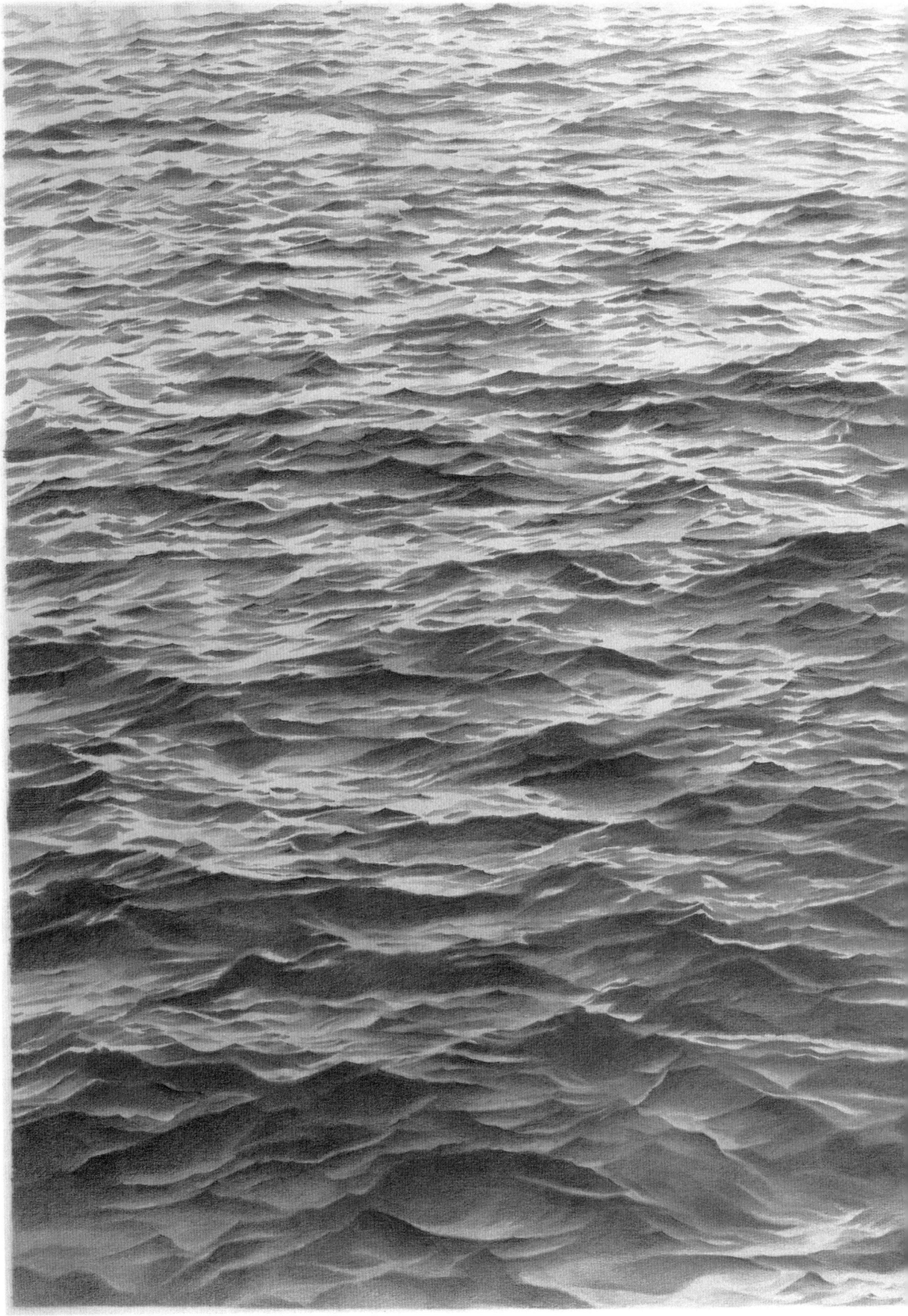

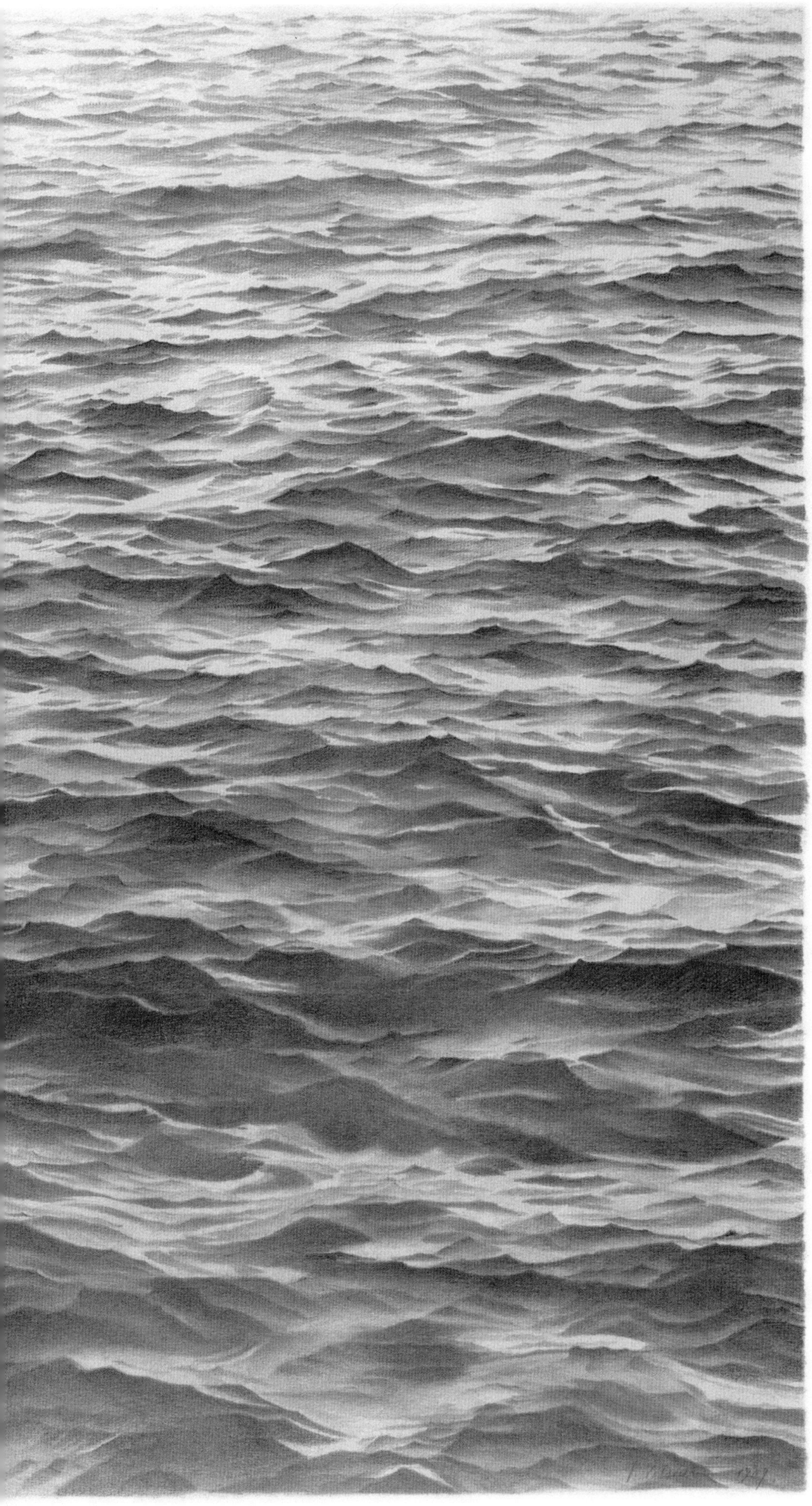

Untitled (Big Sea #1)
1969
Graphite on acrylic ground on paper
86.5 × 115 cm
34.125 × 45.25 in

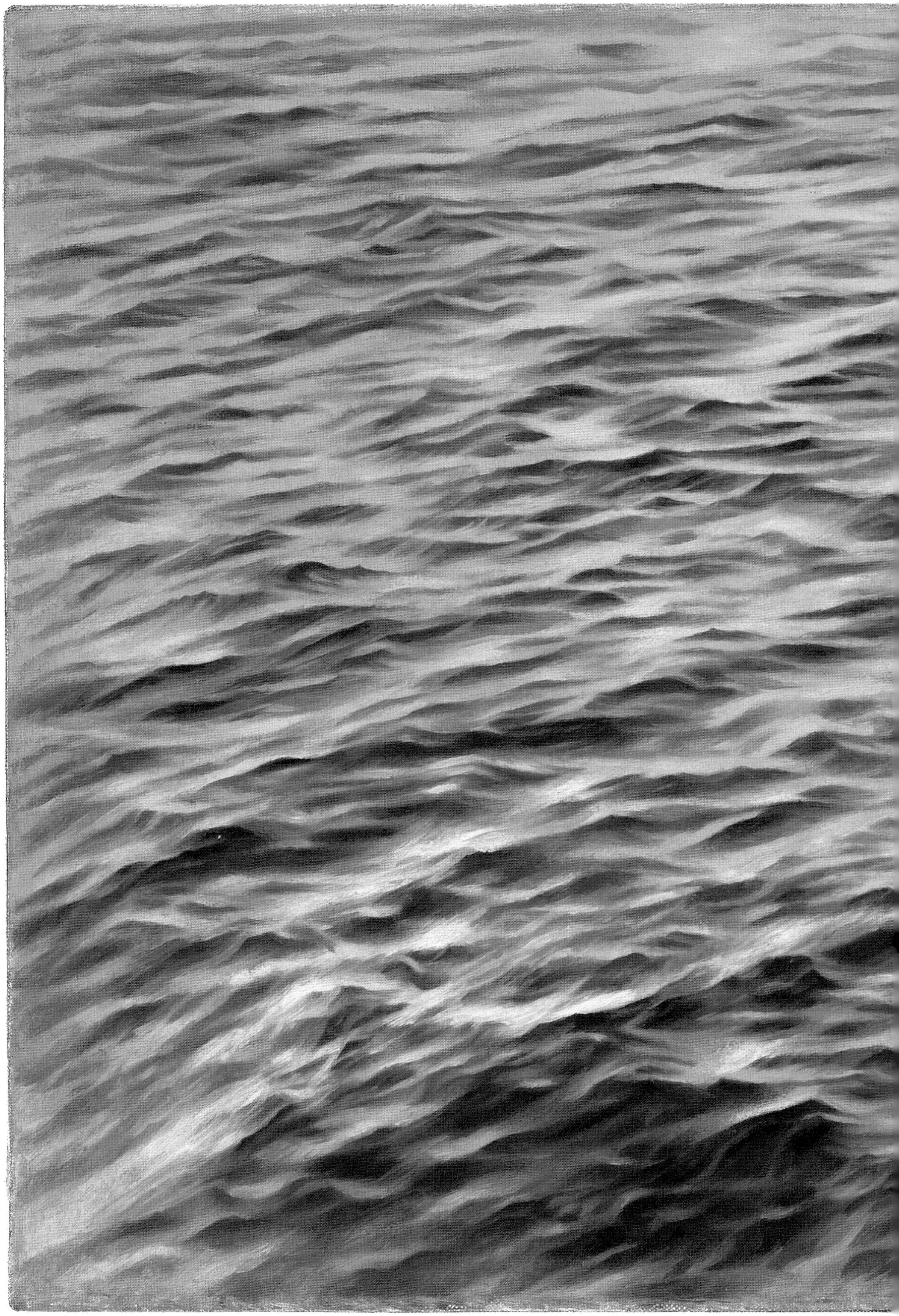

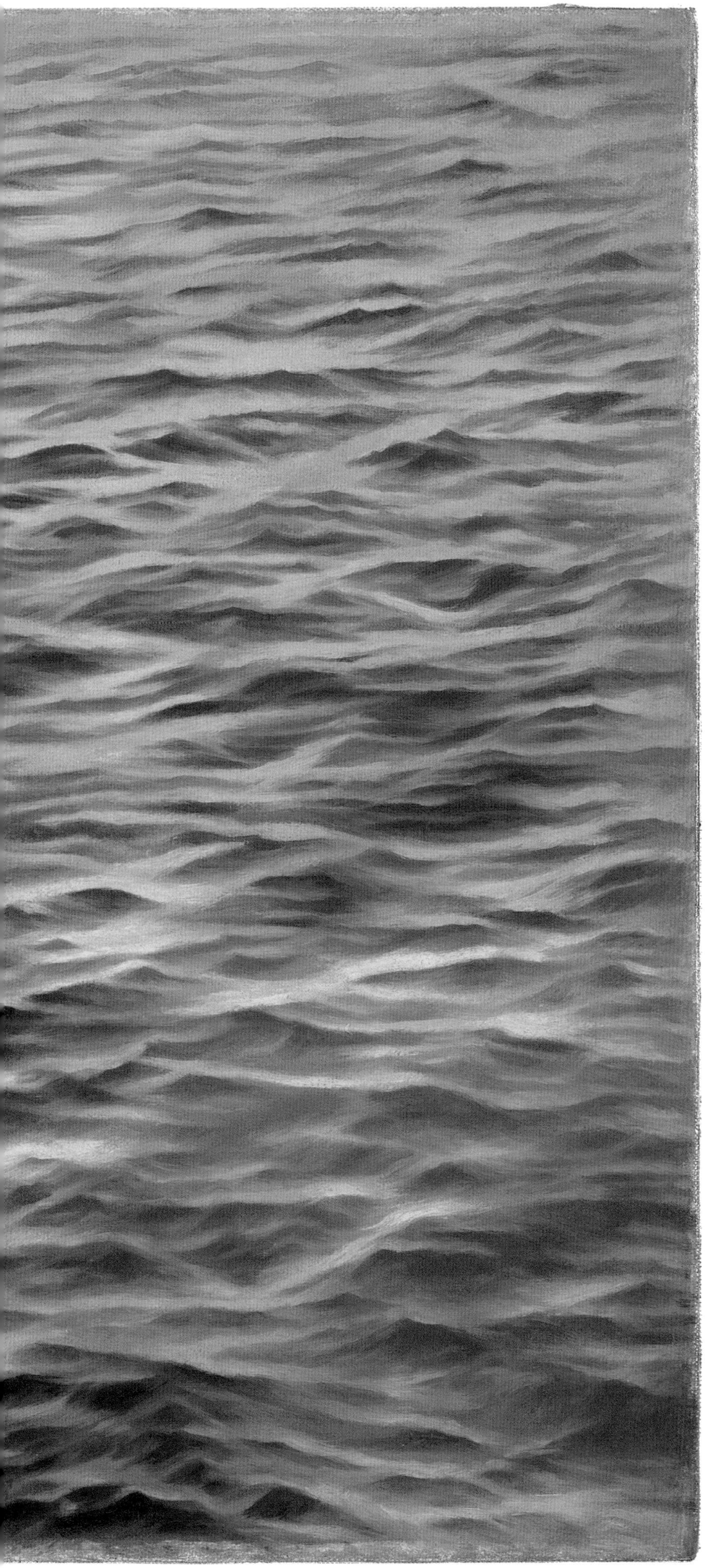

Untitled (Ocean)
1990–95
Oil on linen
38.5 × 47.5 cm
15.25 × 18.75 in

Untitled (Double Desert)
1974
Graphite on acrylic ground on paper
31 × 61 cm
12.25 × 24 in

the object. Instead, such art sought to manifest a transcendent opticality, to bring human vision *per se* into fuller possession of itself; the fields it unscrolled were described as accessible 'to eyesight alone', as offering no lingering allusions to material, tactile things. Indeed, Fried would pit field painting in stark opposition to what he called the 'objecthood' of much 1960s art, particularly Minimalist sculpture. The priority that field painting gave to colour meant inversely that it needed to abolish any suggestion of value distinctions, of modelling with lights and darks, precisely the opposite of Celmins' approach. But not only did Celmins subtract nearly all colour from her fields, she also jettisoned paint itself. At the very moment when she decided to move from rendering objects to rendering surfaces, she also changed media, and began working primarily with graphite on paper. It's as if she were trying to emulate more closely the photograph's fine grain, its balance of density and fragility, choosing not to spread paint with a brush since, while useful for making a field painting, this risked building up a sumptuous presence too disengaged from her photographic source. Once again Celmins deflates her means, constrains it as a way to get outside herself. Obviously she wanted a utensil with a more precise point, as if she were intending to perform a very specific task, a kind of surgery, to operate on her source exactly and not gesture towards it vaguely. Celmins takes up drawing as a way through which to identify the field of her work more strongly with the photograph, and to identify the photograph's field all the more as a resistant

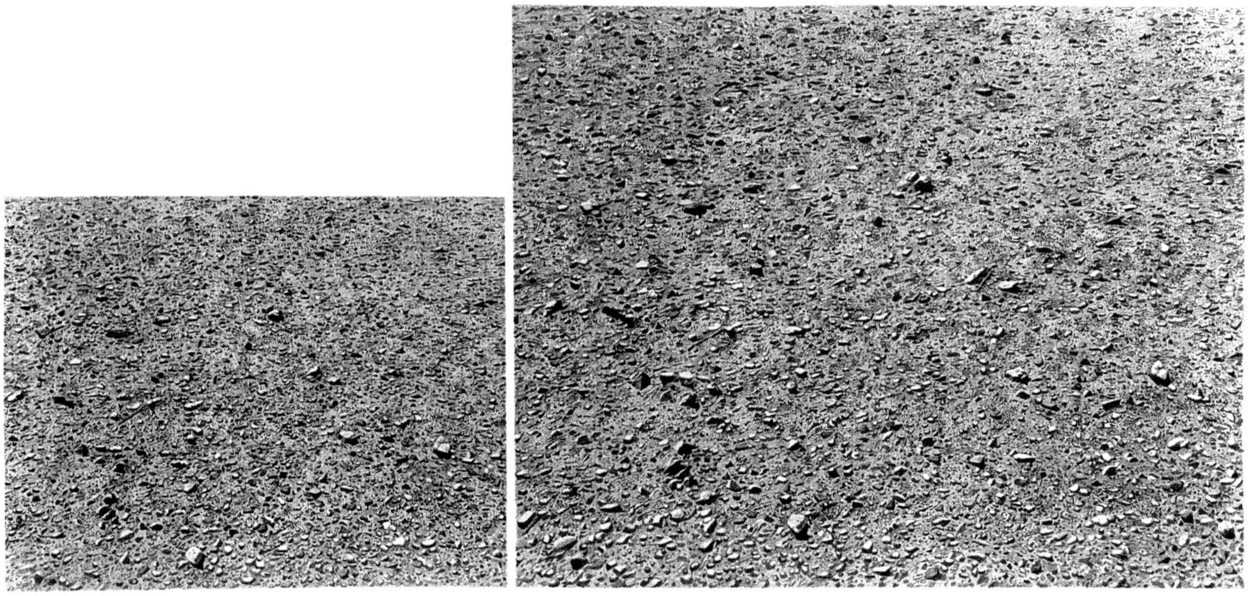

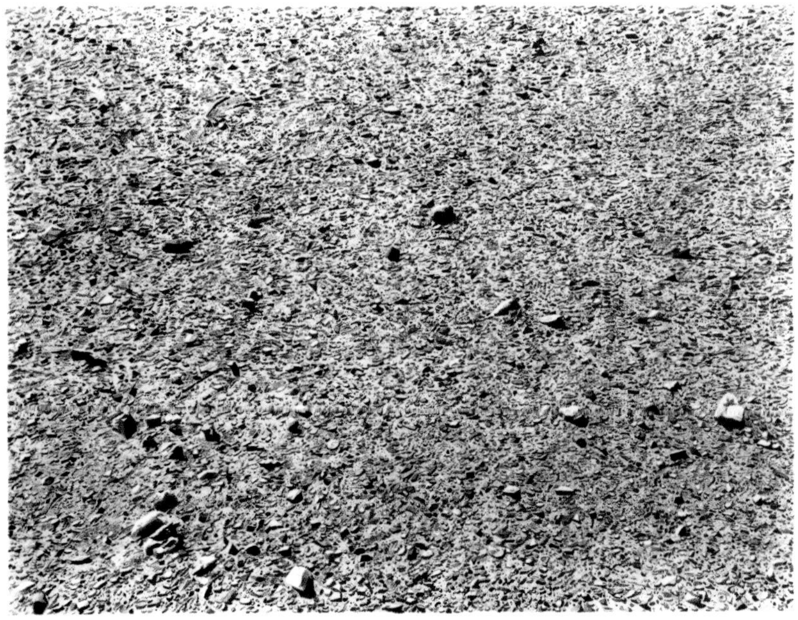

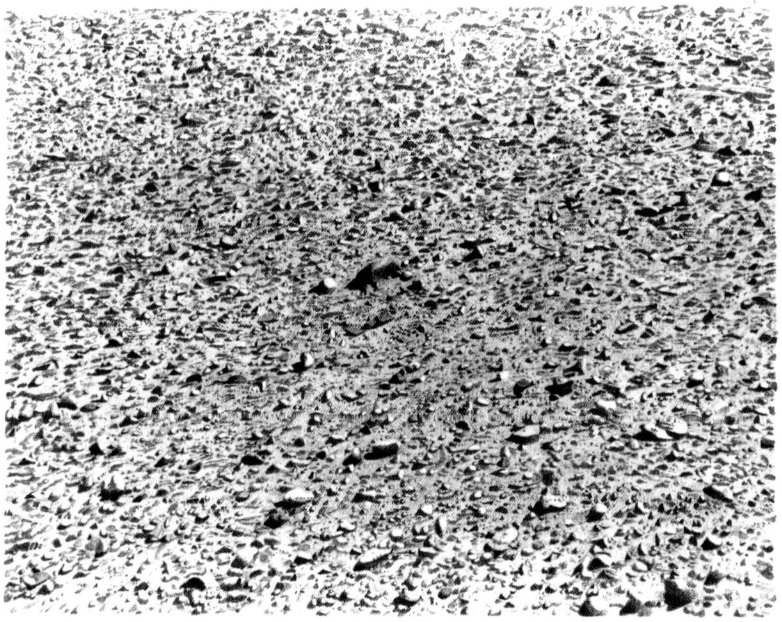

object confronting her.

From 1969 to the present, as the swaying seas yield to motionless archaic deserts that in turn give way to timeless faraway skies, Celmins' pictures increasingly level out and calm down, but never does the imagery coincide exactly with the work's actual hard, still surface. The more insistently the images press against the picture plane, revealing themselves to be only deposited graphite or oil, the farther away they nevertheless appear, 'constantly out of reach', to quote Robbe-Grillet again. A dialectic of sorts can be found undergoing rehabilitation here, even if it's not the barrel-chested version for which Rosenberg had pined. Celmins' use of drawing is a case in point: it's long been a staple of art education that drawing, more than painting and sculpture, approximates most closely to the artist's mind, that it's least burdened by the stubbornness and particularity of materials and therefore reveals ideas and inspiration more transparently. Thus it's heavily identified with the creative subject; indeed, draughtsmanship, the ability to bestow beautiful form through line and contour, is often treated as synonymous with artistic genius itself. But Celmins doesn't use drawing in this way; in fact, she only devotes herself to the medium once line has completely vanished from her pictures, once her images have grown most formless. Line ends up migrating to her sculptures (think of *Comb*), making them more like drawings, while her drawings in turn become all the more material,

above, left, **Untitled (Large Desert)**
1974–75
Graphite on acrylic ground on paper
48.5 × 62 cm
19 × 24.5 in

above, right, **Untitled (Regular Desert)**
1973
Graphite on acrylic ground on paper
30.5 × 38 cm
12 × 15 in

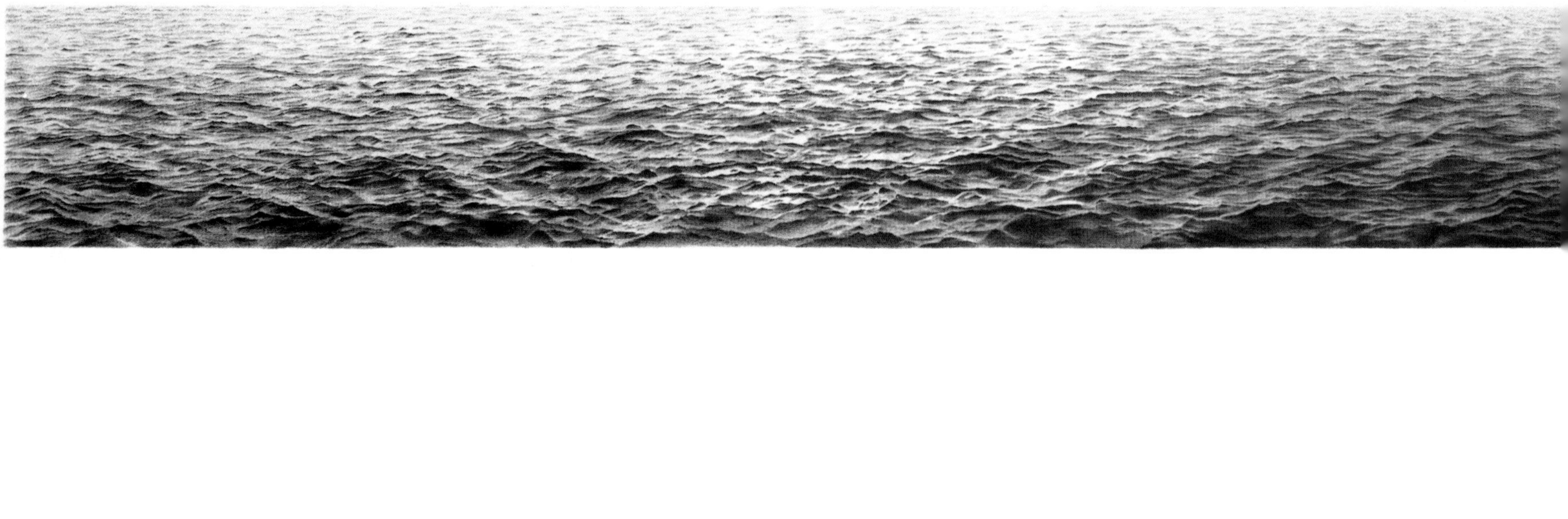

almost sculptural, like objects (Celmins describes them as 'really full', 'dense' and 'fat').

But no matter how densely Celmins packs her all-over pictures, the photographic reference always hollows them back out again, by appealing to a reality beyond the material facts of pencil lead or paint. 'Reference', Barthes writes, 'is the founding order of Photography'.[40] And this reference itself always points in two directions, claiming simultaneously its own sudden presence as well as an unavoidable displacement. Like Celmins' painting of the smoking gun, the photograph is simultaneously a bang and a dispersal. 'It has been here', as Barthes reads the photographic image, 'and yet immediately separated; it has been absolutely, irrefutably present, and already deferred'. It could be argued that what Celmins' drawings and paintings depict, what they refer to, is even further split and displaced. On the one hand there is a specific reality, a precise moment in time and location in space, the hyper-detailed character of which has long dissolved back into flux by the time the photograph has captured it indexically and turned over its remains to Celmins' art. And on the other hand there is the image's iconic side, its pared-down conceptual identity, the single noun that comes to mind ('sea', 'desert', 'sky'), which, in opposition to the indexical, is entirely static and general, without specific time or place. The first indexical referent stands on the side of the object and the past – this small parcel of reality as it was constituted in the camera's eye for a split second before perishing forever, and which leaves behind only this skid-mark of abundant particularity imprinted in the photo-emulsion. Meanwhile, the other, iconic referent is weighted on the side of the subject and the present, as a vivid materialization and confirmation of a bit of language and knowledge, a metaphor or figure of speech that we rightly feel is ours to keep. This metaphor, like the photograph, is both all-over and at-once – it springs to mind in a flash but is also a generalization, an all-encompassing term. It 'invites the act of seeing ... and yet gives the eye nowhere to rest once and for all'. Celmins' art could perhaps be taken as trying to match exactly this word to its object and thus to marry the coded and uncoded, to perfectly line up the summarizing umbrella term with the index's all-over and at-once referent. And yet never do the two coincide and possess each other; like a gunshot and its echo, they are always slightly out of synch, no matter how much they seem to come from the same place, no matter how hard they try to reach back towards that sense of shared origin.

Tellingly, it's by rendering endless stretches of deserts and oceans, and eventually the open blankness of the night-time sky, that Celmins most firmly establishes homelessness as a dominant motif. The point of view that her art now assumes, either looking down at the ground or up at the sky, suggests a traveller brought to a standstill, shaken loose from a sense of direction or destination. Here, looking itself is rendered intransitive, cut loose from a horizon line to journey towards, from any drama to participate in or other actors and objects to engage with. There are no spotlit landmarks or relevant deeds on which to fix one's eyes; instead there's a looming abstraction – some

opposite, **Long Ocean #1**
1973
Graphite on acrylic ground on paper
76 × 112 cm
30 × 44 in

below, working photograph the ocean from Venice pier

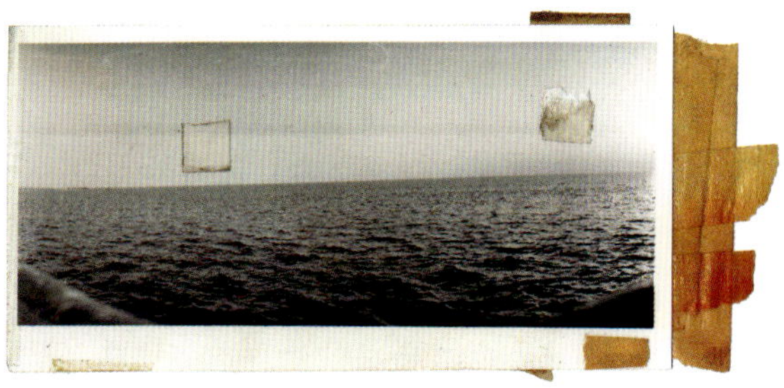

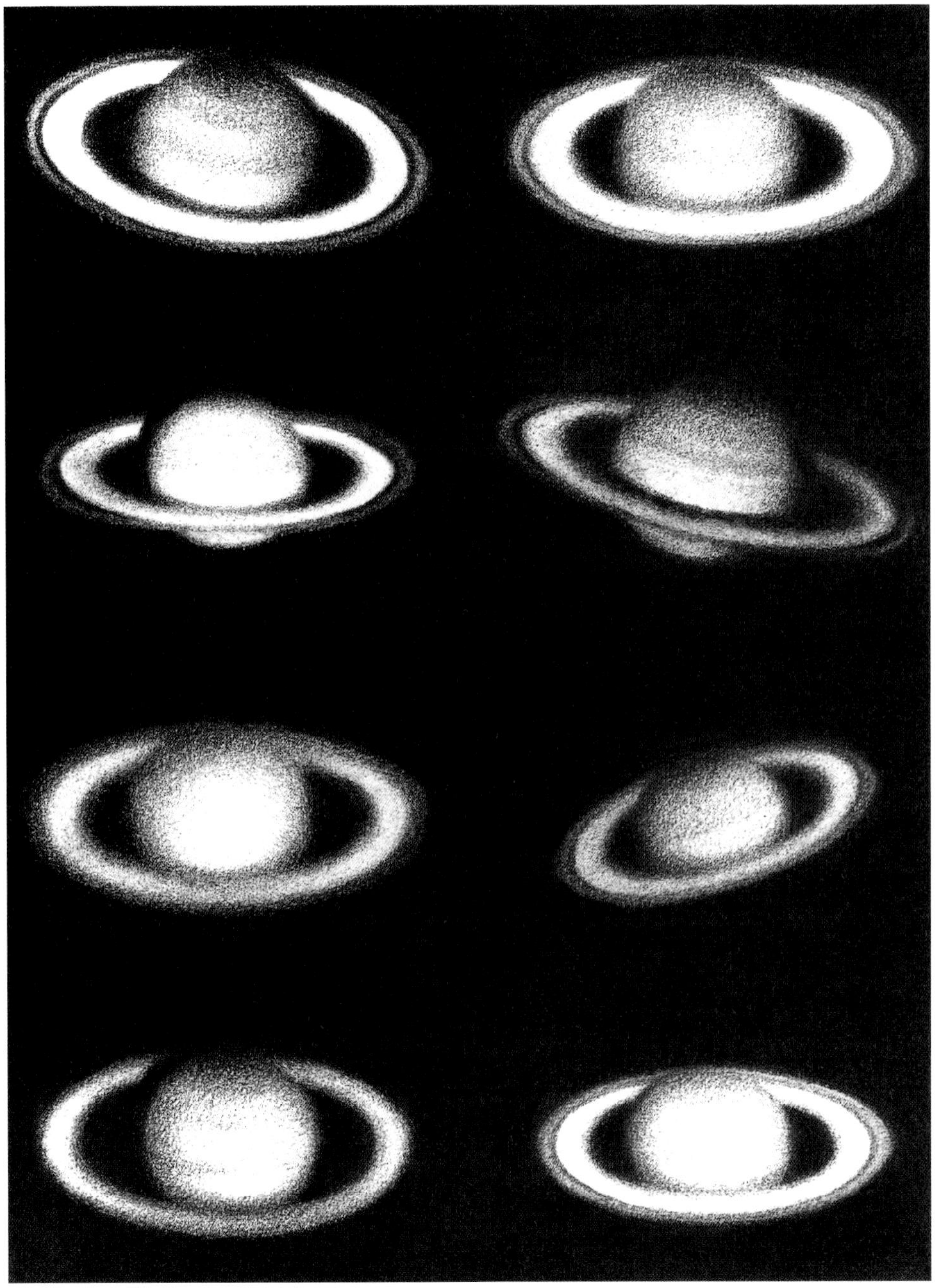

opposite, **Drawing Saturn**
1982
Graphite on acrylic ground on paper
35.5 × 28 cm
14 × 11 in

left, **Star Field I**
1982
Graphite on acrylic ground on paper
53.5 × 70 cm
21 × 27.5 in

ultimate encounter at the farthest end of representation – that belongs as much to a subjective as an objective world, a sense of deliverance and tranquillity at once feared and desired. Celmins' oceans, deserts and starscapes resonate faintly with connotations of high-seas or Saharan adventures, of daring sci-fi space missions, all cultural tropes of risk and discovery. But mostly they evoke primal forms of escape and finality: they promise total submersion, a peaceful blanketing, as well as helplessness, abandonment, loss – at once untold contentment and ultimate desolation.

Perhaps all this applies just as well to Celmins' earlier paintings of domestic objects; in their uncanniness, they too seem to inhabit as much an internal as external realm. But only by travelling so far from the known and familiar, sailing off on

right, **Moving Out (Star Field II)**
1982
Graphite on acrylic ground on paper
53.5 × 68.5 cm
21 × 27 in

opposite, **Star Field III**
1983
Graphite on acrylic ground on paper
53.5 × 68.5 cm
21 × 27 in

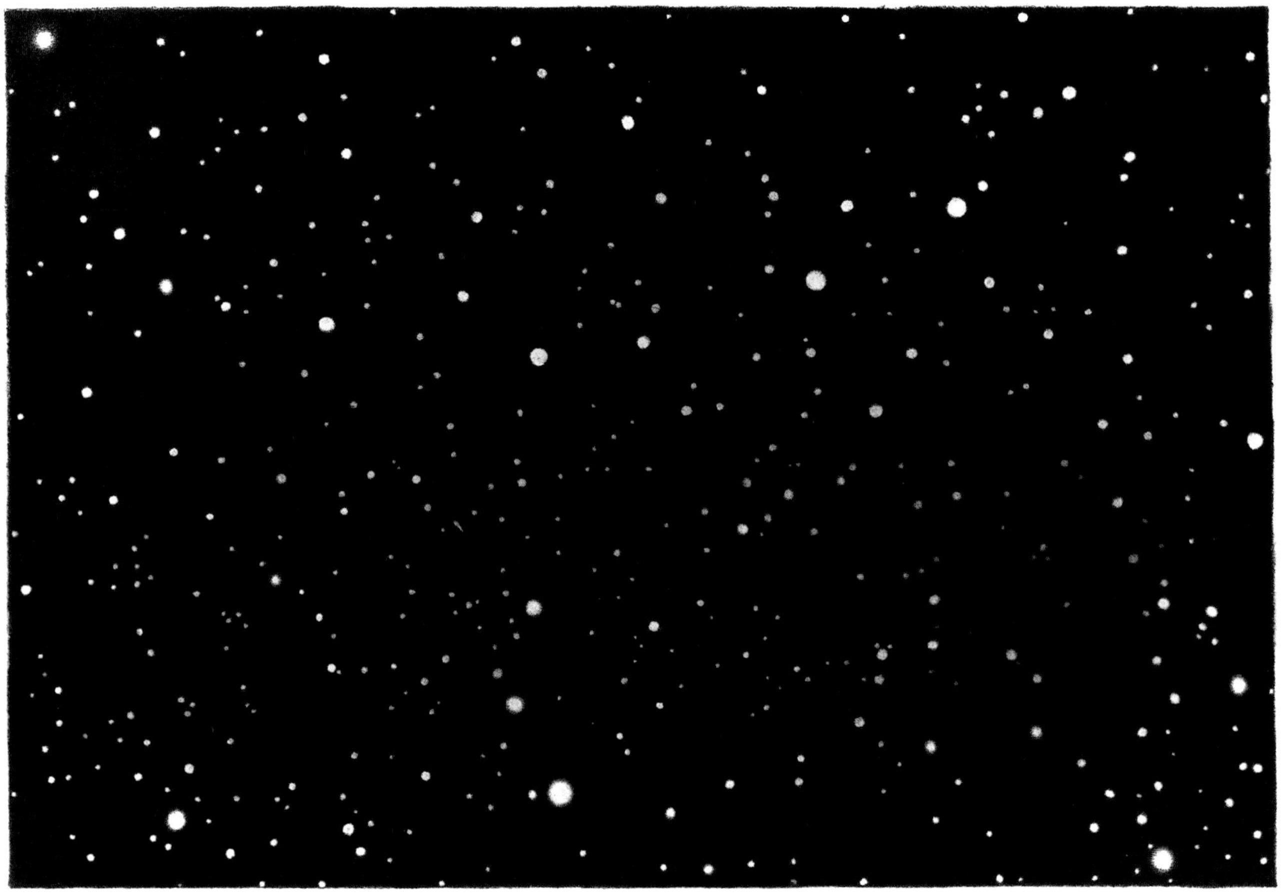

the high seas or into deep space, to the very outskirts of depiction, does Celmins bring into clear view, as if by force of contrast, that sense of a provisional place that her art finally does call its own, a makeshift home-away-from-home that it claims for itself. It's right there in each of her works, discovered amid the strenuous negotiations that constitute their surfaces. Unity and focus emerge at that meeting ground held in place through the dialectics of subject and object, where the artwork and its photographic source each gains definition only by surrendering to its opposite. This is where the photograph comes to the assistance of the drawing or painting, by stopping and framing a world of extension and flux, and also where the artwork in turn comes to stop the extensions of the photograph, its transience and reproducibility, fixing it to a single surface and bestowing on it a unique, one-and-only physical body. This body both resists Celmins and belongs to her; it's made in the likeness of the photograph, which itself is made in the likeness of the word. Celmins reduces to a minimum the space between icon and index, coded and uncoded, as she runs every square inch of the photograph through herself, translates it through eye and hand, gets to know it not as a generality but in its very fibre, its finely grained specificity. She's

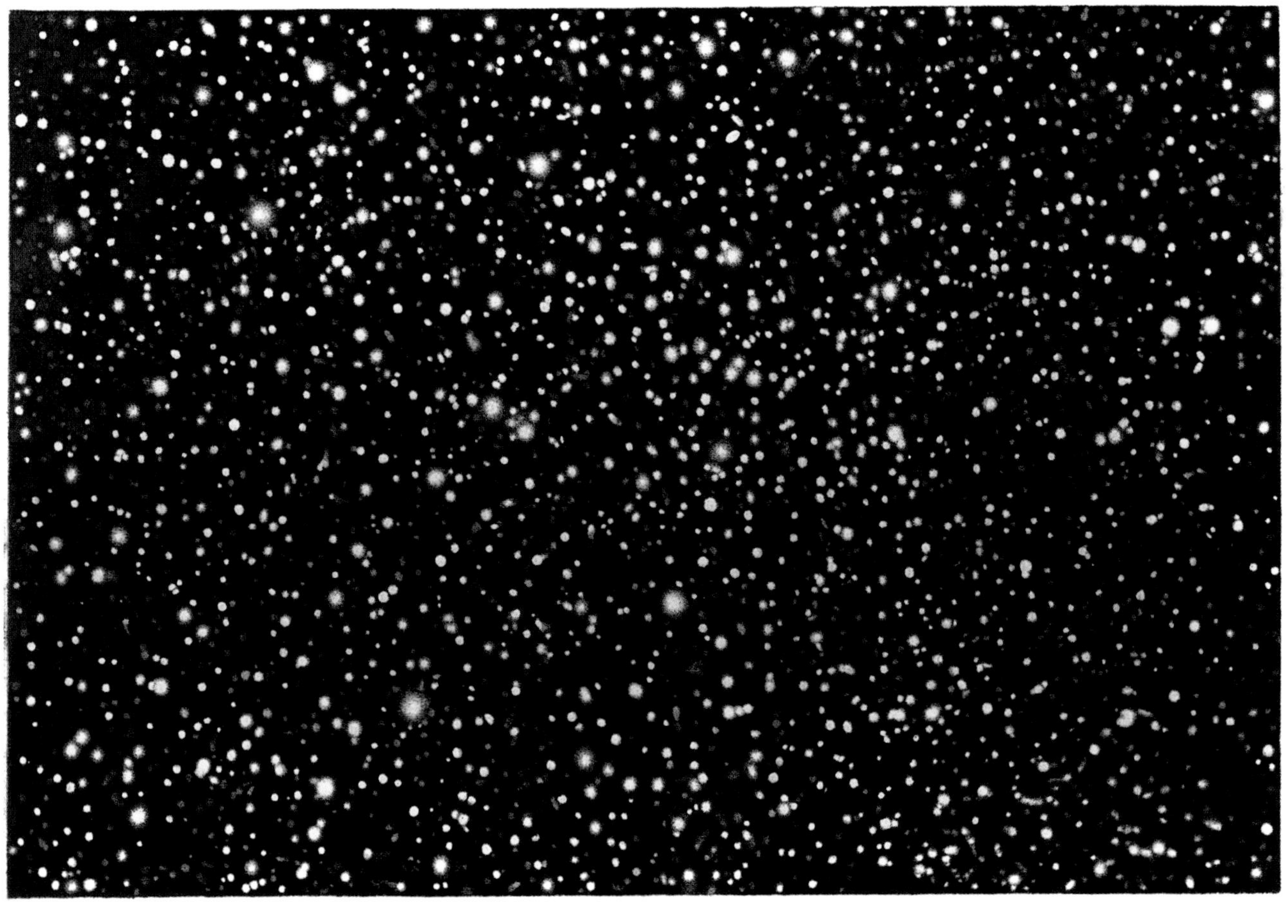

made it over into a lived experience, one that imprints itself on her very being as she paints or draws it as a picture.

Nowhere is this made more apparent than in the eleven painted bronze rocks that Celmins fabricated during 1977–82, and which she calls *To Fix the Image in Memory*. As her title indicates, the piece is heavily influenced by her many collaborations with photography, even though no photographs were actually used in its creation. Taking the place of photographs are the eleven stones that Celmins collected during her excursions through the outlands of northern New Mexico. Each rock is a souvenir from some infinitely larger whole, a cropped and congealed unit broken off from a grander, formless source. The rocks are not that spectacular; they are not unlike the countless stones that Celmins captured in snapshots and used as source material for her many drawings of desert surfaces during the 1970s, except that these rocks are real. But that difference turns out to be negligible: once they've caught the artist's eye, once Celmins picks them out and holds them close up for inspection, there's no going back, no way of returning them to their original home, their natural place in the seamless continuum. They are now exiles. 'I carried them around in the trunk of my car', Celmins recalls. 'I

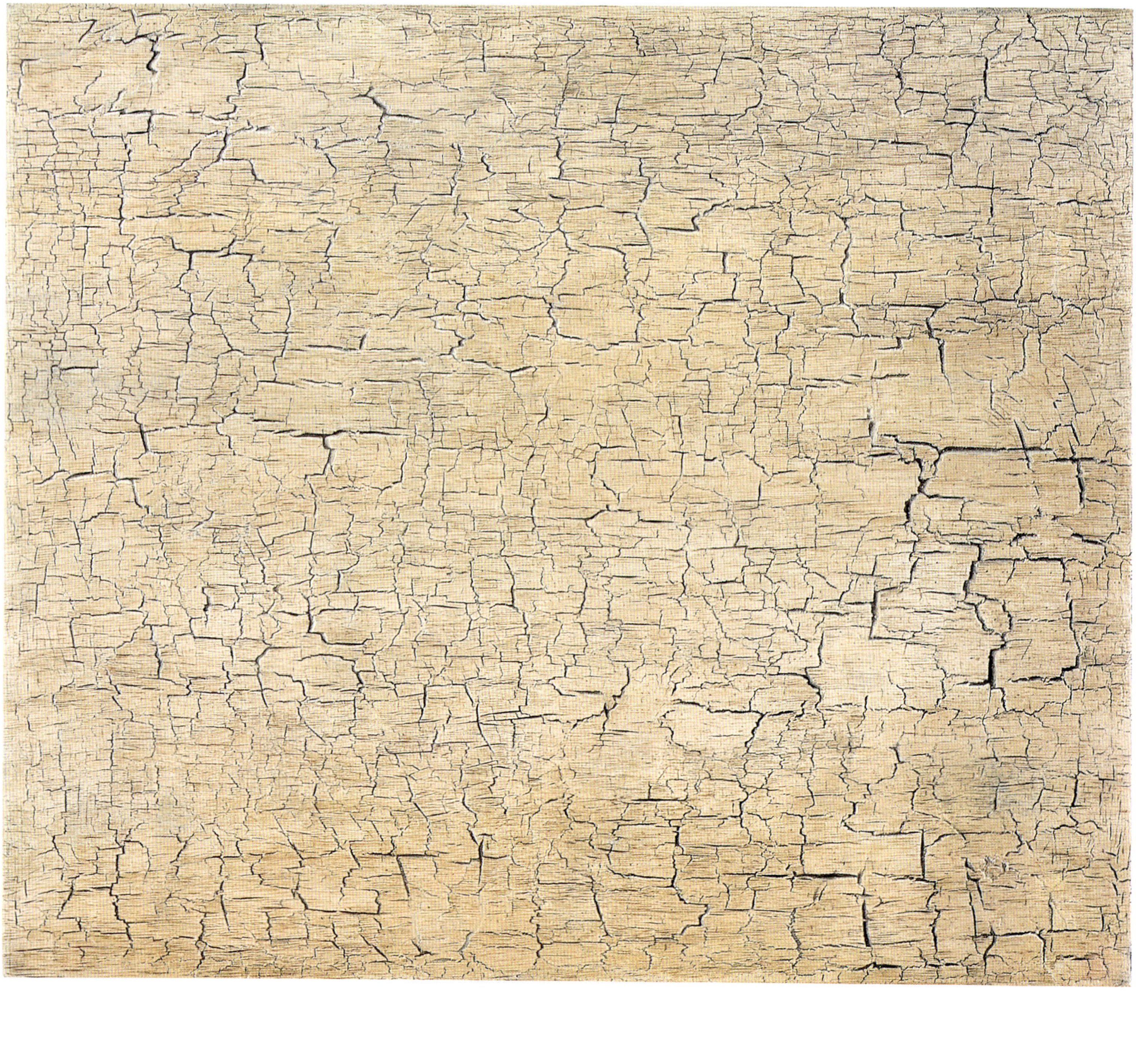

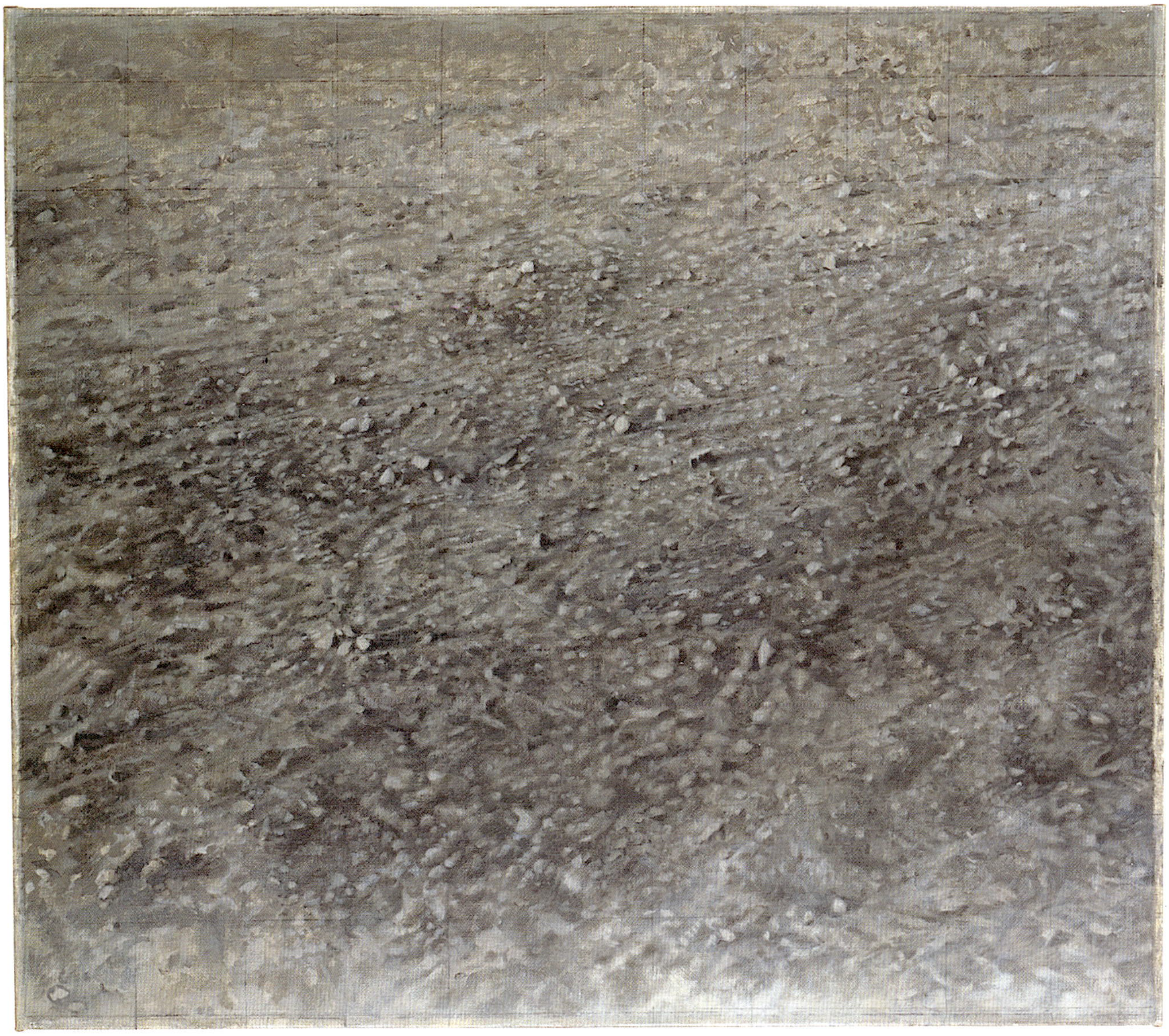

opposite, **Desert Surface #1**
1991
Oil on wood panel
45.5 × 56 cm
18 × 22.125 in

left, **Desert Surface #2**
1992
Oil on canvas
49.5 × 57 cm
19.5 × 22.5 in

put them on window sills. I lined them up. And, finally, they formed a set, a kind of constellation.'[41] The objects are no less unanchored and mobile – each is still only 'a movement whose beginning and character it does not in itself ever altogether reveal' – but they've won temporary lodging in a new gravitational field of concerns, desires and values. This is the kind of lodging that Celmins grants to all the images she laboriously makes over into drawings and paintings. Why Celmins chose to keep and recreate exactly eleven rocks (why not round it off to ten, or make it an even dozen?) is perhaps explained by the way in which the number itself figures that mutual grounding achieved between each found object and its made likeness, as they stand for and against one another and hold each in place through that tension, one to one.

The acrylics with which Celmins painstakingly detailed her bronze rocks marks the only time that she allowed herself to use paint between 1966 and 1985. When she picked up the brush again, it was to make a large starscape called *Barrier* (1985–86). The title is a tip-off that Celmins still felt

Untitled #10
1994–95
Charcoal on paper
43 × 56 cm
17 × 22 in

concerned about evenly spreading out so much oil paint and thus erecting too impassable a surface, with no hint of a fugitive beyond. For the next six years she will give the medium a second chance by testing it out on a number of subjects, not just star fields but also deserts and ocean surfaces. But by 1991 a clear preference emerges, and for the rest of the decade it's the night skies with which Celmins expresses her continuing interest in painting. The choice stands as a classic instance of the artist's approach: like her earlier decision to focus on drawing only after line had exited her imagery, she now settles back into painting by rendering dark heavens, which, unlike ocean surfaces, offer little accommodation to exultant brushwork and painterly technique. Celmins again pledges herself to a subject that showcases her medium and its resistant materiality over and above her confident facility with it. The paint with which she renders the star fields looks not so much stroked on as deposited, poured like concrete. With the earlier ocean waves, it was perhaps their suggestion of back and forth movement that encouraged Celmins to spread the medium more thinly *across* the surface of her pictures, if only to have that emphasis on lateral extension and surface contradict and therefore displace the connotation of depth engrained in every image of "the deep blue sea." But with the night skies there's much less sense that a medium has been applied to the surface of a support. Rather, the paint is so built up that it appears as itself an object with a surface all its own. Yet the same, tell-tale contradiction and displacement results: rather than a surface that depicts depth, now a thick object stands in for infinite space.

It takes Celmins a remarkably long time to make a picture of a truly open night sky, a thoroughly dispersed star field. For over a decade, since her 1973 *Galaxy*, her only drawings of deep space display an object of sorts, a galaxy, at their centre. But by the 1990s her night-sky paintings, especially the blackest ones, could not appear more dense and flat; more significantly, in them the role of photography seems to have all but disappeared. Celmins refines her practice even further, so that the tension she has always sought now exists between a hard surface presence and an image of endless, deepest emptiness. And standing in for the camera flash and its forever deferred moment are the stars themselves, whose weary light reaches us through incomprehensible stretches of space and time, with proof of the existence of worlds likely long deceased. In certain respects Celmins' practice now comes full circle. As she did in the early 1960s, she now switches back and forth between these zoomed-out views and close-up depictions of proximate objects. She reintroduces line and makes pictures of spider webs. But the distance between the star fields and these webs is not as great as may at first appear. Each web can be seen as plotting a system of one-point linear perspective, erecting the armature of an illusion of deep, objectless space; each is both close at hand as well as already departed, at once a nest and a void.

But this again is what Celmins has always done. She makes an image that has too much presence, too much impact and physicality just to be a representation; and yet it also feels too

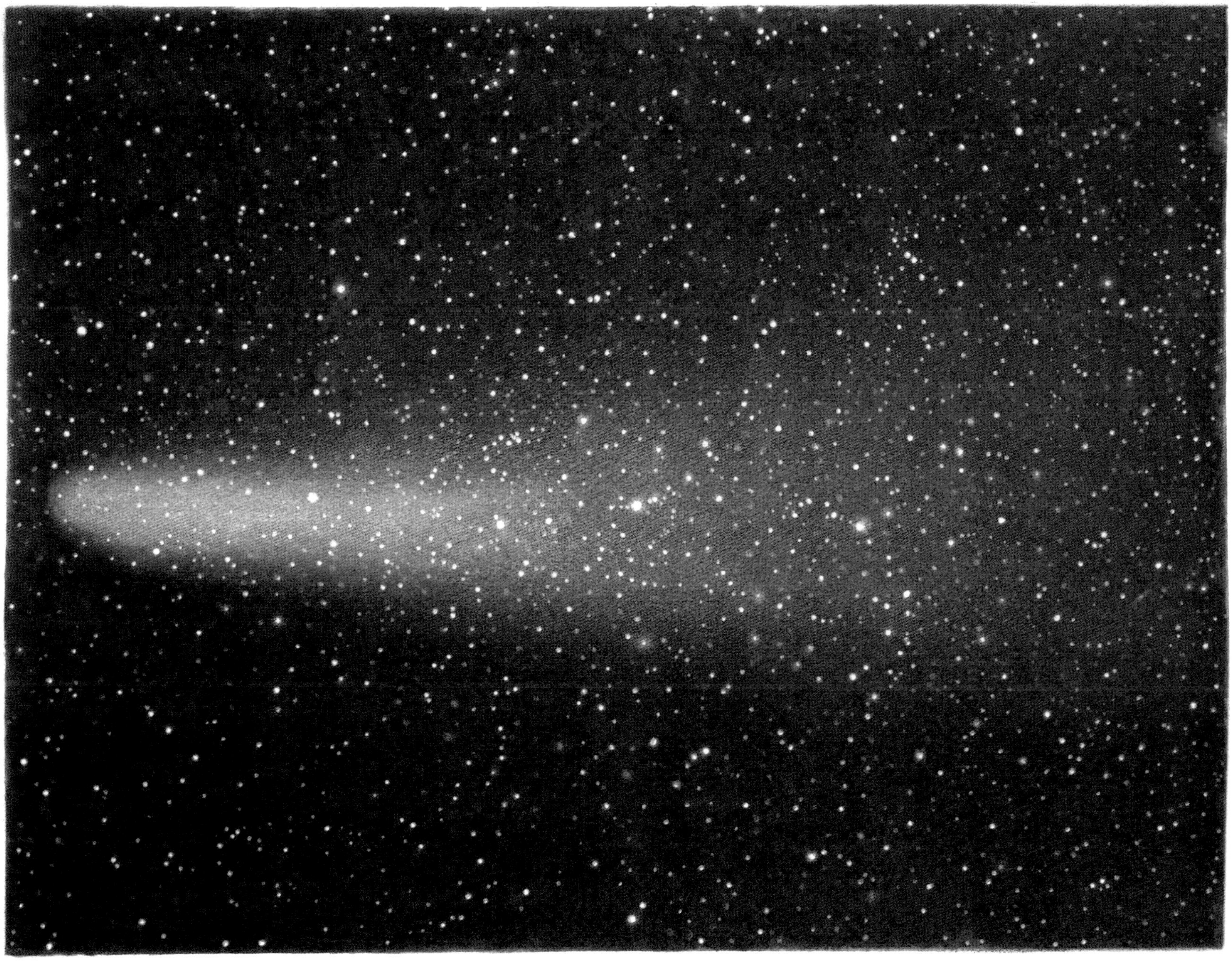

opposite, **Night Sky #6**
1993
Oil on linen mounted on wood
48.5 × 57 cm
19 × 22.5 in
Collection Walker Art Center, Minnesota

below, **Night Sky #7**
1995
Oil on canvas
96.5 × 119.5 cm
38 × 47 in

belated, too poignantly residual to stand as an autonomous entity. Rather, the work exists in the dialectical interplay between the two; neither the dutiful reportings of an already existing object nor the sovereign emanations of a god-like subject. The two impulses keep each other actively in check, at once inviting and resisting the desire for either complete assimilation or complete independence. Each piece by Celmins is just an image, and yet so much more than an image. And each is like an autonomous object, and yet humbly, touchingly less and other than that as well.

1 Roland Barthes, *Image Music Text*, trans. Stephen Heath, Hill and Wang, New York, 1977, p. 44.

2 Brooke Adams, 'Visionary Realist', *Art in America*, Vol. 81, No. 10, October 1993, p. 108.

3 Leo Steinberg, lecture delivered at The Museum of Modern Art, New York, in spring 1960 and published as 'Contemporary Art and the Plight of Its Public', in Gregory Battcock, ed., *The New Art*, E.P. Dutton, New York, 1973, p. 223.

4 Meyer Schapiro, *Modern Art*, George Braziller, New York, 1979, pp. 87, 89.

5 Harold Rosenberg, 'Hans Hofmann: Nature into Action', *ARTnews*, Vol. 56, No. 3, New York, May 1957, pp. 34–36.

6 Harold Rosenberg, 'The American Action Painters', *The Tradition of the New*, Horizon Press, New York, 1959, pp. 25, 29–30.

7 Jane Livingston, 'Four Los Angeles Artists', *Art in America*, Vol. 58, No. 5, New York, September–October 1970, p. 129.

8 Dave Hickey, 'Vija Celmins: The Path Itself', in Judith Tannenbaum, *Vija Celmins*, Institute of Contemporary Art, University of Pennsylvania, Philadelphia, 1992, p. 26.

9 Lucy R. Lippard, 'New York Letter: Recent Sculpture as Escape', *Art International*, Vol. 10, No. 2, Lugano, 20 February 1966, p. 50; Michael Fried, *Art Criticism in the Sixties*, October House, New York, 1967, n.p.

10 Harold Rosenberg, 'Toward an Unanxious Profession', in *The Anxious Object*, The University of Chicago Press, Chicago and London, 1966, p. 13. Given Rosenberg's description of the condition that was dawning at that time, it's not surprising that Alan Sondheim would title his 1977 survey of the preceding decade in art *Individuals: Post Movement Art in America*, E.P. Dutton, New York, 1977.

11 Chuck Close, 'Vija Celmins Interviewed', *Vija Celmins* A.R.T. Press, Los Angeles, 1992, p. 51. In February 1966, eight months after 500 artists and writers signed their names to a full-page ad taken out in *The New York Times* denouncing US intervention in Vietnam and the Dominican Republic, a group of artists organized the erecting of a 'Peace Tower' in Los Angeles. Organized by Judy Chicago, Irving Petlin and Philip Leider among others, the 600-foot pylon was designed by Mark di Suvero and outfitted top-to-bottom with painted panels donated by 418 artists. Celmins donated one of her early still lifes from 1963, a square oil painting of a fishhead on a plate, which she had included in her MA show at UCLA a few years before. Celmins' still life is visible amongst about fifty other contributed panels in a photo of the Peace Tower that ran on the front page of the 4 March 1966 issue of *The Los Angeles Free Press*. A reproduction of this front cover can be found in Francis Frascina, *Art, Politics and Dissent: Aspects of the Art Left in Sixties America*, Manchester University Press, 1999, p. 5.

12 Quoted in Maurice Poirier and Jane Necol, 'The '60s in Abstract: 13 Statements and an Essay', *Art in America*, Vol. 71, No. 9, New York, October 1983, p. 122.

13 Celmins in Close, op. cit., p. 8.

14 Susan Larsen, 'A Conversation with Vija Celmins', *LAICA Journal*, No. 40, Los Angeles, Fall 1984, p. 65.

15 Celmins in Close, op, cit., p. 8; see also Larsen, op. cit., p. 64.

16 Ruscha quoted in Kirk Varnedoe, 'Fire: Johns's Work as Seen and Used by American Artists', in Kirk Varnedoe, *Jasper Johns: A Retrospective*, The Museum of Modern Art, New York, 1996, p. 95.

17 Bechtle quoted in Jean-Claude Lebensztejn, *Malcolm Morley: Itineraries*, trans. Lucy McNair, Reaktion Books, London, 2001, p. 23.

18 Richter quoted in Bruce Ferguson and Jeffrey Spaulding, 'Gerhard Richter', *Parachute*, Montreal, Fall 1979, p. 32.

19 Vija Celmins, 'Chronology,' in *Vija Celmins*, A.R.T. Press, Los Angeles, 1992, p. 61.

20 See Linda Nochlin, 'Some Women Realists,' *Arts Magazine*, Vol. 48, No. 5, New York, February 1974, reprinted in Gregory Battcock, ed., *Super Realism: A Critical Anthology*, E.P. Dutton, New York, 1975, p. 77.

21 Alain Robbe-Grillet, *For a New Novel*, trans. by Richard Howard, Grove Press, New York, 1965.

22 John Ashbery, *Reported Sightings: Art Chronicles, 1957–1987*, Harvard University Press, Cambridge, Massachusetts, 1991, p. 81; Irving Hershel Sandler, 'New York Letter', *Quadrum* 14, 1963, p. 117.

23 Mel Bochner, 'Primary Structures,' *Arts Magazine*, Vol. 40, No. 7, New York, June 1966. p. 34. Brian O'Doherty also cites Robbe-Grillet in a 1966 overview of Minimalism, calling the French novelist 'the theoretician-in-residence' for the new abstract sculpture (see O'Doherty, 'Minus Plato', in Gregory Battcock, ed., *Minimal Art: A Critical Anthology* , E.P. Dutton, New York, 1968, p. 253. From 1958–64 five of Robbe-Grillet's novels were translated into English by Richard Howard and published by New York's Grove Press: *The Voyeur* (1958), *Jealousy* (1959), *In the Labyrinth* (1960), *Last Year at Marienbad* (1962), and *The Erasers* (1964). At the same time, a series of translated critical essays by Robbe-Grillet, as well as appreciations of his work by other authors, appeared in the influential *Evergreen Review*. The very first of these – Robbe-Grillet's 'A Fresh Start for Fiction' – was published in the journal's third issue (1957) alongside a special section devoted to Jackson Pollock.

24 Close quoted in William Dyckes, 'The Photo as Subject: The Paintings and Drawings of Chuck Close', in Gregory Battcock, ed., *Super-Realism*, op. cit., p. 152. An early champion of photo-realism, Linda Chase employs Robbe-Grillet extensively in her *Photo Realism*, Eminent Publications, New York, 1975.

25 Nochlin, op. cit., p. 77.

26 Celmins in Close, op. cit., p. 11.

27 Clement Greenberg, *The Collected Essays and Criticism. Vol. 4: Modernism with a Vengeance, 1957–1969*, ed. John O'Brian, University of Chicago Press, Chicago and London, 1993, p. 126.

28 Steinberg, op. cit., p. 223.

29 Roland Barthes, *Camera Lucida*, trans. Richard Howard, Hill and Wang, New York, 1981, p. 79.

30 Celmins in Close, op. cit., p. 12.

31 Noland quoted in Karen Wilkin, *Kenneth Noland*, Rizzoli, New York, 1990, p. 23.

32 Henry Geldzahler, 'The Art Audience and the Critic', in Gregory Battcock, ed., *The New Art*, op. cit., p. 55.

33 Allan Kaprow, 'Should the Artist become a Man of the World?', *ARTnews*, Vol. 63, No. 6, New York, October 1964, p. 36.

34 Lawrence Alloway, 'Artists and Photographs', originally published in *Artists and Photographs*, Multiples, Inc., New York, 1970, reprinted in Douglas Fogle, ed., *The Last Picture Show*, Walker Art Center, Minneapolis, Minnesota, 2003, p. 21.

35 Dyckes, op. cit., p. 147.

36 Michael Fried, 'Some Notes on Morris Louis,' *Arts Magazine*, Vol. 36, No. 2, New York, November 1963, p. 25.

37 Clement Greenberg, *The Collected Essays and Criticism. Vol. 2: Arrogant Purpose, 1945–1949*, ed. John O'Brian, University of Chicago Press, Chicago, 1986, p. 217.

38 Michael Fried, *Three American Painters*, Fogg Art Museum, Cambridge, Massachusetts, 1965, p. 14.

39 Clement Greenberg, *The Collected Essays and Criticism. Vol. 2*, op. cit., pp. 202, 315; Clement Greenberg, *Collected Essays Vol. 4: Modernism with a Vengeance, 1957–1969*, ed. John O'Brian, University of Chicago Press, Chicago and London, 1993, pp. 80–81.

40 Barthes, *Camera Lucida*, op. cit., p. 77.

41 Celmins in Close, op. cit., p. 17.

Contents

Interview **Robert Gober** in conversation with **Vija Celmins, page 6.** Survey **Lane Relyea** Vija Celmins' Twilight Zone, **page 44.**

Focus **Briony Fer** *Night Sky #19*, 1998, **page 100.**

Artist's Choice

Artist's Writings

Chronology

There is nothing ethereal about Vija Celmins' drawing of a night sky. It is not engulfing. Its surface remains impenetrable despite the constellation of starlight that it holds. A dense layer of charcoal lies on the surface like a blanket of dark. The associations of a night sky filled with showers of stars only increases this sense of there being something unyielding in infinity. Celmins' sense of the infinite is absolutely not transcendental or sublime but material and concrete. Like her webs, which she has said interested her because, not in spite of, their slightly 'corny' connotations,[1] Celmins offers us a spectacular reversal: a vast nebulous sky becomes the material world of a drawing.

If *Night Sky #19* is a drawing of anything, it is a drawing of a photograph culled from an astronomy book. All her work is based on photographs. A drawer in her studio is full of old dog-eared photographs of the sea and the desert that she has taken herself or night skies which she has cut out from books or magazines. Some have the brownish patina of old photographs; many have been used already and have sections cropped with yellowish tape. Although she may adapt a passage here, or edit out a comet there, *Night Sky #19* is a translation of the photograph into the medium of drawing. It is meticulous as a replication and yet the appearance of it is radically unlike its source. Magnified many times over, made of charcoal not printer's ink, its surface is totally matt on coated paper. Made as art not illustration and made to be looked at *as* art not illustration. Whilst I don't think the effect of her work is to make us feel lost in the enormity of a sky we could say that we do get lost in translation between photography and drawing and painting. These are the translations that seem to interest her most.

Vija Celmins has said that she uses photographs in order to impose 'another layer that creates a distance'.[2] She has said that she treats the photograph 'as an object to scan'. Photographs

provide her with a sort of archive of what she has called 'broken-surface images'.[3] *Night Sky #19* is a bit of sky, put together piece by piece. When she talked about beginning the galaxy drawings she said, 'Even though you may think they came from lying under the stars, for me, they came out of loving the blackness of the pencil. It's almost as if I was exploring the blackness of the pencil along with the image that went with it'.[4] Within the dense opacity of the surface, there is infinite variation. The longer you look the more tiny threads of stars or milky ways unfold in the passages that had seemed entirely black. This is not unlike Ad Reinhardt and the slow unfolding of different blacks – but without Reinhardt's mysticism. Taking as she does the elements of earth, sea and sky is a fairly high-risk operation. At first, her move to draw galaxies looks like a dramatic move away from her earlier concerns with painting ordinary things in her studio like a fan or a light. But there is also a continuity in her use of grisaille. In the end night skies are no less part of the visual pattern of our world than the lights of a truck on a freeway in *Truck* from 1966 in which the asymmetric but spreading aureoles of the headlights distort spatial distance. This is reminiscent of what it is like to look into the night and be subjected to the nocturnal distortions of dark and light. The confusion between recession and projection in her galaxies is not so different from her earlier preoccupations with the quotidian. Trucks and constellations are both, for Celmins, to be built up on and as a darkly massive surface. *Night Sky #19* veers between a telescopic view containing a vast surface, to a microscopic one insisting on each highly worked part of the surface and what it yields. As it yields, a different kind of time-field opens up. A dark area becomes mottled. There is an analogy with stars, of course, where what we see is the old light of dead or distant stars, but in this case it is the remains of the paper that we see.

Working in series, small differences and adjustments get made out of repetition. In her more recent work she has tended to edit out the activity of comets to concentrate on endless variation in the grouping and clustering and scattering of a constellation. From one drawing to another, the shift from blacks to greys (as in the shift from *Night Sky #18* to *Night Sky #19*) becomes spectacular in its own highly concentrated way. In the layers of her oil paintings of night skies in the same series, there are traces of colour embedded in the black surface. Celmins shows how many blacks there are in black. She uses the shading colours that in conventional pictorial terms describe shadows and define solid bodies through chiaroscuro – but she uses them instead to differentiate a flat all-over surface, varying from

previous pages, **Night Sky #19**
1998
Charcoal on paper on acrylic ground
48.5 × 58.5 cm
19.125 × 23 in

opposite, **Night Sky #18**
1998
Charcoal on paper on acrylic ground
48.5 × 58.5 cm
19.125 × 23 in

jet-black through a silvery or a leaden grey. Grisaille colours thought to be sombre are enlivened in this way to animate a surface as we might expect colour to do. The charcoal is velvety and matt and absorbent. Black is a palette. If there is an analogy with night viewing it is this: the slow adjustment to seeing in the dark, to making out the slightest gradation.

Celmins' drawing does not consist of line. Charcoal is rubbed on to the surface evenly and painstakingly. Adding more layers darkens it. Rubbing it in and spreading it across the paper lightens it. In others in the series the pressure of rubbing in is increased to a maximum to get the blackest black. The smudge of the charcoal is rigorously controlled. Even when she draws with pencil her drawing is not concerned with linear inscription, but is built up with shading. The physical labour involved in making a surface like this takes time. It is a slow process. This kind of layering is also how she makes her paintings, adding layer upon layer and sanding off and adding on, to create in some of them an almost pumiced surface.

In *Night Sky #19* Celmins has laid on the charcoal ground and then used an eraser to take out the points of light. If the dark sky is constructed by rubbing in the charcoal, the constellations of light are made by rubbing out. She uses an electric eraser in addition to a fine pencil eraser to get the different degrees of brightness. The fields of stars are drawn by erasing. In the pencil drawings, on the other hand, the stars are drawn by leaving the paper bare. So the drawing is itself a kind of negative. This relates to the recent paintings Celmins has made of negative galaxies, with the stars black and the ground light. The erased points in the charcoal are like a negative touch – a touch which takes away. So touch has a double: the eraser. The concern with doublings goes right back to earlier drawings like her *Letter* from 1968. Her drawings and paintings after photographs could be seen as doubles too – except of course that the result is not mere replication. But in a way that misses the point, because the most pervasive doubling seems to occur between her works, in translation *between* drawings or *between* drawing and painting. She sometimes works on paintings in pairs.

Celmins has said 'Drawing is kind of like a dry world, a dry world of graphite and pieces of charcoal'.[5] She has talked about her drawing being more about charcoal and 'a certain kind of dustiness'.[6] I think she redeems touch for that dry world and sets it against the kind of touch associated conventionally with gesture – what we could call in this context, liquid gesture. The fluid brushstroke dries of course but maintains the material trace of its former liquidity. A fluid stroke or line invokes a whole metaphorics of expressive feeling. Post-Pollock the drip takes on that mantle, then the stain. Celmins rejects the liquid gesture in favour of the dry world of her drawing table: charcoal and graphite and dusty, powdery possibilities. From this point of view, she might draw night skies or she might draw oceans, but the subject that reflects on her medium most directly is the desert floor. A parched ground, endlessly differentiated.

Robert Smithson once speculated on the 'climate of sight' that changes 'from wet to dry and from dry to wet in one's mental weather'. Paint was a kind of liquefaction (all pools and stains). He preferred the dry of his non-sites. He enlists Malevich in his support for daring to imagine a kind of dryness that burns hot.[7] Another artist to explore the wet and dry was Ed Ruscha, with his liquid paintings and his gunpowder drawings. But it seems to me that Celmins proposes another kind of dry world. One less concerned with the dynamics of sight than with the circuits of sight and touch. Liquid gesture never interested her. Even her early paintings of objects are chalky dry – a dryness that burned red only occasionally, like the fluorescent glow of *Hot Plate* (1964). Rather than maintain hard and fast distinctions between drawing and painting, Celmins' work and working methods tends to blur them. Painting becomes like drawing and *vice versa*.

Celmins creates a perceptual field of uncertain distances but certain materiality. In the 'Night Sky' series, it becomes clear that the distances involved are not those measuring our relation to the universe. They are much closer to home. There is a huge distance or gap between

Celmins' surface which is a terrain of touch and an intangible, vast sky; in between, closer, but not too close, is the strange surface of the photographs of constellations, whose surfaces clearly absorb her. Or rather, she has said, she had 'an affection for certain little areas in the photographs ... that I re-examined all the time'.[8] These distances are also detachments of subject from object. Rather than present touch as the utopian antidote to a dystopian vision of modernity, Celmins' touch is also a means of detachment and estrangement. It is touch that is being charted in all its complexity here rather than the astral bodies. Charting touch ends up being as vast and infinite and as sensual as charting a night sky.

There is no linear trace of the hand, no texture. Only at the edges is there the slightest lightening of tone that reveals the charcoal worked faintly over a textured paper. And yet Celmins herself talks of her surfaces in terms of touch. The compression seems to squeeze out the spectator's gaze, just as Celmins' methods of making seem to squeeze out the normal cognates of touch. From this point of view, liquid gesture, pools of feeling, obey the arid conventions which codify the expressive according to established aesthetic models. Celmins makes touch strange again – intractable in its way yet the more affecting for its being harder won. It seems to me that what makes Celmins' work compelling is precisely this, that she effects a kind of pure touch that is detached from trace or texture. Celmins' dry touch is set against the liquid gesture. Whilst it might empty the work of expressive gesture as it has normally been understood, touch erupts on this surface as if it were the raw, unmediated material of this dry world.

1 In conversation with the artist, New York, February, 2003.

2 'Vija Celmins Interviewed by Chuck Close at her New York Loft on September 26 and 27, 1991', Vija Celmins, A.R.T. Press, New York, 1992, p. 12.

3 Ibid, p. 14.

4 Ibid, p. 36.

5 Interview with Ann Seymour, *Vija Celmins Drawings of the Night Sky*, Anthony d'Offay, London, 2003.

6 Interview with Chuck Close, op. cit.

7 Robert Smithson , 'A Sedimentation of the Mind: Earth Projects' (1968), *The Collected Writings*, University of California Press, 1996, p. 108.

8 Interview with Chuck Close, op. cit., p. 49.

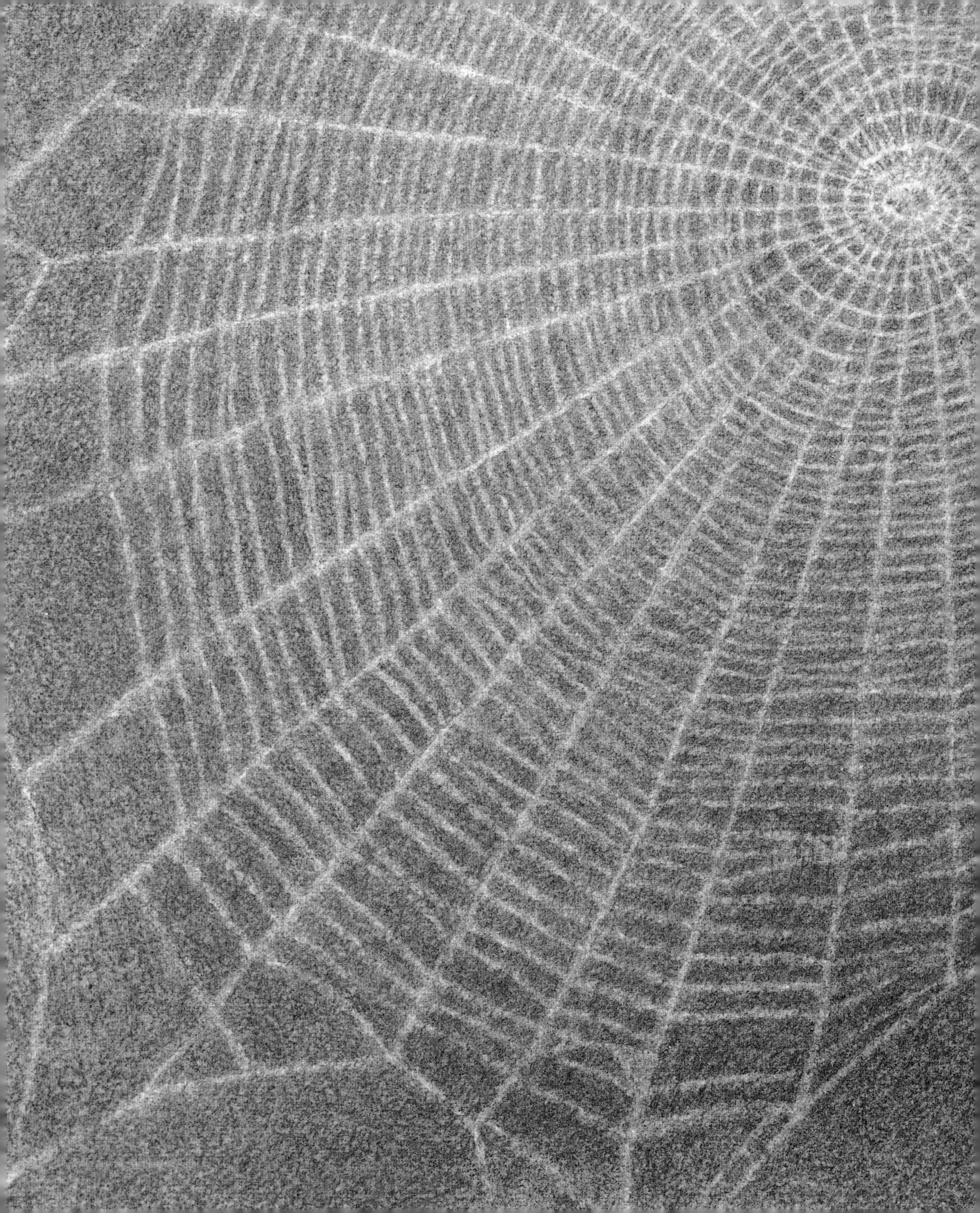

Artist's Choice

Jorge Luis Borges Funes the Memorious (extracts), 1941, **page 108.**

Web #8
2004
Charcoal on paper
51.5 × 41.5 cm
20.25 × 16.25 in

I remember him (I have no right to utter this sacred verb, only one man on earth had that right and he is dead) with a dark passion flower in his hand, seeing it as no one has ever seen it, though he might look at it from the twilight of dawn till that of evening, a whole lifetime. I remember him, with his face taciturn and Indian-like and singularly *remote*, behind the cigarette. I remember (I think) his angular, leather-braiding hands. I remember near those hands a maté gourd bearing the Uruguayan coat of arms; I remember a yellow screen with a vague lake landscape in the window of his house. I clearly remember his voice: the slow, resentful, nasal voice of the old-time dweller of the suburbs, without the Italian sibilants we have today. I never saw him more than three times; the last was in 1887 ...

[...] My first memory of Funes is very perspicuous. I can see him on an afternoon in March or February of the year 1881. My father, that year, had taken me to spend the summer in Fray Bentos. I was returning from the San Francisco ranch with my cousin Bernardo Haedo. We were singing as we rode along and being on horseback was not the only circumstance determining my happiness. After a sultry day, an enormous slate-coloured storm had hidden the sky. It was urged on by a southern wind, the trees were already going wild; I was afraid (I was hopeful) that the elemental rain would take us by surprise in the open. We were running a kind of race with the storm. We entered an alleyway that sank down between two very high brick sidewalks. It had suddenly got dark; I heard some rapid and almost secret footsteps up above; I raised my eyes and saw a boy running along the narrow and broken path as if it were a narrow and broken wall. I remember his baggy gaucho trousers, his rope-soled shoes, I remember the cigarette in his hard face, against the now limitless storm cloud. Bernardo cried to him unexpectedly: 'What time is it, Ireneo?' Without consulting the sky, without stopping, he replied: 'It's four minutes to eight, young Bernardo Juan Francisco.' His voice was shrill, and mocking.

I am so unperceptive that the dialogue I have just related would not have attracted my attention had it not been stressed by my cousin, who (I believe) was prompted by a certain local pride and the desire to show that he was indifferent to the other's tripartite reply.

He told me the fellow in the alleyway was one Ireneo Funes, known for certain peculiarities such as avoiding contact with people and always knowing what time it was, like a clock. He added that he was the son of the ironing woman in town, María Clementina Funes, and that some people said his father was a doctor at the meat packers, an Englishman by the name of O'Connor, and others that he was a horse tamer or scout from the Salto district. He lived with his mother, around the corner from the Laureles house.

During the years eighty-five and eighty-six we spent the summer in Montevideo. In eighty-seven I returned to Fray Bentos. I asked, as was natural, about all my acquaintances and, finally, about the 'chronometrical' Funes. I was told he had been thrown by a half-tamed horse on the San Francisco ranch and was left hopelessly paralyzed. I remember the sensation of uneasy magic the news produced in me: the only time I had seen him, we were returning from San Francisco on horseback and he was running along a high place; this fact, told me by my cousin Bernardo, had much of the quality of a dream made up of previous elements. I was told he never moved from his cot, with his eyes fixed on the fig tree in the back or on a spider web. In the afternoons, he would let himself be brought out to the window. He carried his pride to the point of acting as if the blow that had felled him were beneficial ... Twice I saw him behind the iron grating of the window, which harshly emphasized his condition as a perpetual prisoner: once, motionless, with his eyes closed; another time, again motionless, absorbed in the contemplation of a fragrant sprig of santonica [...]
Not without a certain vaingloriousness, I had begun at that time my methodical study of Latin. My valise contained the *De viris illustribus* of Lhomond, Quicherat's *Thesaurus*, the commentaries of Julius Caesar and an odd volume of Pliny's *Naturalis historia*, which then exceeded (and still exceeds) my moderate virtues as a Latinist. Everything becomes public in a small town; Ireneo, in his house on the outskirts, did not take long to learn of the arrival of these anomalous books. He sent me a flowery and ceremonious letter in which he recalled our encounter, unfortunately brief, 'on the seventh day of February of the year 1884', praised the glorious services my uncle Gregorio Haedo, deceased that same year, 'had rendered to our two nations in the valiant battle of Ituzaingó' and requested the loan of any one of

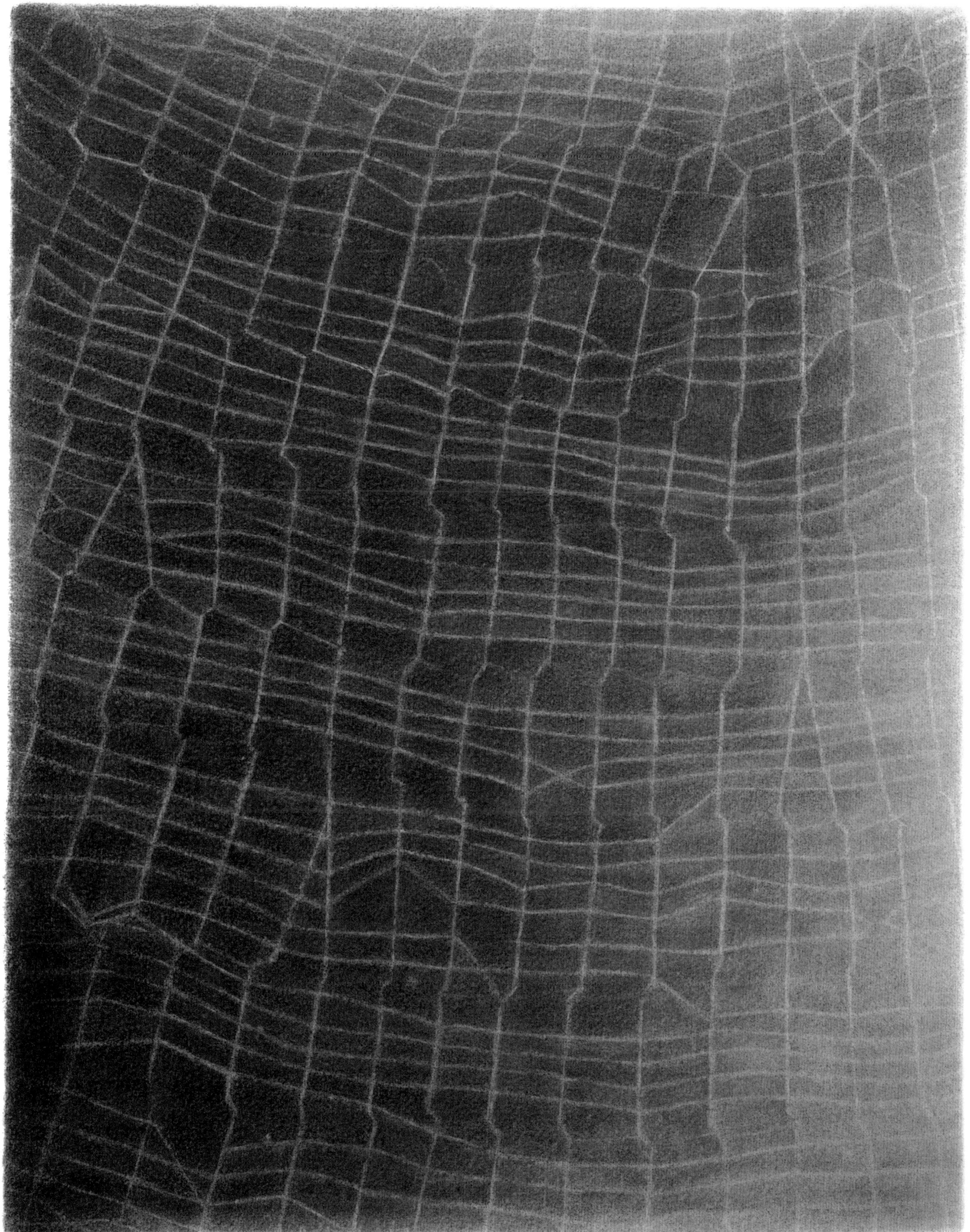

Web #1
1998
Charcoal on paper
56.5 × 65 cm
22.25 × 25.5 in

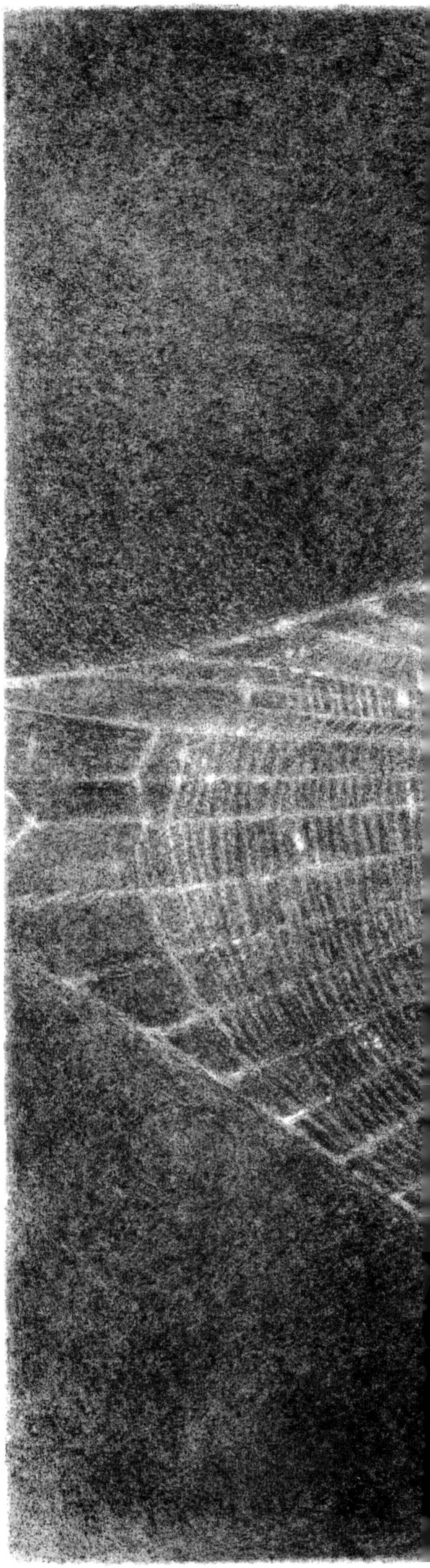

my volumes, accompanied by a dictionary 'for the proper intelligence of the original text, for I am as yet ignorant of Latin'. He promised to return them to me in good condition, almost immediately. His handwriting was perfect, very sharply outlined; his orthography, of the type favoured by Andrés Bello: *i* for *y*, *j* for *g*. At first I naturally feared a joke. My cousins assured me that was not the case, that these were peculiarities of Ireneo. I did not know whether to attribute to insolence, ignorance or stupidity the idea that the arduous Latin tongue should require no other instrument than a dictionary; to disillusion him fully, I sent him the *Gradus ad Parnassum* of Quicherat and the work by Pliny.

On the fourteenth of February, I received a telegram from Buenos Aires saying I should return immediately, because my father was 'not at all well'. May God forgive me; the prestige of being the recipient of an urgent telegram, the desire to communicate to all Fray Bentos the contradiction between the negative form of the message and the peremptory adverb, the temptation to dramatize my suffering, affecting a virile stoicism, perhaps distracted me from all possibility of real sorrow. When I packed my valise, I noticed the *Gradus* and the first volume of the *Naturalis historia* were missing. The *Saturn* was sailing the next day, in the morning; that night, after supper, I headed towards Funes' house. I was astonished to find the evening no less oppressive than the day had been.

At the respectable little house, Funes' mother opened the door for me.

She told me Ireneo was in the back room and I should not be surprised to find him in the dark, because he knew how to pass the idle hours without lighting the candle. I crossed the tile patio, the little passageway; I reached the second patio. There was a grape arbour; the darkness seemed complete to me. I suddenly heard Ireneo's high-pitched, mocking voice. His voice was speaking in Latin; his voice (which came from the darkness) was articulating with morose delight a speech or prayer or incantation. The Roman syllables resounded in the earthen patio; my fear took them to be indecipherable, interminable; afterwards, in the enormous dialogue of that night, I learned they formed the first paragraph of the twenty-fourth chapter of

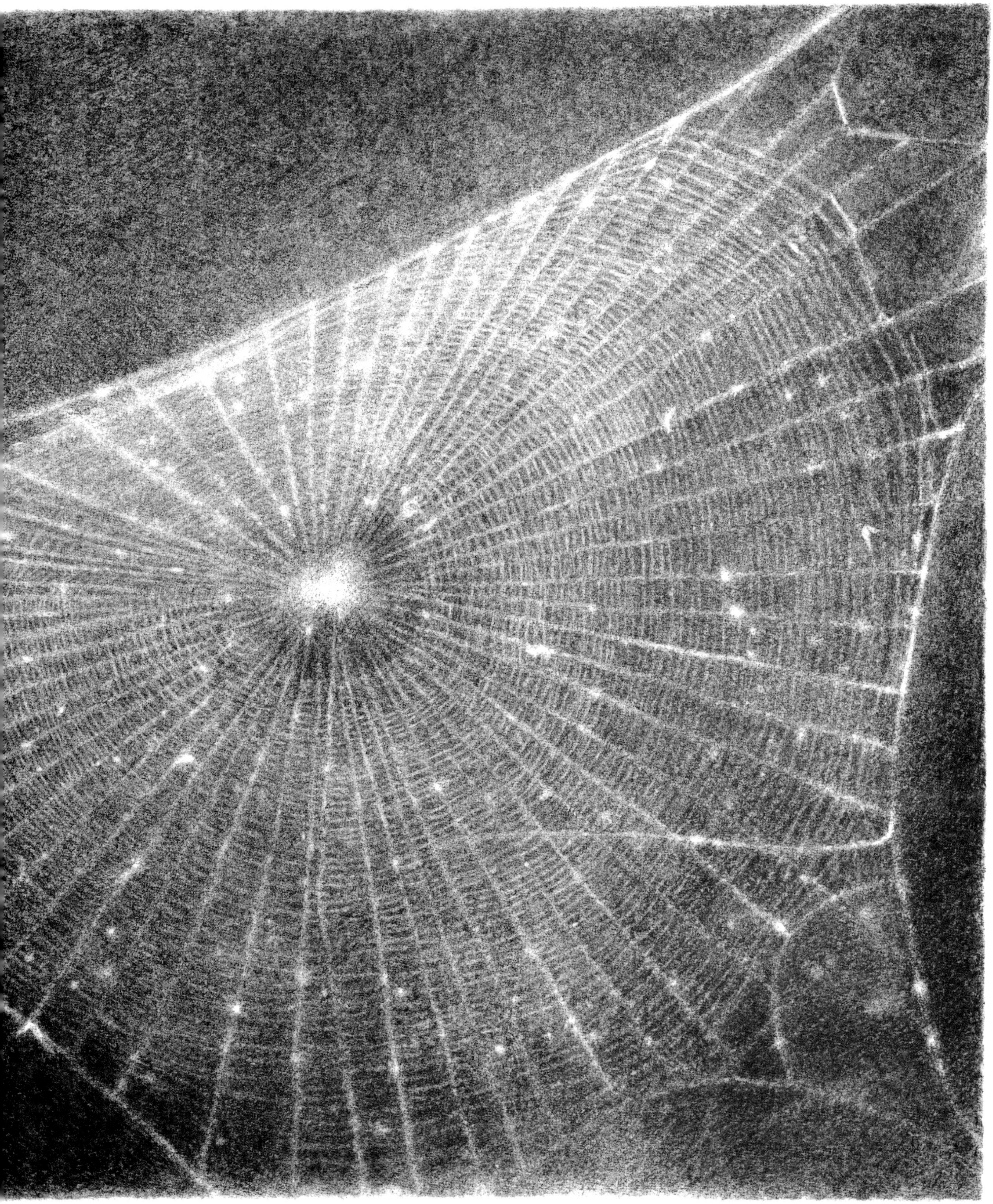

the seventh book of the *Naturalis historia*. The subject of that chapter is memory; the last words were *ut nihil non iisdem verbis redderetur auditum*.

Without the slightest change of voice, Ireneo told me to come in. He was on his cot, smoking. It seems to me I did not see his face until dawn; I believe I recall the intermittent glow of his cigarette. The room smelled vaguely of dampness. I sat down; I repeated the story about the telegram and my father's illness. I now arrive at the most difficult point in my story. This story (it is well the reader know it by now) has no other plot than that dialogue which took place half a century ago. I shall not try to reproduce the words, which are now irrecoverable. I prefer to summarize with veracity the many things Ireneo told me. The indirect style is remote and weak; I know I am sacrificing the efficacy of my narrative; my readers should imagine for themselves the hesitant periods which overwhelmed me that night.

Ireneo began by enumerating, in Latin and in Spanish, the cases of prodigious memory recorded in the *Naturalis historia*: Cyrus, king of the Persians, who could call every soldier in his armies by name; Mithridates Eupator, who administered the law in the twenty-two languages of his empire; Simonides, inventor of the science of mnemonics; Metrodorus, who practised the art of faithfully repeating what he had heard only once. In obvious good faith, Ireneo was amazed that such cases be considered amazing.

[Ireneo] told me that before that rainy afternoon when the blue-grey horse threw him, he had been what all humans are: blind, deaf, addle-brained, absent-minded. (I tried to remind him of his exact perception of time, his memory for proper names; he paid no attention to me.) For nineteen years he had lived as one in a dream: he looked without seeing, listened without hearing, forgetting everything, almost everything. When he fell, he became unconscious; when he came to, the present was almost intolerable in its richness and sharpness, as were his most distant and trivial memories. Somewhat later he learned that he was paralyzed. The fact scarcely interested him. He reasoned (he felt) that his immobility was a minimum price to pay. Now his perception and his memory were infallible.

We, at one glance, can perceive three glasses on a table; Funes, all the leaves and tendrils and fruit that make up a grape vine. He knew by heart the forms of the southern clouds at dawn on the 30th April, 1882, and could compare them in his memory with the mottled streaks on a book in Spanish binding he had only seen once and with the outlines of the foam raised by an oar in the Río Negro the night before the Quebracho uprising. These memories were not simple ones; each visual image was lined to muscular sensations, thermal sensations, etc. He could reconstruct all his dreams, all his half-dreams. Two or three times he had reconstructed the whole day; he never hesitated, but each reconstruction had required a whole day. He told me: 'I alone have more memories than all of mankind has probably had since the world has been the world.' And again: 'My dreams are like you people's waking hours.' And again, towards dawn: 'My memory, sir, is like a garbage heap'. A circle drawn on a blackboard, a right triangle, a lozenge – all these are forms we can fully and intuitively grasp; Ireneo could do the same with the stormy mane of a pony, with a herd of cattle on a hill, with the changing fire and its innumerable ashes, with the many faces of a dead man throughout a long wake. I don't know how many stars he could see in the sky.

These things he told me; neither then nor later have I ever placed them in doubt. In those days there were no cinemas or phonographs; nevertheless, it is odd and even incredible that no one ever performed an experiment with Funes. The truth is that we live out our lives putting off all that can be put off; perhaps we all know deep down that we are immortal and that sooner or later all men will do and know all things.

Out of the darkness, Funes' voice went on talking to me.

He told me that in 1886 he had invented an original system of numbering and that in a very few days he had gone beyond the twenty-four thousand mark. He had not written it down, since anything he thought of once would never be lost to him. His first stimulus was, I think, his discomfort at the fact that the famous thirty-three gauchos of Uruguayan history should require two signs and two words, in place of a single word and a single sign. He then applied this absurd principle to the other numbers. In place of seven thousand thirteen, he would say (for example)

Máximo Pérez; in place of seven thousand fourteen, *The Railroad*; other numbers were *Luid Melián Lafinur*, *Olimar*, *sulphur*, *the reins*, *the whale*, *the gas*, *the cauldron*, *Napoleon*, *Agustín de Vedia*. In place of five hundred, he would say *nine*. Each word had a particular sign, a kind of mark; the last in the series were very complicated ... I tried to explain to him that this rhapsody of incoherent terms was precisely the opposite of a system of numbers. I told him that saying 365 meant saying three hundreds, six tens, five ones, an analysis which is not found in the 'numbers' *The Negro Timoteo* or *meat blanket*. Funes did not understand me or refused to understand me.

Locke, in the seventeenth century, postulated (and rejected) an impossible language in which each individual thing, each stone, each bird and each branch, would have its own name; Funes once projected an analogous language, but discarded it because it seemed too general to him, too ambiguous. In fact, Funes remembered not only every leaf of every tree of every wood, but also every one of the times he had perceived or imagined it. He decided to reduce each of his past days to some seventy thousand memories, which would then be defined by means of ciphers. He was dissuaded from this by two considerations: his awareness that the task was interminable, his awareness that it was useless. He thought that by the hour of his death he would not even have finished classifying all the memories of his childhood.

The two projects I have indicated (an infinite vocabulary for the natural series of numbers, a useless catalogue of all the images of his memory) are senseless, but they betray a certain stammering grandeur. They permit us to glimpse or infer the nature of Funes' vertiginous world. He was, let us not forget, almost incapable of ideas of a general, Platonic sort. Not only was it difficult for him to comprehend that the generic symbol *dog* embraces so many unlike individuals of diverse size and form; it bothered him that the dog at three fourteen (seen from the side) should have the same name as the dog at three fifteen (seen from the front). His own face in the mirror, his own hands, surprised him every time he saw them. Swift relates that the emperor of Lilliput could discern the movement of the minute hand; Funes could continuously discern the tranquil advances of corruption, of decay, of fatigue. He could note the progress of death, of dampness. He was the solitary and lucid spectator of a multiform, instantaneous and almost intolerably precise world. Babylon, London and New York have overwhelmed with their ferocious splendour the imaginations of men; no one, in their populous towers or their urgent avenues, has felt the heat and pressure of a reality as indefatigable as that which day and night converged upon the hapless Ireneo in his poor South American suburb. It was very difficult for him to sleep. To sleep is to turn one's mind from the world; Funes, lying on his back on his cot in the shadows, could imagine every crevice and every moulding in the sharply defined houses surrounding him. (I repeat that the least important of his memories was more minute and more vivid than our perception of physical pleasure or physical torment.) Towards the east, along a stretch not yet divided into blocks, there were new houses, unknown to Funes. He imagined them to be black, compact, made of homogenous darkness; in that direction he would turn his face in order to sleep. He would also imagine himself at the bottom of the river, rocked and annihilated by the current.

With no effort, he had learned English, French, Portuguese and Latin. I suspect, however, that he was not very capable of thought. To think is to forget differences, generalize, make abstractions. In the teeming world of Funes, there were only details, almost immediate in their presence.

The wary light of dawn entered the earthen patio.

Then I saw the face belonging to the voice that had spoken all night long. Ireneo was nineteen years old; he had been born in 1868; he seemed to me as monumental as bronze, more ancient than Egypt, older than the prophecies and the pyramids. I thought that each of my words (that each of my movements) would persist in his implacable memory; I was benumbed by the fear of multiplying useless gestures.

Ireneo Funes died in 1889, of congestion of the lungs.

Translated by James E. Irby

Brown top. white front big)

(14) - all red black wings - & tail. (like scarlet tanager)

- tern. yellow bill

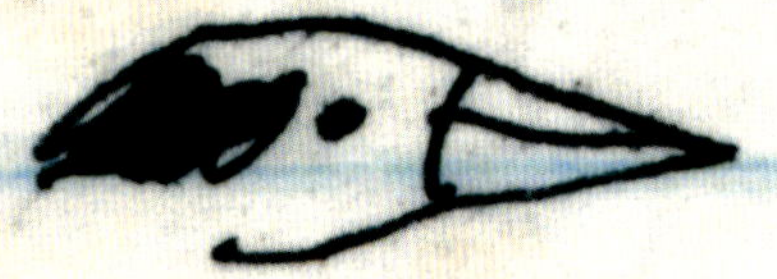

• hooded oriole black cap

toucan → green bill red
hind end -

small like warbler
black hed

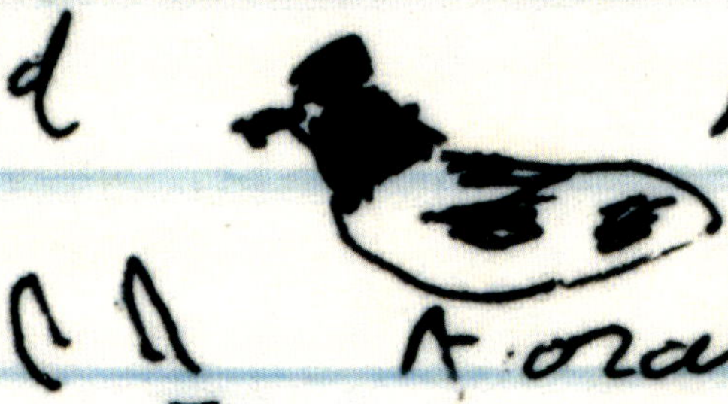

Cota • Jamaica • beak yellow

• ani

• warbler. bl. head yellow

Contents

Interview **Robert Gober** in conversation with **Vija Celmins**, **page 6**. Survey **Lane Relyea** Vija Celmins' Twilight Zone, **page 44**. Focus **Briony Fer** *Night Sky #19*, 1998, **page 100**. Artist's Choice **Jorge Luis Borges** Funes the Memorious (extracts), 1941, **page 108**.

Artist's Writings

Vija Celmins Interview with Chuck Close (extracts), 1991, **page 116**.

Chronology page 144 & Bibliography, List of Illustrations, page 158.

Interview with Chuck Close (extracts) 1991

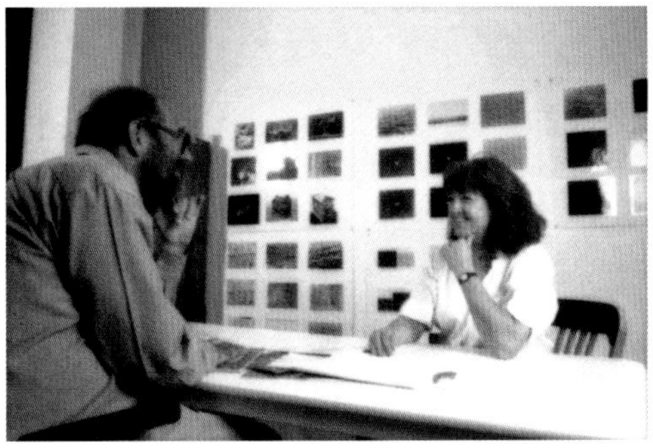

Vija Celmins […] **In retrospect I have detached myself from my work somewhat. Now I can sort of see it as if I had nothing to do with it, which is perhaps one of the most interesting things that has happened as I have gotten older – that I am able to look back and say, what is this? So when I'm forced to look at imagery this way, the imagery has an intensity, especially in the early things. They have an ominous, kind of dangerous strangeness.**

Chuck Close I think those [early object paintings] are the most violent-looking paintings. What appear to be …

Celmins **Benign.**

Close That's right. It is the most dangerous hot plate, or the most dangerous heater, or whatever, that I have ever seen. And they are scary for some reason.

Celmins **Oh, I don't know, do you think so? They do have that ominous feeling that there is something going on besides just still lifes. I think that it came about because I had been painting in an Abstract Expressionist manner and I had been trying to make my strokes – the painting space – meaningful. I had tried to do passionate kinds of paintings because I was full of this energy, like I think you were, like we were when we were twenty years old. A couple of years later, I began to feel that there was no meaning in it for me. I lost my way, I rejected it. I couldn't resolve the stroke-making with the essential stillness of the painting. So then I went back to some basic thing, like looking at simple objects and painting them straight, trying to rediscover if there was anything there that might be more authentic. But the object paintings came out sort of twisted, with more energy in them than was needed.**

Close Do you think that we rejected Abstract Expressionism because we were coming to it so late, sort of fourth-generation junior Abstract Expressionists? We were imitating the look – it's what we learned art looks like.

Celmins **It was hard not to make it at that time.**

Heater
1964
Oil on canvas
122 × 122 cm
48 × 48 in
Collection Whitney Museum of American Art, New York

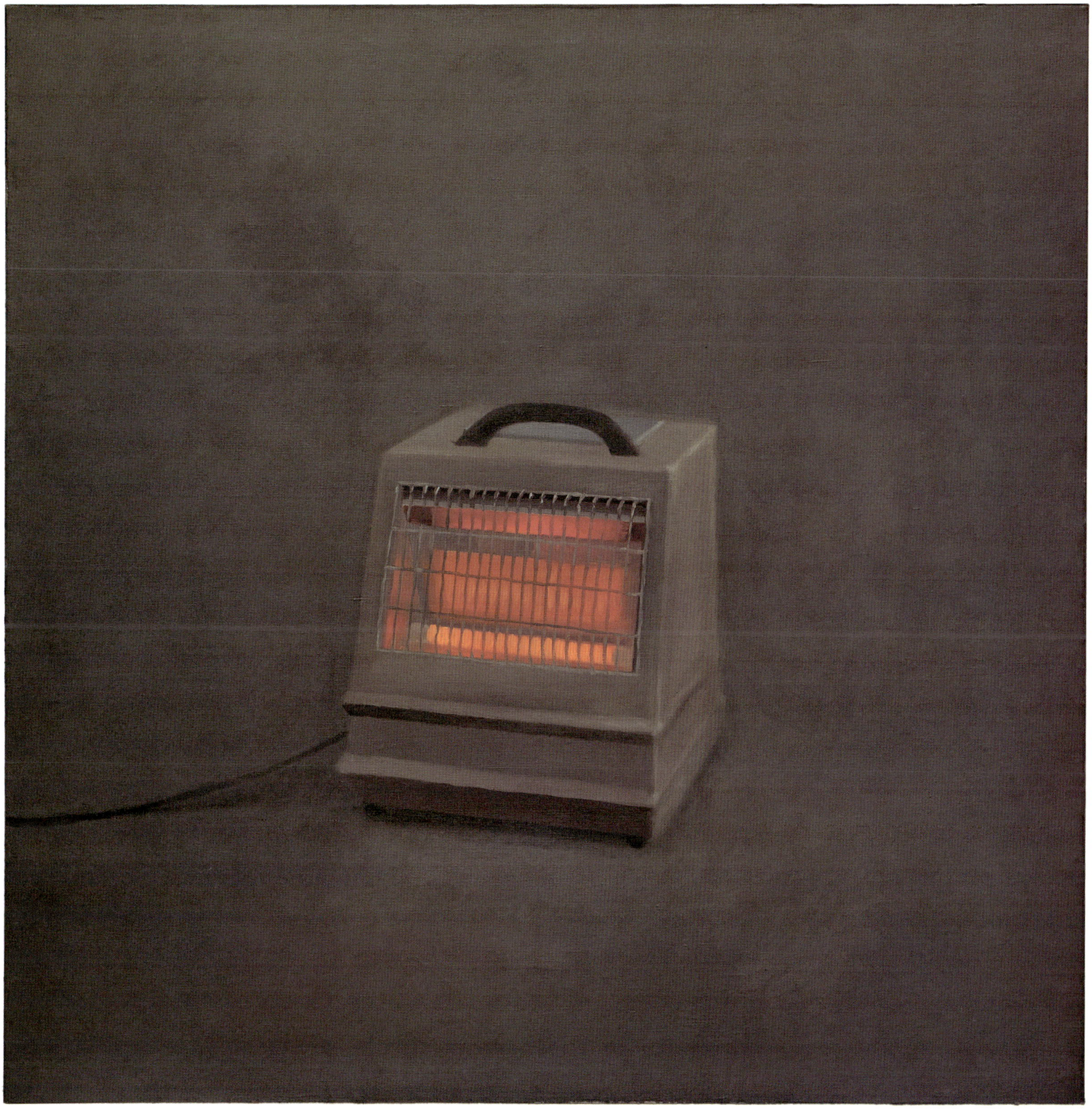

below, **Hot Plate**
1964
Oil on canvas
63.5 × 89 cm
25 × 35 in

opposite, **Pan**
1964
Oil on canvas
63.5 × 89 cm
25 × 35 in

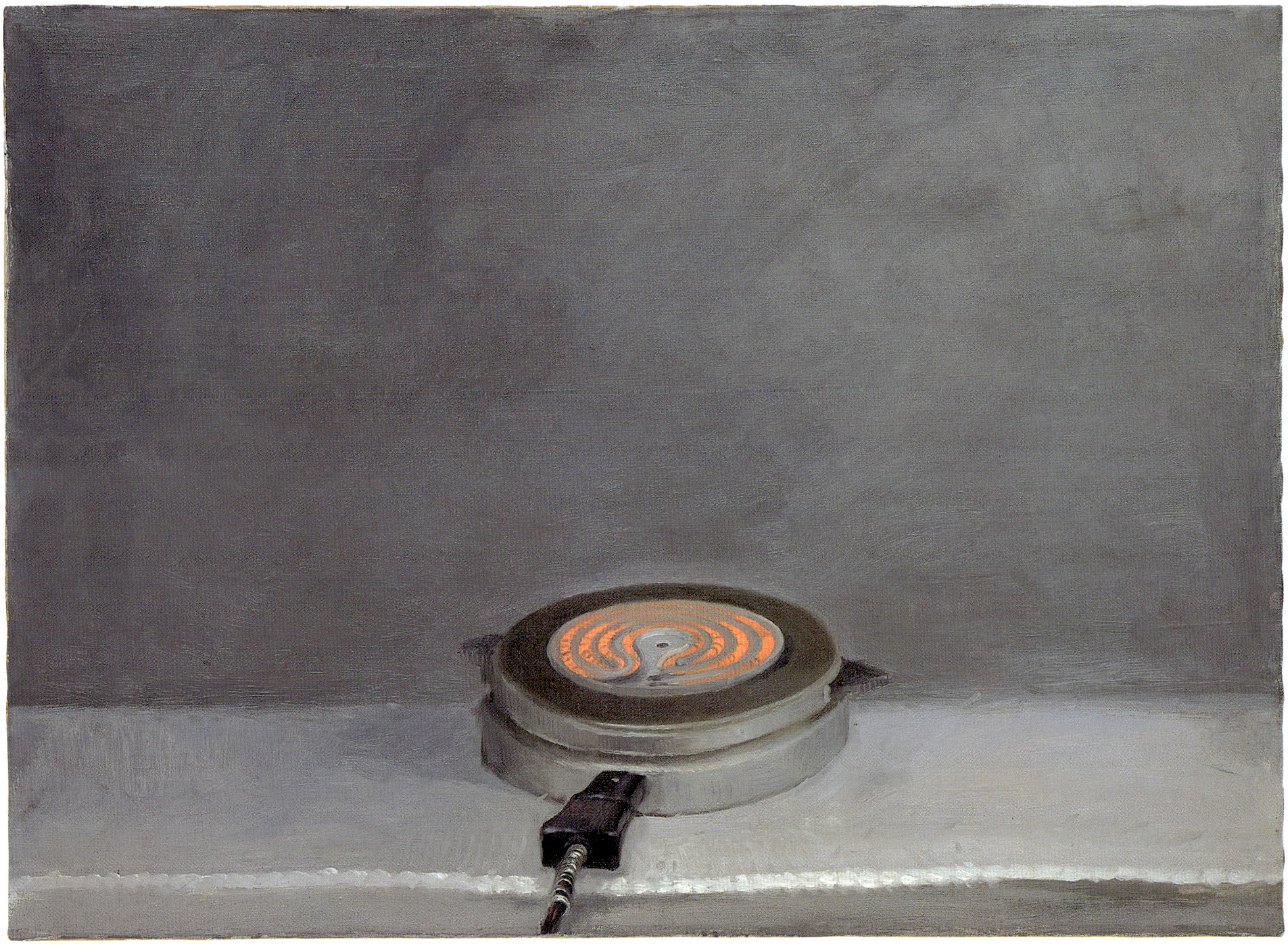

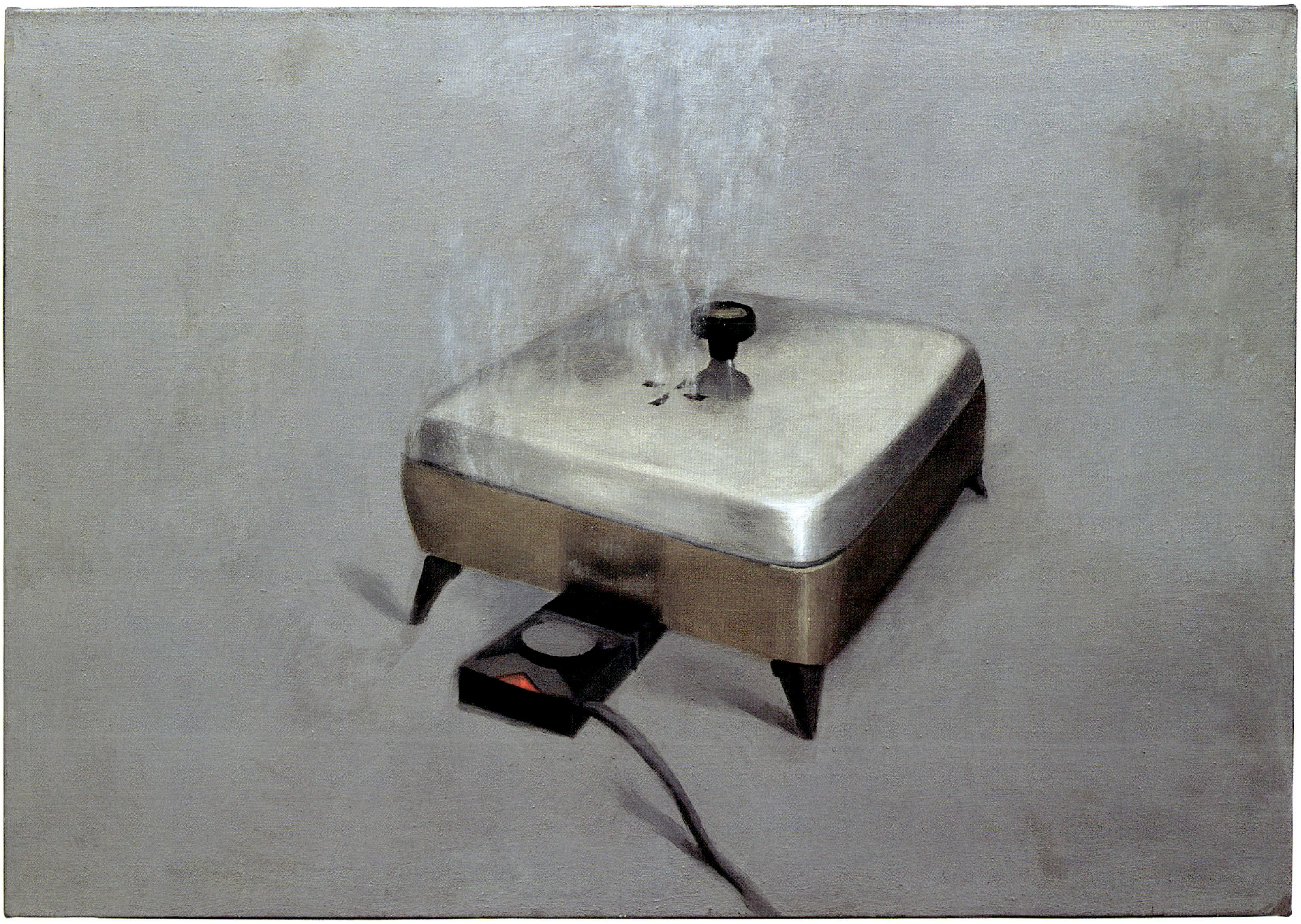

Close That's right. Do you feel that you purposely pushed yourself into some corner where you had something more specifically personal to do?

Celmins **The truth is that I have always had a lot of stops and starts in my work. So sometimes it's hard to see a logical development. When I realized that this painting that I was doing was getting so decorative and meaningless, probably for reasons you said – that I hadn't really originated it and received most of this information from magazines – I had to leave it. I had to back up and find a place where I felt more comfortable.**

Close In the 1940s and 1950s art magazines were in black and white. Growing up in Seattle, I went over these magazines with magnifying glasses. As far as I was concerned, all these de Koonings and stuff were black and white. I had never seen any of the originals; I didn't know what colour they were. And it wasn't until about 1961, when the magazine *It Is* came out, that I saw the first reproductions in colour to see what these paintings actually looked like. Both of us have spent a lot of time making black-and-white work.

Celmins **I think I probably dropped the colour for other reasons.**

Close Well, me too.

Celmins **I was dissatisfied. As I remember, many people moved on from Abstract-Expressionist painting – so did I. I decided to go back to looking at something outside of myself. I was also going back to what I thought was this basic, stupid painting. You know: there's the surface, there's me, there's my hand, there's my eye, I paint. I don't embellish anymore, I don't compose, and I don't jazz up the colour.**

One of the things that I remember being very struck by was an Ad Reinhardt article. I think it came out in 1957, in *ARTnews* or something. Remember that article on twelve things not to do? I'm just going to read the very first one because I believe that I had never seen Reinhardt's work, and I don't think I've ever been influenced by his painting, but I have been influenced by his writing. He wrote twelve technical rules, or how to achieve the twelve things to avoid – I loved that. No texture, no brushwork or calligraphy, no sketching or drawing. Now you see I drew but I didn't sketch. What I

Zeppelin
1968
Graphite on acrylic ground on paper
35 × 47 cm
13.75 × 18.5 in

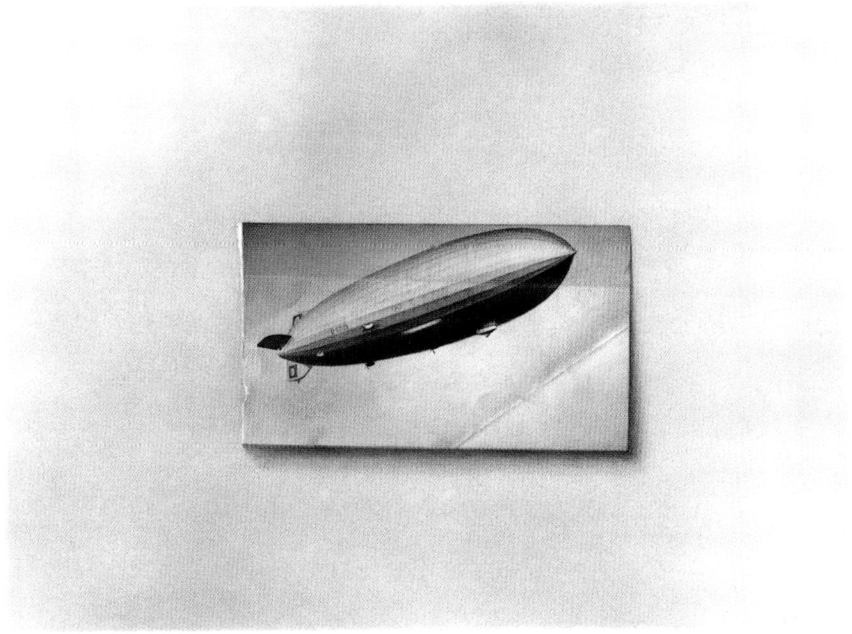

finally did was to leave painting: forms, design, colour, and, I thought, invention.

I remember discussing this article in Indiana, of all places, in this very traditional studio where older students had their own little, messy workplaces. I remember being inspired to imagine what is art if you remove all these things. What was left was a kind of poetic reminder of how little a work of art really is art, and how elusive it is to chase the part that excites you and turns one thing into something else. And how tiny that part is, and how hard it is to define. So I was inspired to throw away as much as I could.

Close Actually, we were on opposite coasts purging our work.

Celmins **Did you do that too?**

Close Absolutely, severe self-imposed limitations: I am not going to do this. I can't do that. I am not going to use this material. Get colour out of there.

Celmins **Were your first things black and white?**

Close Yeah, I didn't work in colour for several years.

Celmins **There were a lot of changes going on in the late 1950s and early 1960s. Johns, Warhol, Rauschenberg, Morley ... all those people that started doing dumb objects, dumb painting, commercial-art painting, whatever you call it. I began to look at Morandi, too, because he was showing up in magazines [...]**

Close As much as your work is purged of a lot – trying to get the handwriting out of there, trying to get the brushwork out of there, get the colour out of there, and all that stuff – it is amazingly physical. There is a tremendous amount of physicality to it. It is not just ethereal. I think that is one of the dichotomies that is really riveting and so engaging in the work. At once they look like they just happened and yet there's this physicality. The drawings are incredibly physical as well.

Celmins **Sometimes I'm convinced that there is nothing else but the physical act of making the art. Sometimes I refine it too much which makes it seem ethereal, which of**

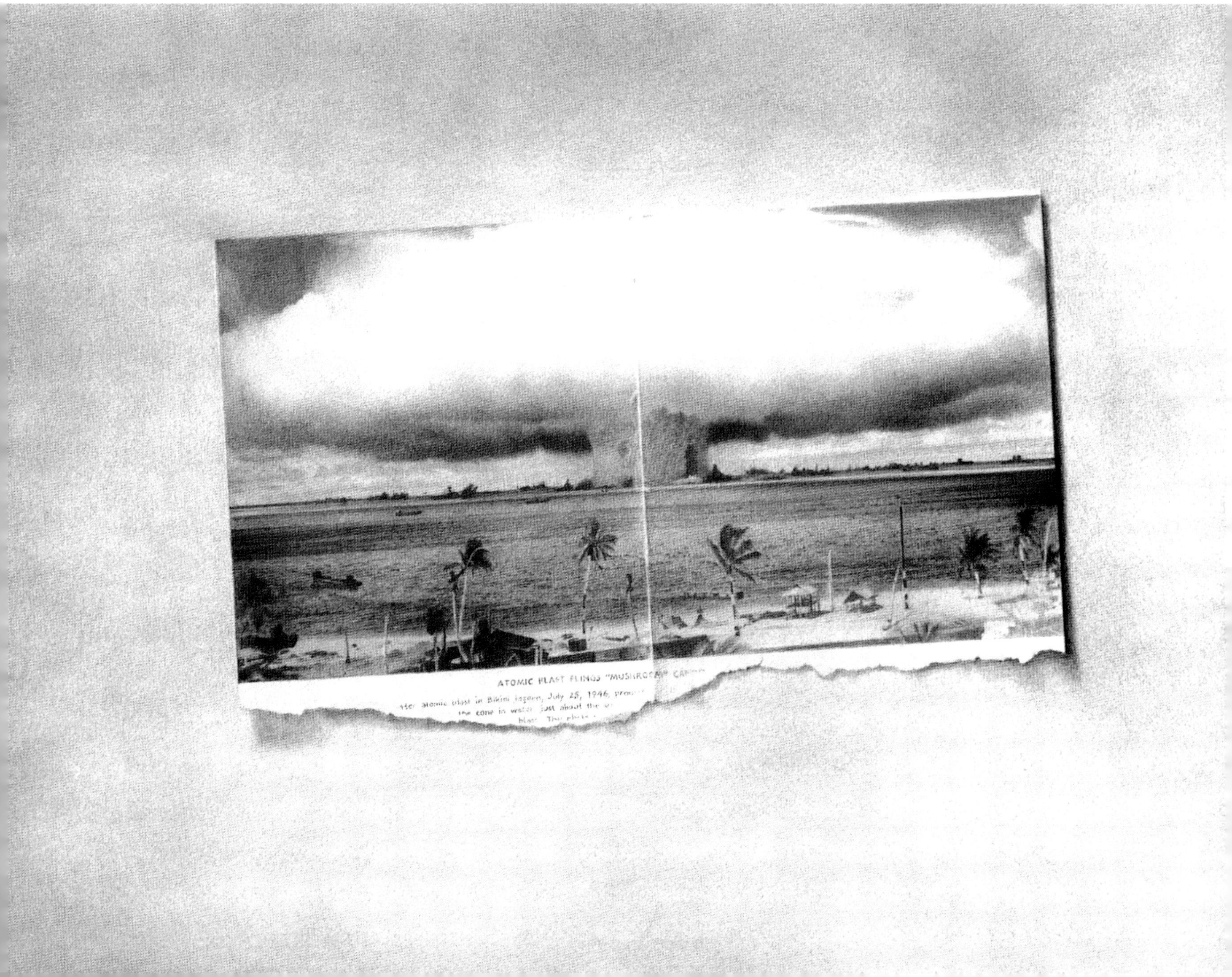
ATOMIC BLAST FLINGS
atomic blast in Bikini lagoon, July 25, 1946,
cone in water just about the

opposite, **Bikini**
1968
Pencil on paper
34.5 × 47 cm
13.5 × 18.5 in

right, **Plane**
1968
Graphite on acrylic ground on paper
35 × 45.5 cm
13.75 × 18 in
Collection Fogg Art Museum, Cambridge, Massachusetts

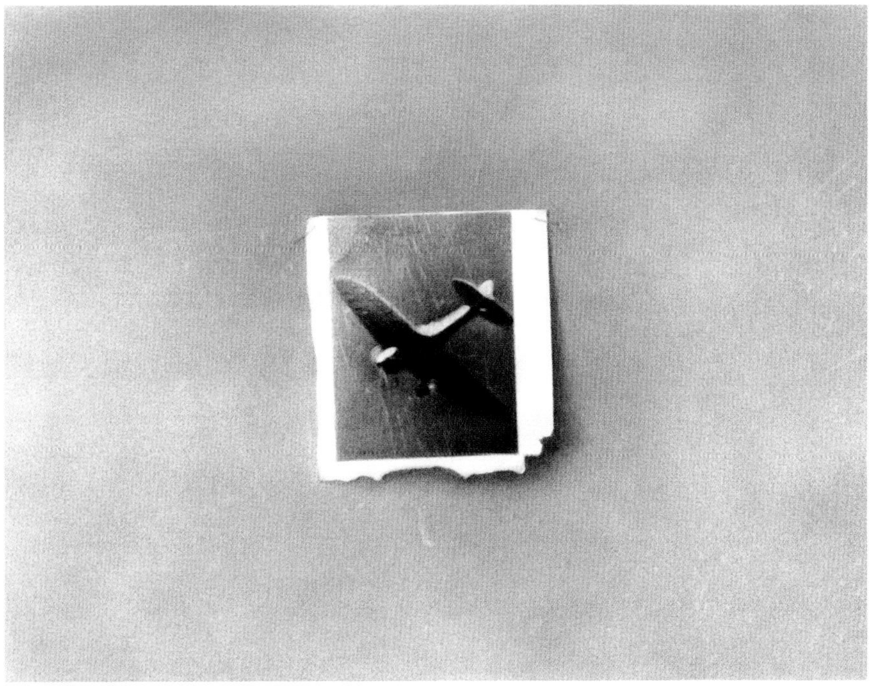

course it's not.

Close You're talking about how conceptual drawing with graphite is. There isn't so much there, just decisions, just a record of decisions having been made.

Celmins **That's because I see drawing as thinking, as evidence of thinking, evidence of going from one place to another. One draws to define one thing from another. Draws proportions, adjusts scale. It is impossible to paint without drawing. I see the drawing in your painting, too.**

Going back to the object paintings I started in 1963–64, I dropped scale and composition altogether and painted the objects one by one, life-sized: hot plate, lamps, refrigerator, radio … I made some of the objects three-dimensional like the *Comb*. I think of them as having fallen out of the picture plane. They are not really sculpture.

Close I don't think of your sculpture as sculpture, but more like painting that comes out of the room and occupies the space with us.

Celmins **That's a nice way to put it. I was grappling with what it meant to work on a two-dimensional plane, and come out of it and go back into it.**

Close I think all this has a lot to do with artifice and the artificial. In a sense you are decorating a surface with paint, but then there is the desire to actually paint around something. It makes me think of your choice of photographs because you say in your notebook, 'My eyes were honed in nature. I practised seeing the desert.' Some people think that you're not looking if you're looking at a photograph.

Celmins **Oh, that's ridiculous.**

Close Why do you put this artificial layer between you and what you're looking at?

Celmins **The photo is an alternative subject, another layer that creates distance. And distance creates an opportunity to view the work more slowly and to explore your relationship to it. I treat the photograph as an object, an object to scan. Actually, the**

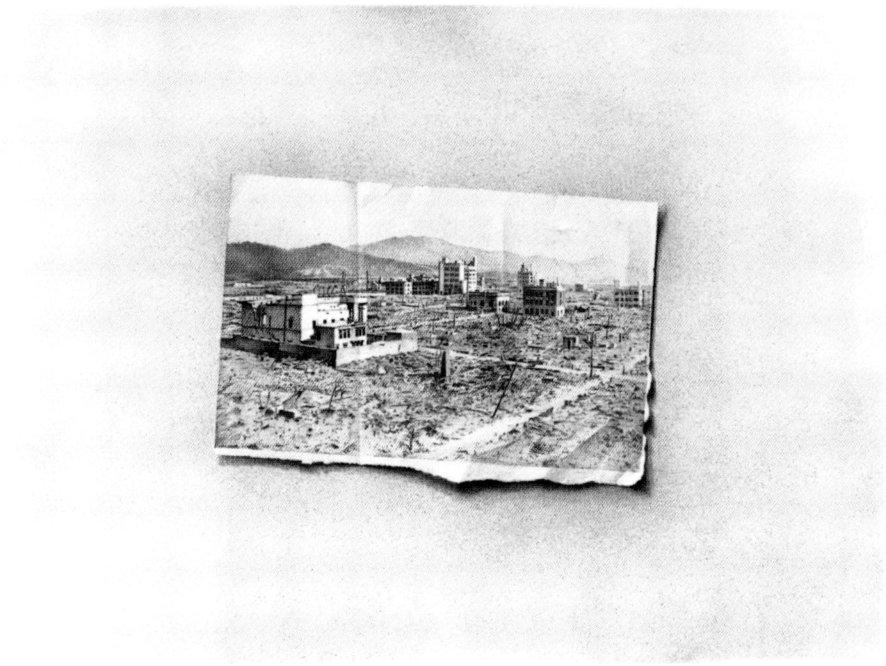

left, **Hiroshima**
1968
Graphite on acrylic ground on paper
34.5 × 45.5 cm
13.5 × 18 in

opposite, artist's source material in studio drawer

first time I used photographs was really because I had been away from my family and was lonely. I had been going through bookstores finding war books and tearing out little clippings of aeroplanes, bombed out places – nostalgic images. At first I painted them, later I decided the clippings were this wonderful range of greys for me to explore with graphite. Then I started to do these moon drawings from photographs taken by a machine that had recorded the range of greys on the moon and had transmitted them back. Then they had been photographed and printed in a book, and then ...

Close There was a layering in between.

Celmins **I thought of it as putting the images that I found in books and magazines back in the real world – in real time. Because when you look at the work you confront the here and now. It's right there.**

Close So you approach these photographs as an object in the same way as the lamp had been an object?

Celmins **Right, I did at first. I think you can see that the whole idea at first was that it might be possible to put something in a two-dimensional plane, or on it, or somehow solve that problem. You can see that the photographs had the same kind of single-object imagery, like the objects that I had been painting earlier. In a way, the photograph helps unite the object with the two-dimensional plane. Although I think that with aeroplanes there is kind of wonderful place where they really float, and then they become dimensional, and they take off as well as staying flat. I did not realize it then, but now I can see that the subject matter has a kind internal tension that also exists in the work. The paintings tend to have an internal feeling, as if there was something behind what you see.**

Close The paintings are very lush and, at the same time, they're incredibly restrictive. That is a funny dichotomy.

Celmins **I'm always aware of the limits of painting, and have come to think that the limits are what give it more meaning. Of course, one has to find the limits. I painted so**

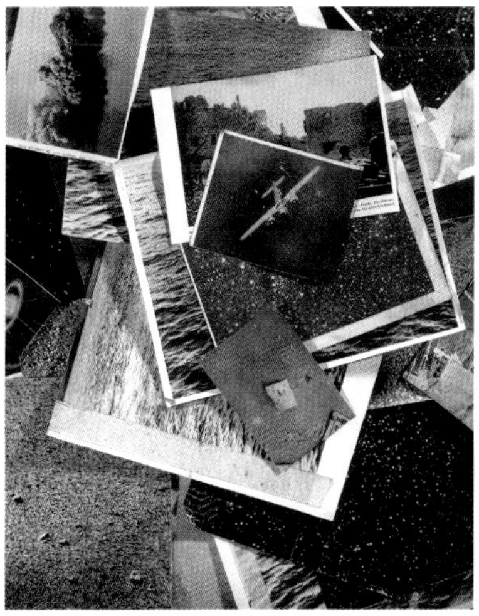

much between 1961 and 1964 that I probably went through five lifetimes of different sorts of painting: Matisse, Hoffman, Gorky, and de Kooning. I think you can also see quite a bit of a Morandi influence, as well.

Close More in the early colour work. It's a world of colour but it's really approached monochromatically. Later, when you got colour totally out of the picture, the viewer fills in the colour in his/her mind. I always thought that black-and-white photographs of war, for instance, were far more scary than colour photographs of war because colour photographs of war always look wrong – the blood doesn't look like blood, it looks like ketchup or something. But in a black-and-white photograph of war you fill in the colour in your mind and make blood blood-coloured. In a way, it's sort of less artificial. By purging the work of colour it actually makes them more naturalistic.

Celmins **Yeah, but naturally I didn't think of that either. What I know is that I didn't just wake up one day and say, I'm not going to use colour. I slipped into it through drawing the photographs, which were black and white, because those were the only photographs available at the time. The second thing is that I do believe I wanted a more sombre note and I thought that colour was an extra, as if I were decorating something.**

Close I understand that. I got rid of colour because I felt I depended too much on it. I'd been told that I had a good sense of colour and all that. It just occurred to me that the colour I was using was learned colour, was art colour, it had something to do with other people's paintings. I could see wanting to get it out because it was reminiscent of a certain kind of art.

Celmins **That's right, though I often think that my thing of removing things was going too fast. Part of it was an intellectual series of decisions to remove stuff arrived at intuitively. Then I think it may just be my nature to throw stuff away.**

Close Let's talk about your nature. At one time, you described yourself as lazy. To look at your work, the last word to describe you as is lazy. When we started talking about compulsion you said that everyone would assume you're a very compulsive person. I don't think you're a very compulsive person, nor do I think I am. A compulsive person is driven

Letter
1968
Graphite on acrylic ground on paper
33.5 × 46 cm
13.25 × 18.125 in

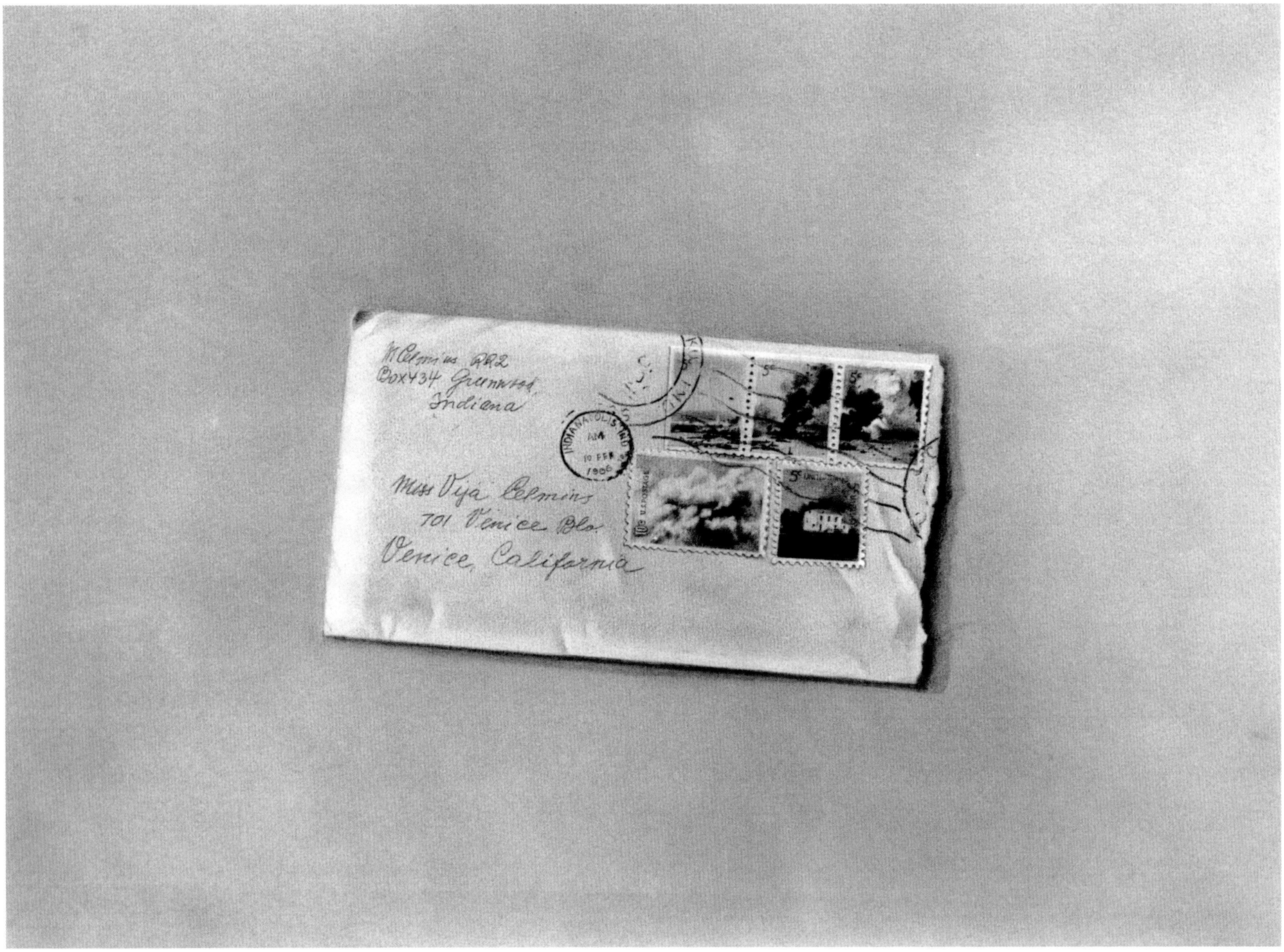

to do things whether they want to do them or not. They have almost no control over themselves.

Celmins **Oh no, I'm not like that.**

Close I don't see you that way at all. I see that you force yourself to behave in a compulsive manner, that is, to sit there and keep doing it. But it doesn't come from some kind of compulsive drive.

Celmins **No, I don't think it's mindless compulsion.**

Close Do you think that people like your work for the wrong reasons?

Celmins **Who knows why people like work. At a certain point, you're very happy that people look at it at all; in that way it's good. My feeling is, however, that often people only look at the image. I feel that the image is just a sort of armature on which I hang my marks and make my art. The early imagery, especially the war things, had a more specific emotional tension, but most of my later imagery developed without choosing any specific kind of symbolic meaning. I don't use the ocean in any kind of symbolic way. These first broken-surface images were a way to articulate the surface of the drawing in a Cubist way: with individual marks that break up the surface and then build up into a whole.**

Close In your notebook you talk about building a painting: 'I build the work like a house, like a construction. Hah, all the materials put together – When I was young I had mechanical ability.' You could build whatever you wanted [...] I like to think the way I work is almost like knitting a painting, or something like that. I don't think of it as painting in layers, the way you talk about finding a way to get down to an armature for the individual marks to build upon. That's something that interests me a great deal.

Celmins **I have long been interested in building a form in the painting. It's hard to define the word *form*, but I wanted to make a work that was multidimensional and that went back and forth in space yet remained what it was: a small, concentrated area that was**

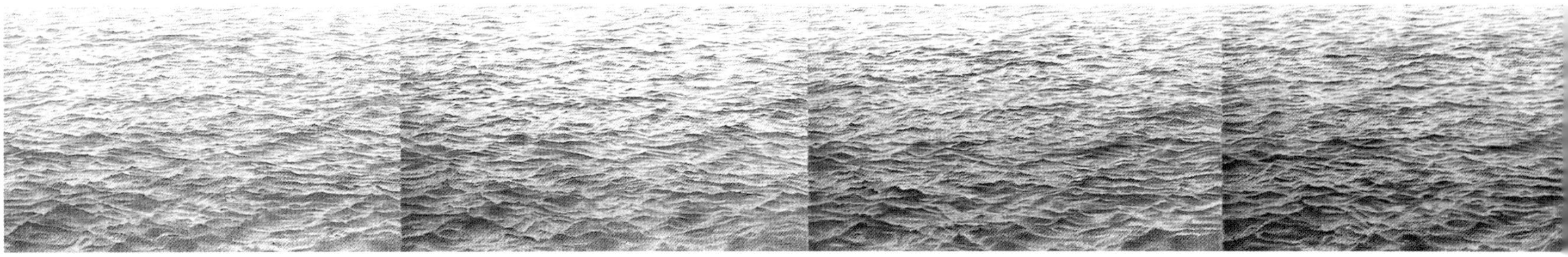

Ocean: 7 Steps #1
1972–73
Graphite on acrylic ground on paper
29 × 249 cm
11.5 × 98 in
Collection Whitney Museum of American Art, New York

essentially flat. Who knows why you want to do this. So, in a way, I thought of painting as building a dense and multi-levelled structure. Now I tend to think of it only in physical terms, but you could say that it alludes to a denser experience of life. You have to re-imagine it in other terms, which is lead [graphite], paper, paint and canvas. My feeling is that we all do essentially the same thing. I like to talk about it in terms of structuring because when I'm working, my instinct is to try to build and to fill. To fill something until it is really full [...]

Close The last time we were together we were talking about how important the Abstract Expressionists had been for us – how we thought we learned from de Kooning, what we thought we learned from them. Now, most people looking at your work would not assume these people had played any seminal role in your deciding to make the kind of work that you make. Yet I see it as absolutely integral to what you do.

Celmins **Good, 'cause I do too.**

Close Whether it's the all-overness of the American painting: doing away with foreground, middle distance, background, and making the whole surface ...

Celmins **Right, although, I don't think that started with Abstract Expressionists. Another artist I looked at carefully is Cézanne. Cézanne recognized and gave value to the space that is in front of you, here and now. It is not just an illustration of absent events, he did it self-consciously. The mark was a mark on the mountain; and that mark also indicated that atmosphere in which the mountain existed; and, finally, it is also a mark on the canvas. At a certain point I realized that this work, which can only allude to so much outside of itself, nevertheless remains comprehensible only through the organization of that flat arena. This is no limitation but an essential expressive element of painting. I think that the abstract expressionists, certainly de Kooning, knew that and used it. They added another subject, however, which was the unconscious – but, of course, that's the subject you like to keep bringing up.**

Close I'm sorry, I'm the last person in the world to keep bringing this stuff up. I feel like I've really failed you. I hate it when people ask who my subjects are looking at, and what

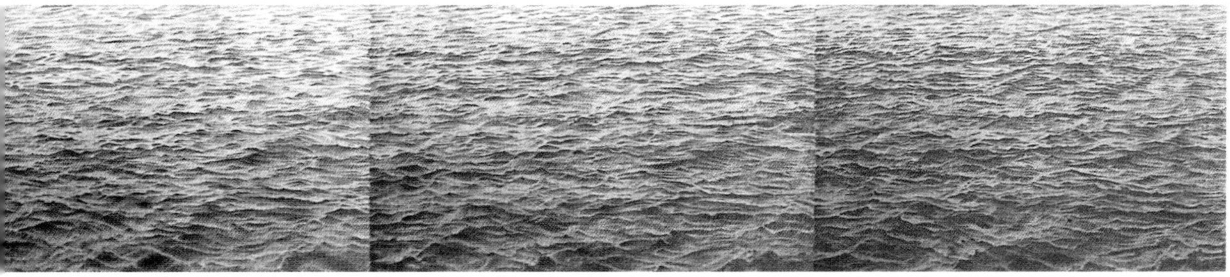

are they thinking, and who are these people. The whole is greater than the sum of its parts. There is a transcendent quality to your work and to all great art.

Celmins **What do you mean by transcendent?**

Close It's the magic of art that makes graphite more than just graphite. Look at her face, she's going to ask for another interviewer! I don't see anything corny in that.

Celmins **So look at your work, maybe that's the nature of art. You do one thing and then something else always comes through.**

Close You stack up the bricks, and you build something that is more than just a pile of bricks. That's what you're doing; the approach is bricklaying. It is something that I respond to in your work.

Celmins **I would say that the work, beginning with ocean drawings, is more like that. It really went into kind of a rigorous building, and letting the material be the material. Letting the image be more and more like an armature. In some of these the image is almost nothing. It just holds you and it articulates the picture all over. See, I'm really interested in that. For some reason I'm able to do that over and over again without getting bored.**

Close Well, maybe because I know what it's like to build a picture. I see the delight in what seems laborious and the pleasure that one takes in small things having occurred. I find it very life-affirming, finally.

Celmins **I guess it is life-affirming [...]**

Close Let's talk about the difference between drawing with a pencil and painting. Even the smallest brush is a clutzier, clumsier tool; then you use this very sharp thing.

Celmins **You can pin the drawing to the paper on the point. Each point is like a point of consciousness. So it is like a record of having been there, which is probably what you**

Untitled (Ocean with Cross #1)
1971
Graphite on acrylic ground on paper
44 × 58 cm
17.25 × 22.75 in

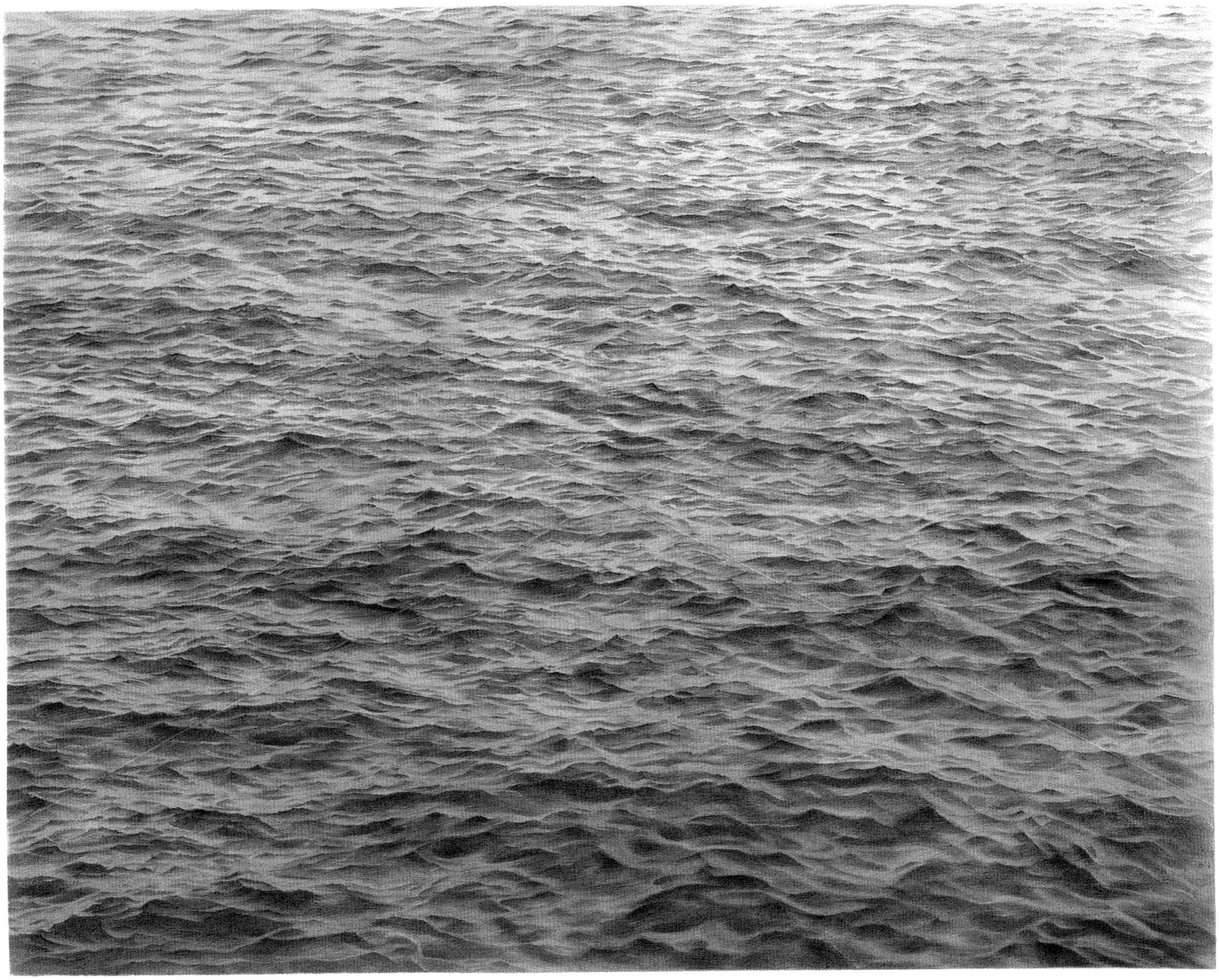

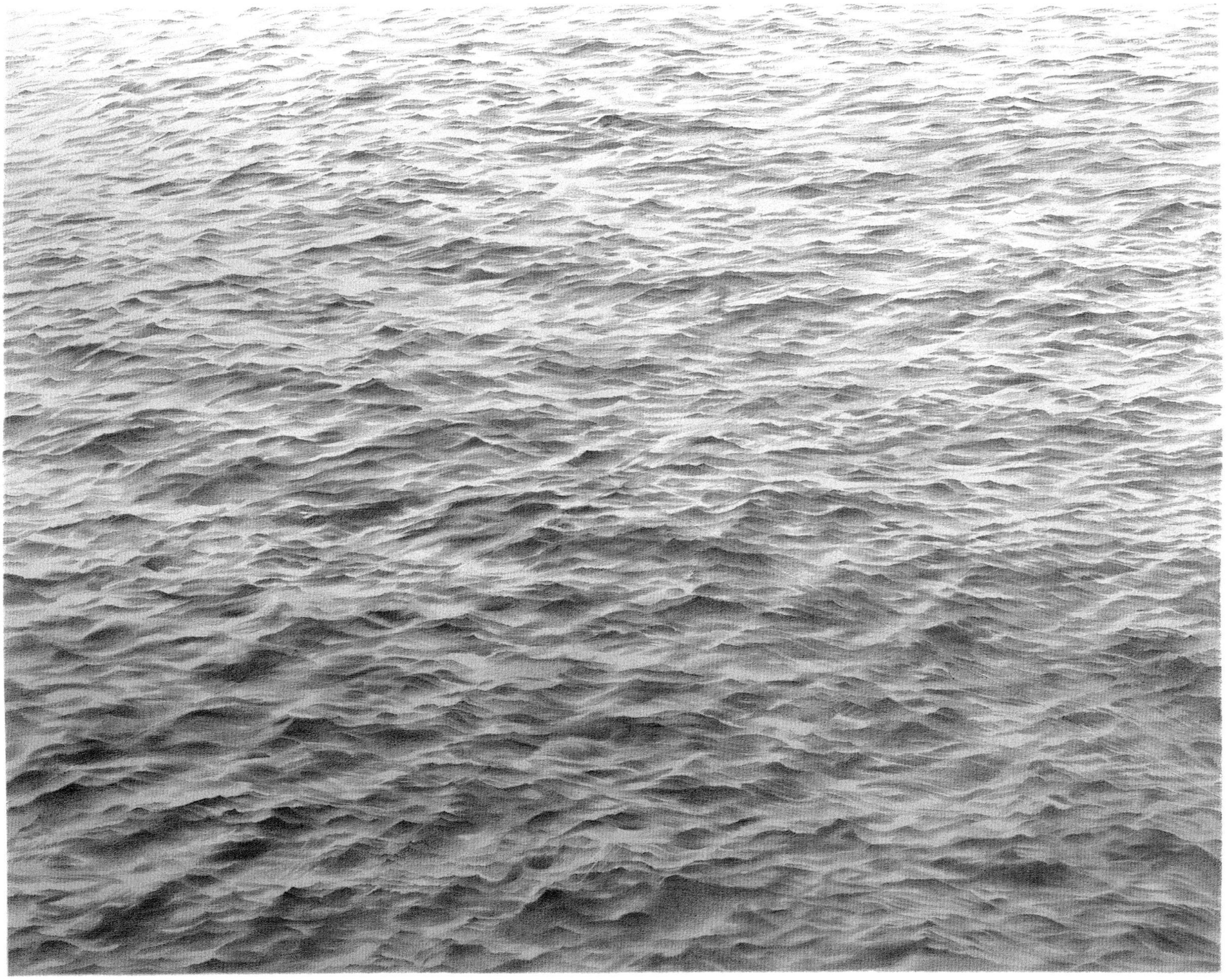

Untitled (Ocean with Cross #2)
1972
Graphite on acrylic ground on paper
47 × 59.5 cm
18.5 × 23.5 in

below, **Galaxy (Cassiopeia)**
1973
Graphite on acrylic ground on paper
30.5 × 38 cm
12 × 15 in
Collection The Baltimore Museum of Art, Maryland

opposite, **Untitled (Snow Surface)**
1977
Graphite on acrylic ground on paper
30.5 × 38 cm
12 × 15 in

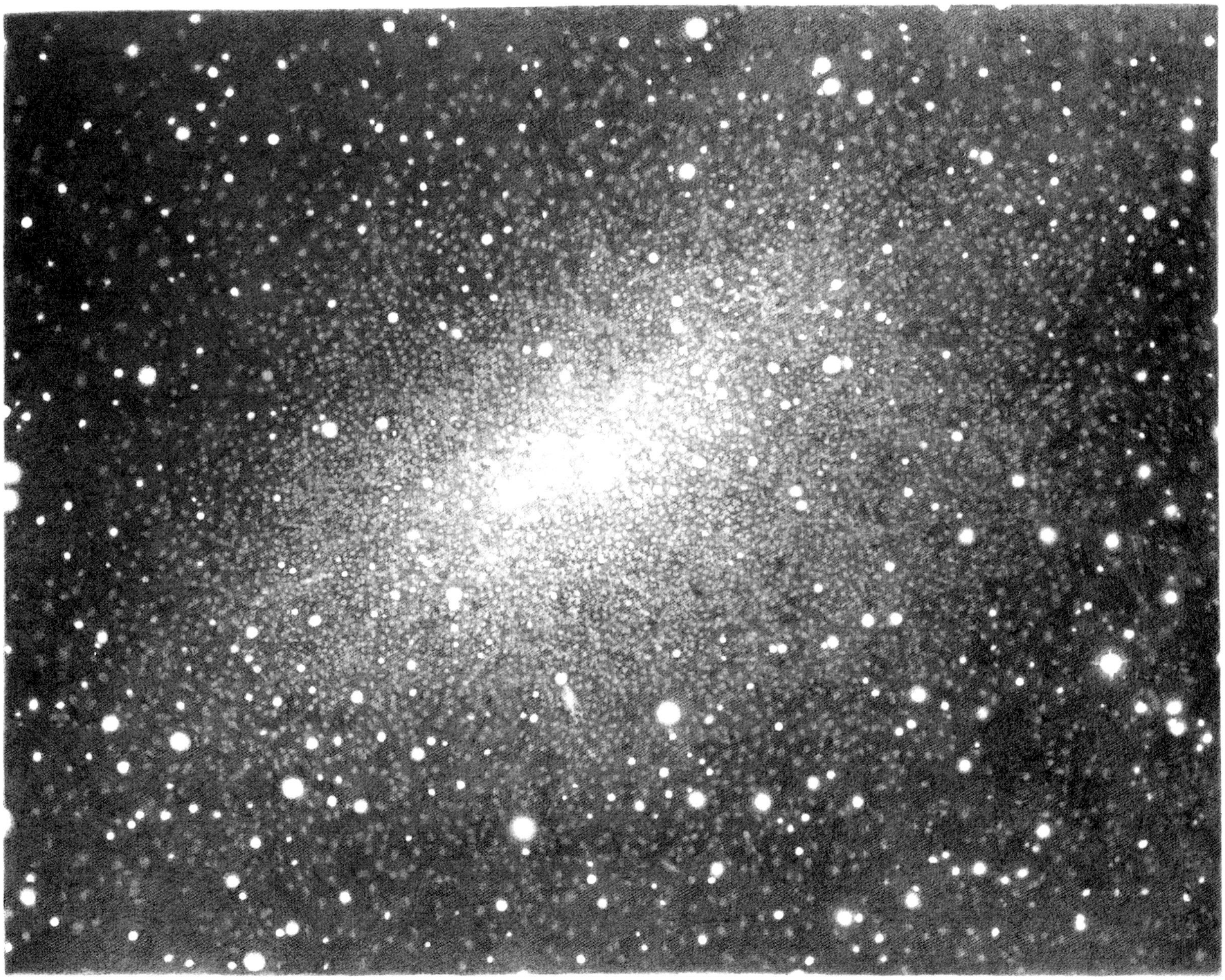

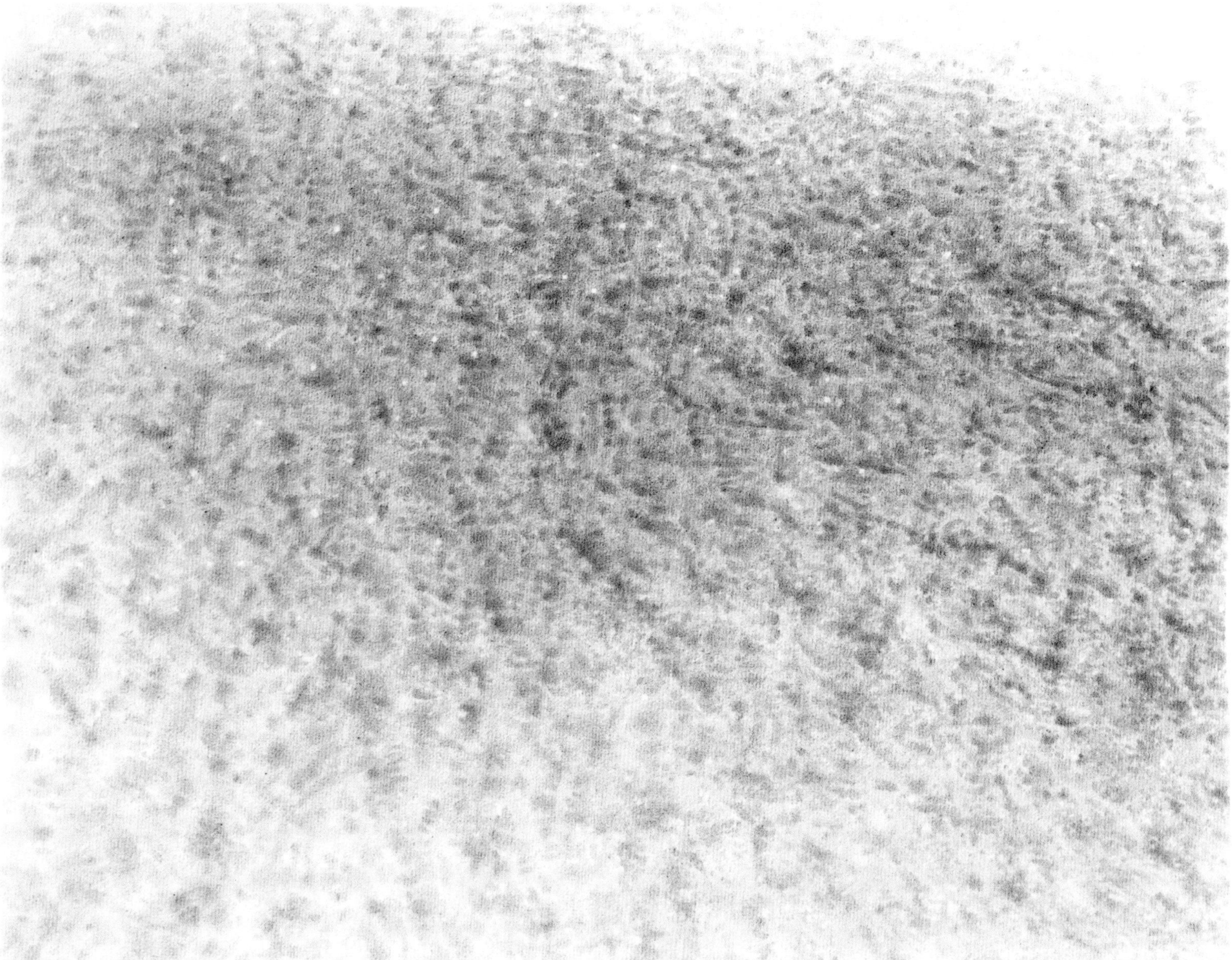

left, **Night Sky #16**
2000–01
Oil on linen mounted on wood
78.5 × 96.5 cm
31 × 38 in

opposite, **Holding onto the Surface**
1983
Graphite on acrylic ground on paper
53.5 × 53.5 cm
21 × 21 in

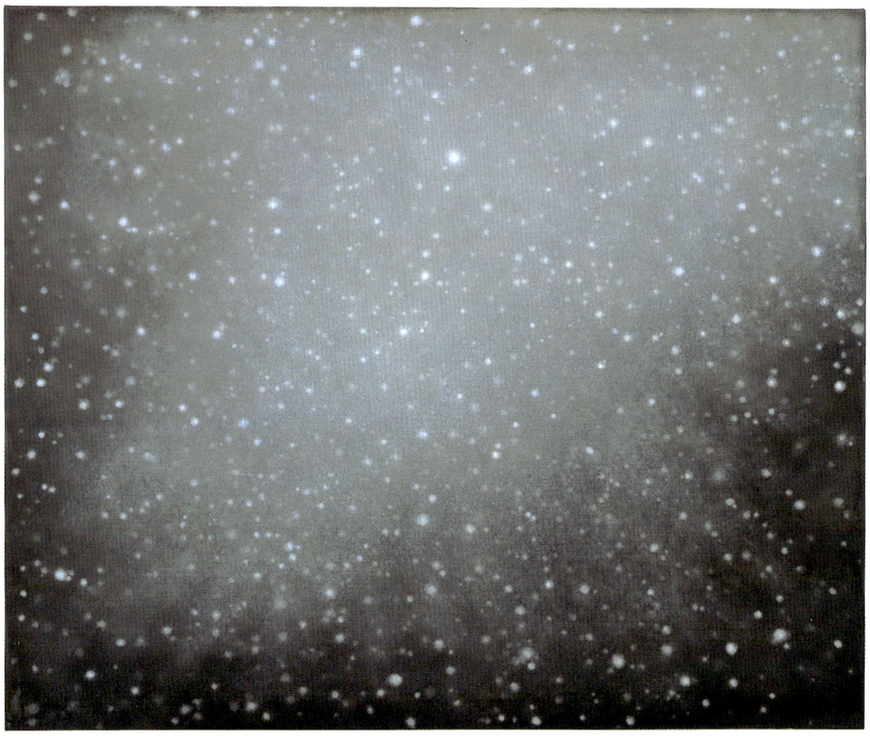

like because we're both artists. You get to be very intimate with the process of putting down the point of the pencil. I like it at that moment. I like the fact that I didn't have to smudge or erase, or push or pull.

Close So what happened when you came back to painting? I would like to continue talking about the difference between pencil and paint.

Celmins **When I started painting again in the mid-1980s, I couldn't finish anything. I painted on this one painting for about six months, scraping off the paint and putting it back on. The paint looked like an old rubber tyre. I layered the paint on dozens of times trying to reach some place in the painting that I could accept, one layer on top of the other. I feel that painting permits a more complicated spatial experience. I like the experience but I felt like a baby crawling on my hands and knees. I should have called this first painting *Start Over*, but I called it *The Barrier* (1985–86) because it was an obstacle to overcome and the overworked surface became a barrier to the image.**

Close Do you work all over?

Celmins **Yeah, I work all over. But in layers, one on top of the other.**

Close Which is the really old, Abstract Expressionist way of working. Slowly bringing the whole surface up at once.

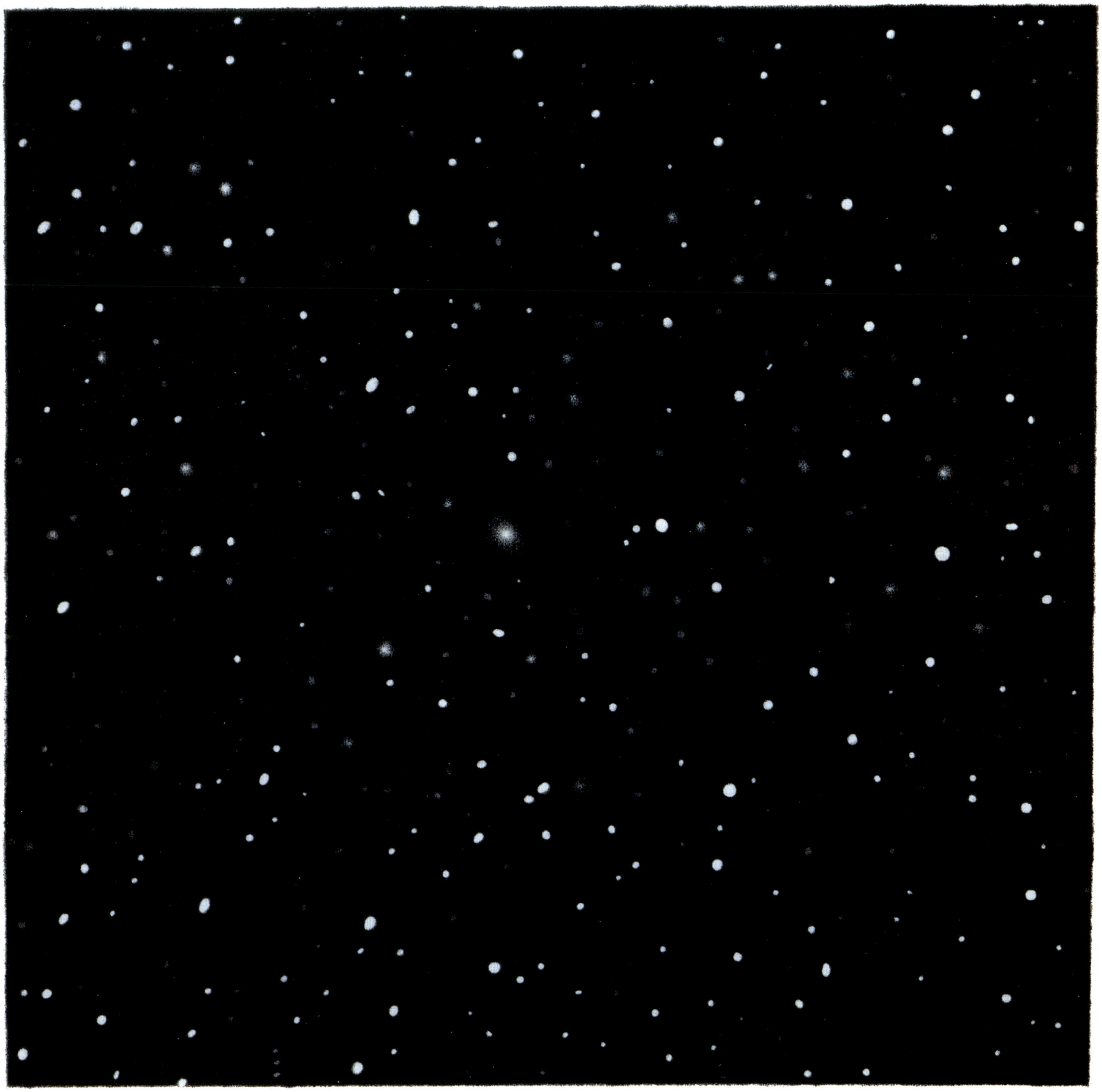

Untitled (Divided Rectangle)
1986–87
Oil on canvas
35.5 × 45.5 cm
14 × 18 in

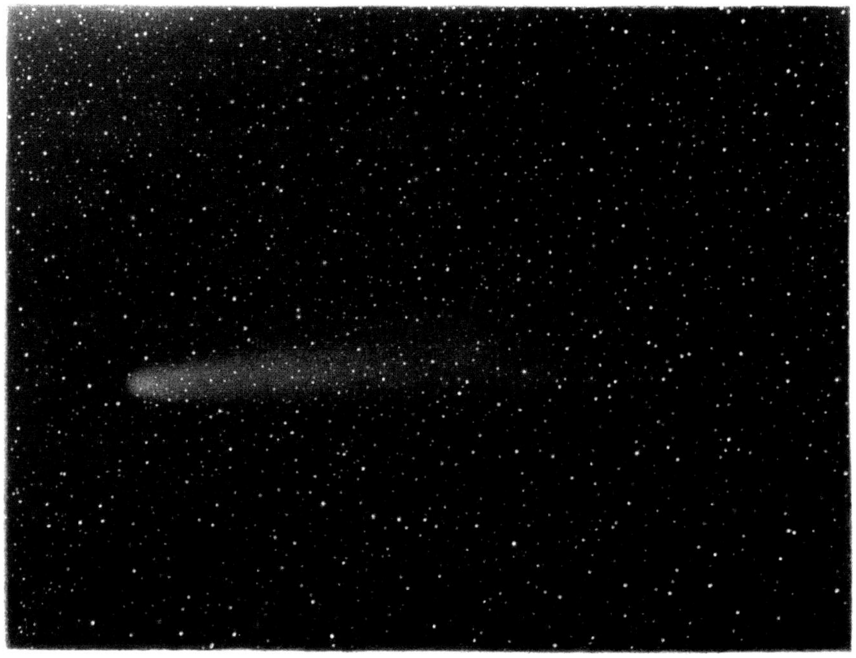

left, **Untitled #9 (For Felix)**
1994–95
Charcoal on paper
43.5 × 56 cm
17.125 × 22.125 in

opposite, **Night Sky #18**
2000–01
Oil on linen mounted on wood
50 × 57 cm
19.75 × 22.5 in

following pages, **Night Sky #12** (detail)
1994–95
Oil on canvas mounted on wood panel
78.5 × 95.5 cm
31 × 37.5 in
Collection Carnegie Museum of Art, Pittsburgh, Pennsylvania

Celmins **I went back to painting because I wanted more form, I wanted the work to carry more weight. I have this feeling the work has more meaning when it is fuller and richer and has what I call 'more form'. I think I'd taken that pencil lead as far as it could go. I think all the last drawings were really my wish to paint and I just hadn't switched to the brush yet. They were as heavy as they could be with lead. They were really about mass and weight but they couldn't carry anymore form. I had a longing for more dimension.**

Close Another way that I think the painting is different is that every square inch of one of these paintings has paint on it. So white areas are painted as well as dark areas. White is reflecting off the outside skin no matter how much is underneath it.

Celmins **There are more possibilities with paint. I like to show the support, yet it is harder to do with paint. I've been leaving the canvas showing on the edges, but that's such a common solution.**

Close Somehow the way the light bounces off the paintings is a lot different than the way the light bounces off the drawings.

Celmins **These paintings that I've just done are matt, so that they don't have light bouncing off them. In fact, the graphite has more light bouncing off it because it's shiny. The white is not painted on black: both the white and the black develop together. I layer them until they become what I call 'fat', so they're like marble. There are more possibilities with painting because I have a feeling that somehow the form is bigger just because there's more layering. There are more shifts in the work. It just is a more complicated spatial experience […]**

'Vija Celmins Interviewed by Chuck Close at her New York Loft on September 26 and 27, 1991', *Vija Celmins*, A.R.T. Press, New York, 1992.

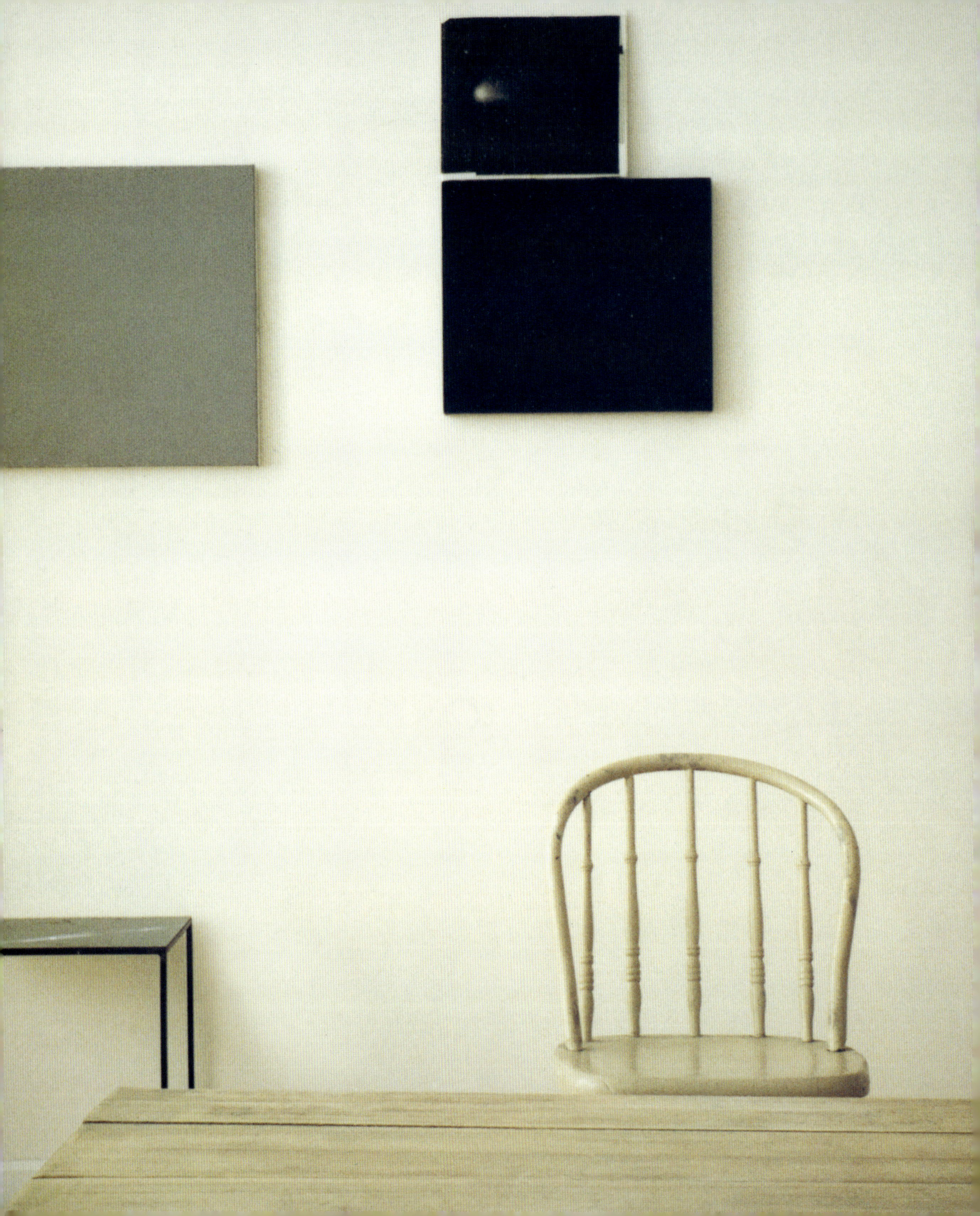

Contents

Interview **Robert Gober** in conversation with **Vija Celmins, page 6.** Survey **Lane Relyea** Vija Celmins' Twilight Zone, **page 44.** Focus **Briony Fer** *Night Sky #19*, 1998, **page 100.** Artist's Choice **Jorge Luis Borges** Funes the Memorious (extracts), 1941, **page 108.** Artist's Writings **Vija Celmins** Interview with Chuck Close (extracts), 1991, **page 116.**
Chronology **page 144** & Bibliography, List of Illustrations, **page 158.**

Selected exhibitions and projects

1948–71

1948
Arrives in New York

1949
Family settles in Indianapolis, Indiana

1961
Receives fellowship to Yale University Summer Session

1962
Receives BFA from John Herron Institute, Indianapolis

1962–80
Lives and works in Venice, California

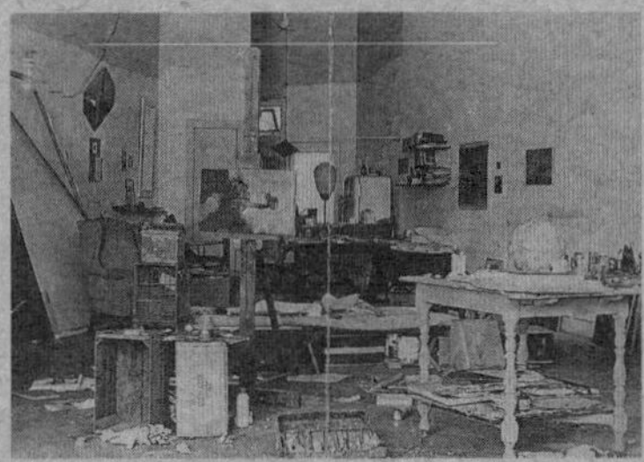

Artist's studio, Venice, California, 1965

1965
Receives MFA from University of California at Los Angeles

Dickson Art Center, University of California at Los Angeles (MFA exhibition, solo)

1965–66
Instructor, California State College, Los Angeles

1966
David Stuart Galleries, Los Angeles (solo)

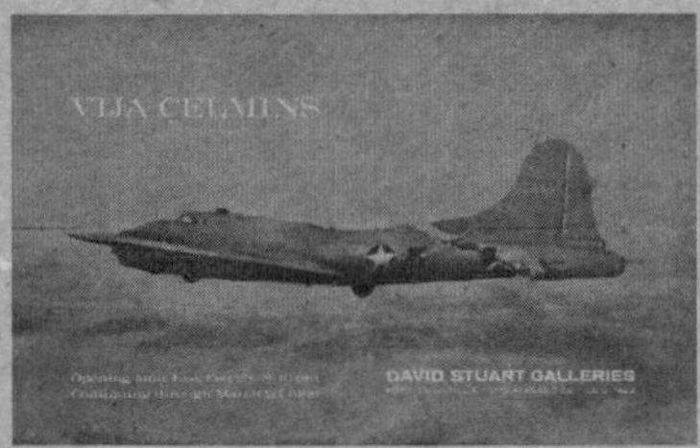

1967–72
Instructor, University of California, Irvine

1968
Receives Cassandra Foundation Award

1969
Riko Mizuno Gallery, Los Angeles (solo)

'Contemporary American Drawings',
Modern Art Museum of Fort Worth, Texas (group)
Cat. *Contemporary American Drawings*, Modern Art Museum of Fort Worth, Texas, text Peter Plagens

1970
'Annual of Contemporary American Sculpture',
Whitney Museum of American Art, New York (group)
Cat. *Annual of Contemporary American Sculpture*, Whitney Museum of American Art, New York

1971
Receives Artist's Fellowship from National Endowment for the Arts

'Twenty-Four Young Los Angeles Artists',
Los Angeles County Museum of Art (group)
Brochure, *Twenty-Four Young Los Angeles Artists*, Los Angeles County Museum of Art, texts Jane Livingston, Maurice Tuchman

Selected articles and interviews

1948–71

1964
Wholden, Rosalind G., 'Los Angeles', *Arts Magazine*, New York, December

1966
Snyder, S.R., 'Los Angeles', *Artforum*, New York, May

Lippard, Lucy (ed.), *Pop Art*, Praeger Publishers, New York

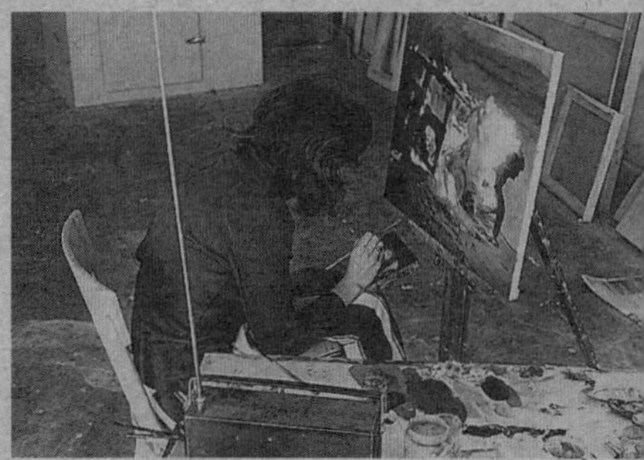

The artist with **Burning Man** (in progress), 1967

1970

Plagens, Peter, 'Exhibitions in Los Angeles', *Artforum*, New York, March
Livingston, Jane, 'Four Los Angeles Artists', *Art in America*, No. 5, New York, September–October

1971

Baker, Elizabeth, 'Los Angeles', *ARTnews*, New York, September

Selected exhibitions and projects

1972–77

1972
'California Prints',
The Museum of Modern Art, New York (group)

'L.A.',
San Francisco Art Institute, California (group)

'Eighteenth National Print Exhibition',
Brooklyn Museum, New York, toured to **California Palace of the Legion of Honor**, San Francisco (group)
Cat. *Eighteenth National Print Exhibition*, Brooklyn Museum, New York, text Jo Miller

1973
Riko Mizuno Gallery, Los Angeles (solo)

Whitney Museum of American Art, New York (solo)
Brochure, *Vija Celmins*, Whitney Museum of American Art, New York, text Elke M. Solomon

'American Drawings 1963–1973',
Whitney Museum of American Art, New York (group)
Cat. *American Drawings 1963–1973*, Whitney Museum of American Art, New York, text Elke M. Solomon

1974
'Seventy-First American Exhibition',
Art Institute of Chicago, Illinois (group)
Cat. *Seventy-First American Exhibition*, Art Institute of Chicago, Illinois, text A. James Speyer

1975
Felicity Samuel Gallery, London (solo)

Broxton Gallery, Los Angeles (solo)

'Recent Drawings',
organized by the American Federation of the Arts, New York
Huntsville Museum of Art, Alabama, toured to **Princeton University**, New Jersey; **Cummer Gallery of Art**, Jacksonville, Florida; **State University of New York**, Stony Brook (group)
Cat. *Recent Drawings*, American Federation of the Arts, New York, text Elke M. Solomon

Receives, Artist's Fellowship from National Endowment for the Arts

1976–77
Instructor, California Institute of the Arts, Valencia

Selected articles and interviews

1972–77

1972

McCann, Cecile, 'Los Angeles Artists', *ArtWeek*, New York, 9 December

van Deren, Coke, *The Painter and the Photograph*, University of New Mexico Press, Albuquerque

1973

Borden, Lizzie, 'Art Economics and the Whitney Drawing Show', *Artforum*, New York, October

Montgomery, Cara, 'West Coast Report', *Arts Magazine*, New York, September

1974

Kozloff, Max, 'Vija Celmins', *Artforum*, New York, March
Plagens, Peter, *Sunshine Muse: Contemporary Art on the West Coast*, Praeger Publishers, New York

1975
Crichton, Fenella, 'London: Vija Celmins at Felicity Samuels', *Art International*, Bogotá, June
Kent, Sarah, 'Vija Celmins: Drawings', *Studio International*, London, July–August

Rush, David, 'Cirrus Editions Prints', *ArtWeek*, New York, 1 November

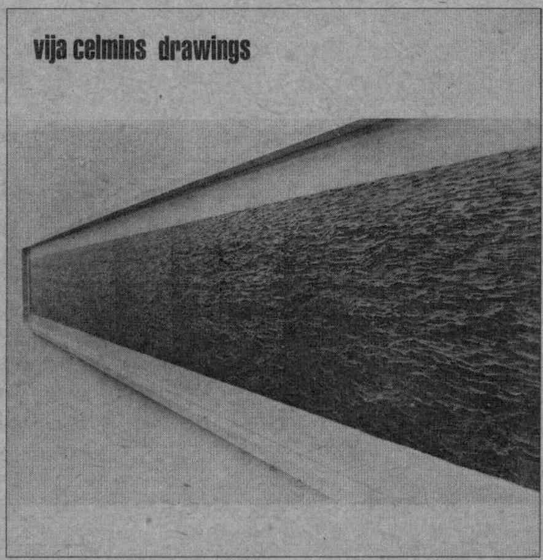

Invitation card, 'Vija Clemins', Whitney Museum of American Art, New York

Selected exhibitions and projects

1976–80

1976

'America 1976',
Corcoran Gallery of Art, Washington, D.C., toured to **Wadsworth Athenaeum**, Hartford, Connecticut; **Fogg Art Museum**, Cambridge, Massachusetts; **The Minneapolis Institute of Arts**, Minnesota; **Milwaukee Art Center**, Wisconsin; **Art Museum of Forth Worth**, Texas; **San Francisco Museum of Modern Art**; **High Museum of Art**, Atlanta, Georgia; **Brooklyn Museum of Art**, New York (group)
Cat. *America 1976*, Corcoran Gallery of Art, Washington, D.C., text Robert Rosenblum

1977

'American Artists: A New Decade',
Detroit Institute of Arts, Michigan, toured to **Modern Art Museum of Fort Worth**, Texas; **Grand Rapids Art Museum**, Michigan (group)
Cat. *American Artists: A New Decade*, Detroit Institute of Arts, Michigan, texts Jay Belloli, Barbara Haskell

'Painting and Sculpture in California: The Modern Era',
San Francisco Museum of Modern Art, toured to **National Collection of Fine Arts**, Smithsonian Institution, Washington, D.C. (group)

'1977 Biennale Exhibition',
Whitney Museum of American Art, New York (group)
Cat. *1977 Biennale Exhibition*, Whitney Museum of American Art, New York

1978

Security Pacific National Bank, Los Angeles (solo)

1979

'The Decade in Review: Selection of the 1970's',
The Museum of American Art, New York (group)
Cat. *The Decade in Review: Selection of the 1970's*, The Museum of American Art, New York, text Patterson Sims

'Vija Celmins: A Survey Exhibition',
Newport Harbor Art Museum, Newport Beach, California, toured to the **Arts Club of Chicago**; **Hudson River Museum**, Yonkers, New York; **Corcoran Gallery of Art**, Washington, D.C. (solo)
Cat. *Vija Celmins: A Survey Exhibition*, Fellows of Contemporary Art, Los Angeles, text Susan C. Larsen

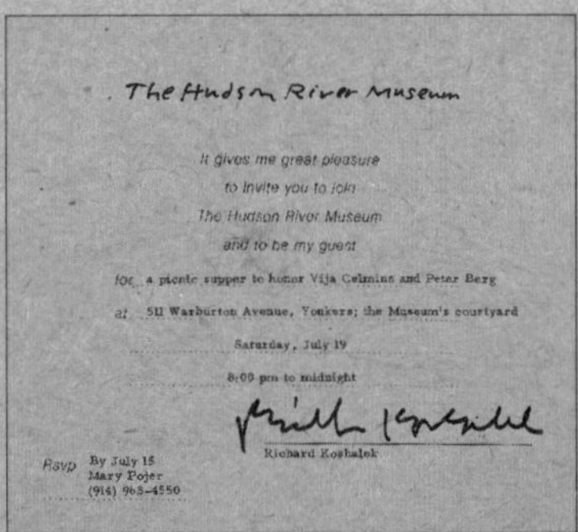
The Hudson River Museum

It gives me great pleasure
to invite you to join
The Hudson River Museum
and to be my guest
for a picnic supper to honor Vija Celmins and Peter Berg
at 511 Warburton Avenue, Yonkers; the Museum's courtyard
Saturday, July 19
8:00 pm to midnight

Richard Koshalek

Rsvp By July 15
Mary Pojer
(914) 963-4550

Selected articles and interviews

1976–80

1976

Perlmutter, Elizabeth, 'A Hotbed of Advanced Art', *ARTnews*, New York, January
Wortz, Melinda, 'New Editions', *ARTnews*, New York, March
Kutner, Janet, 'The Visceral Aesthetic of a New Decade's Art', *Arts Magazine*, New York, December
Stebbins, Theodore E., *American Master Drawings and Watercolors*, Harper & Row, New York

1978

Hazlett, Gordon J., 'Vija Celmins: A Reductionist by Nature', *ARTnews*, New York, February

Larsen, Susan, 'A Conversation with Vija Celmins', *LAICA Journal*, Los Angeles Institute of Contemporary Art, October–November

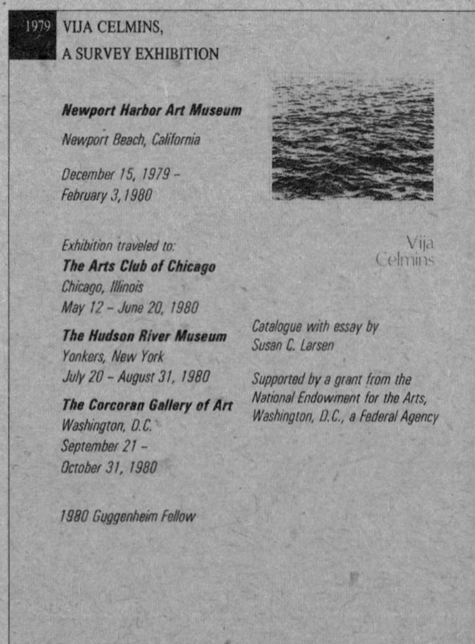
1979 VIJA CELMINS,
A SURVEY EXHIBITION

Newport Harbor Art Museum
Newport Beach, California

December 15, 1979 –
February 3, 1980

Exhibition traveled to:
The Arts Club of Chicago
Chicago, Illinois
May 12 – June 20, 1980
The Hudson River Museum
Yonkers, New York
July 20 – August 31, 1980
The Corcoran Gallery of Art
Washington, D.C.
September 21 –
October 31, 1980

1980 Guggenheim Fellow

Vija
Celmins

Catalogue with essay by
Susan C. Larsen

Supported by a grant from the National Endowment for the Arts, Washington, D.C., a Federal Agency

Muchnic, Suzanne, 'Fellows Get Shows on the Road', *Los Angeles Times*, 24 December
Lewis, Roger, 'Newport Art Museum Moves Up', *Santa Ana Register*, 30 December
Wilson, William, 'Vija Celmins' Expressions of Anxiety', *Calendar*, New York, 6 January 1980
Ball, Mandette, 'Vija Celmins: Objects and Illusions', *ArtWeek*, New York, 12 January 1980
Knight, Christopher, 'Vija Celmins, Newport Harbor Art Museum', *Artforum*, New York, March 1980
Wortz, Melinda, 'Autobiographical Erasers', *ARTnews*, New York, April 1980
Butterfield, Jan, 'Vija Celmins: A Survey Exhibition',

Selected exhibitions and projects

1979–85

1980
Receives Guggenheim Fellowship, New York

1981
Moves to New York City

Resident artist, Skowhegan School of Painting and Sculpture, Maine

1983
'Drawings and Painted Bronzes',
David McKee Gallery, New York (solo)

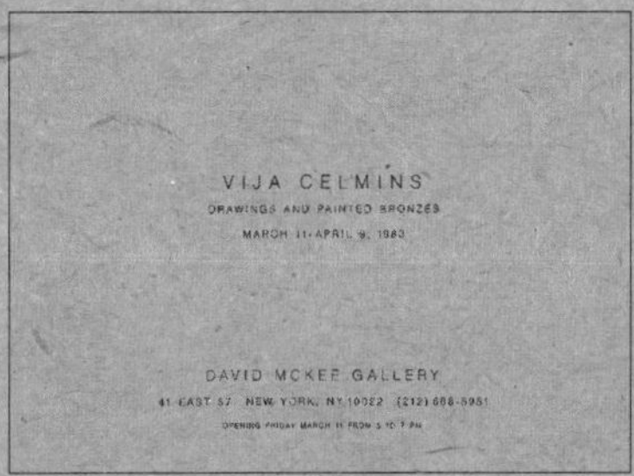

'The American Artist as Printmaker: 23rd National Print Exhibition',
Brooklyn Museum of Art, New York (group)
Cat. *The American Artist as Printmaker: 23rd National Print Exhibition*, Brooklyn Museum of Art, New York, text Barry Walker

'American Still Life 1945–1983',
Contemporary Arts Museum, Houston, Texas, toured to **Albright-Knox Art Gallery**, Buffalo, New York; **Columbus Museum of Art**, Ohio; **Neuberger Museum of Art**, Purchase, New York; **Portland Art Museum**, Oregon (group)
Cat. *American Still Life 1945–1983*, Contemporary Arts Museum, Houston, Texas, text Linda Cathcart

1984
Teaches, Cooper Union, New York

'Gemini, G.E.L., Art and Collaboration',
New York Academy for the Sciences, New York;
National Gallery of Art, Washington, D.C. (group)
Cat. *Gemini, G.E.L., Art and Collaboration*, Abbeville Press, New York, texts Ruth E. Fine, J. Carter Brown

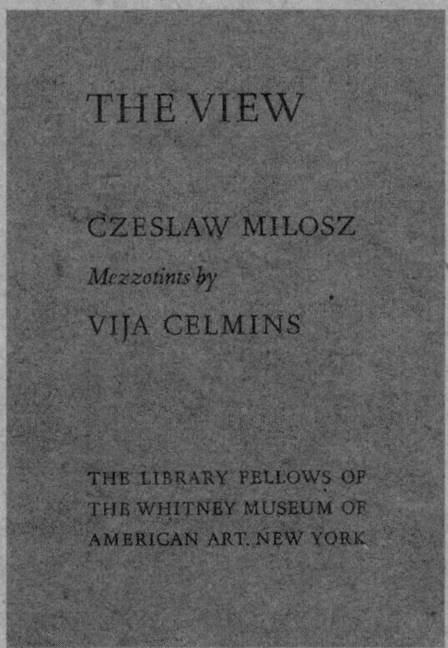

1985
'Focus on Realism: Selections from the Collection of Glenn C. Janss',
Boise Gallery of Art, Idaho, toured to **San Francisco Museum of Modern Art** (group)

Book, Czeslaw Milosz, *The View*, Whitney Museum of American Art, New York, with mezzotints by the artist

Selected articles and interviews

1979–85

Images and Issues, Santa Monica, Summer 1980
Russell, John, 'A Remarkable Museum Debut', *The New York Times*, 28 July 1980

1980

1981

Armstrong, Richard, 'Of Earthly Objects and Stellar Sights: Vija Celmins', *Art in America*, New York, May

1983
Russell, John, 'The Sea and Stars as Seen by Vija Celmins', *The New York Times*, 18 March
Baker, Kenneth, 'A Landscape Beyond Reference Points', *The Christian Science Monitor*, Boston, 20 May
Westfall, Stephen, 'Vija Celmins', *Arts Magazine*, New York, June
Armstrong, Richard, 'Vija Celmins', *Artforum*, New York, Summer
Baker, Kenneth, 'Vija Celmins: Drawing Without Withdrawing', *Artforum*, New York, November

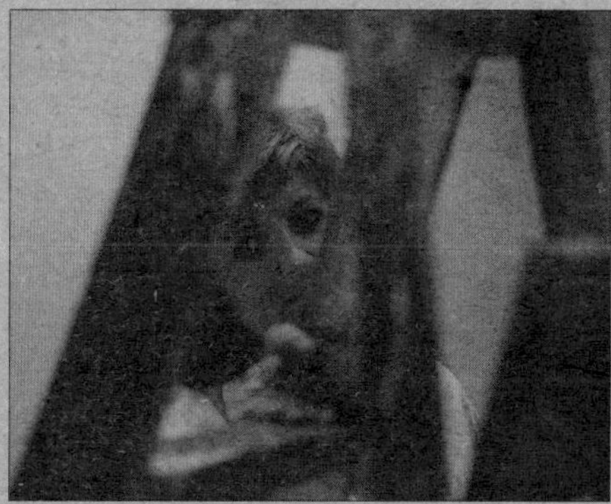
The artist, 1983

Larson, Kay, 'Prints for the Present', *New York Magazine*, 28 November

Raynor, Vivien, 'Traveling Show of American Still Lives Is at the Neuberger', *The New York Times*, 19 August 1984

1984

Ratcliff, Carter, 'Vija Celmins: An Art of Reclamation', *Print Collector's Newsletter*, New York, January–February

1985

'Vija Celmins and Czeslaw Milosz', *Print Collector's Newsletter*, New York, January–February 1986

'Vija Celmins: Concentric Bearings A,B,C,D', *Print Collector's Newsletter*, New York, May–June

Selected exhibitions and projects
1986–90

1986
'Individuals: A Selected History of Contemporary Art, 1945–1986',
Museum of Contemporary Art, Los Angeles (group)
Cat. *Individuals: A Selected History of Contemporary Art, 1945–1986*, Museum of Contemporary Art, Los Angeles, texts Kate Linker, et al.

1987
Teaches, Yale Graduate School, New Haven, Connecticut

'A Graphic Muse: Prints by Contemporary American Women',
Mount Holyoke College Art Museum, South Hadley, Massachusetts (group)
Cat. *A Graphic Muse: Prints by Contemporary American Women*, Mount Holyoke College Art Museum, South Hadley, Massachusetts, texts Richard S. Field, Ruth E. Fine

'Collaborative American Printmaking from Whistler to the Present',
Joe and Emily Lowe Art Gallery, Syracuse, New York (group)

1988
'Vija Celmins, New Paintings',
David McKee Gallery, New York (solo)

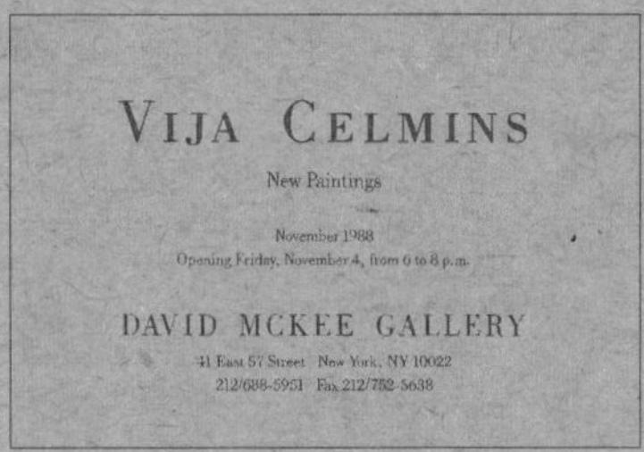
VIJA CELMINS
New Paintings
November 1988
Opening Friday, November 4, from 6 to 8 p.m.
DAVID MCKEE GALLERY
41 East 57 Street New York, NY 10022
212/688-5951 Fax 212/752-5638

1989
'Making Their Mark: Women Artists Move into the Mainstream',
Cincinnati Art Museum, Ohio, toured to **New Orleans Museum of Art**, Louisiana; **Denver Art Museum**, Colorado; **Pennsylvania Academy of the Fine Arts**, Philadelphia (group)
Cat. *Making Their Mark: Women Artists Move into the Mainstream*, Cincinnati Art Museum, Ohio, texts Judith Stein, Ann-Sargent Wooster

'L.A. Pop in the Sixties',
Newport Harbor Art Museum, Newport Beach, California, toured to **Henry Art Gallery**, University of Washington, Seattle; **Palm Springs Desert Museum**, California; **Neuberger Museum**, State University of New York at Purchace; **Pheonix Art Museum**, Arizona (group)
Cat. *L.A. Pop in the Sixties*, Newport Harbor Art Museum, Newport Beach, California, texts Anne Ayres, Jay Belloli

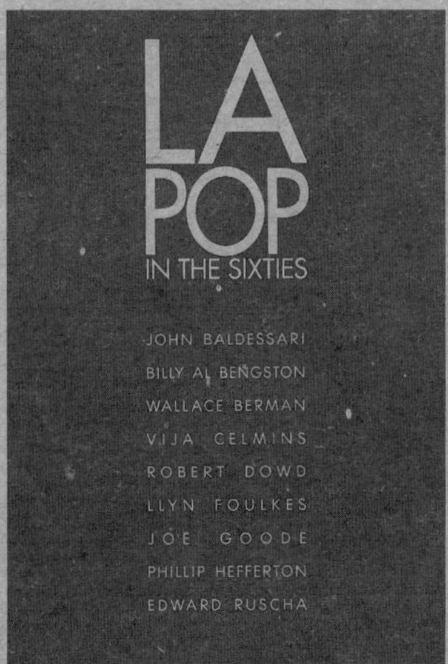

1990
'Vija Celmins: Drawings and Prints',
Pence Gallery, Santa Monica (solo)

'The Persistence of Vision',
Tibor de Nagy Gallery, New York (group)

Selected articles and interviews
1986–90

1986

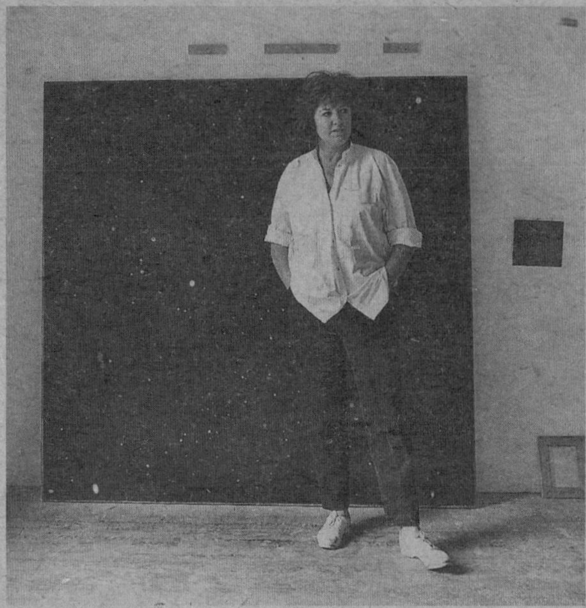
The artist with **Barrier** (1985–86)

1988
Cooper, Dennis, 'New York Letter', *Art issues*, Los Angeles, February
Cooper, Dennis, 'Vija Celmins', *Artforum*, New York, February
Haggerty, Gerard, 'Vija Celmins', *Arts Magazine*, New York, March
Brenson, Michael, 'Vija Celmins', *The New York Times*, 2 December
Johnson, Ken, 'Vija Celmins at David McKee', *Art in America*, New York, March 1989

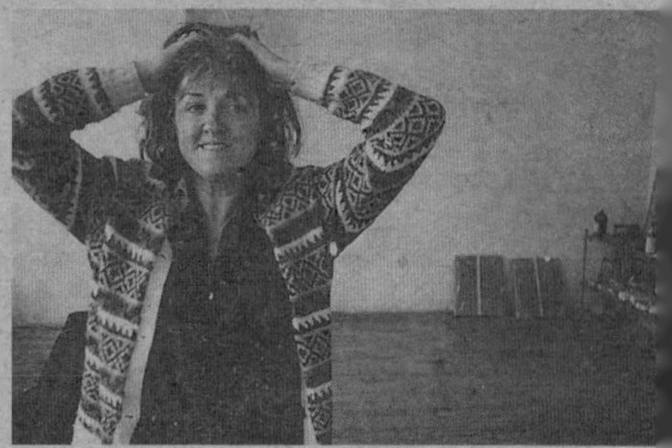
The artist, 1987

1989
Frank, Peter, 'L.A. Pop', *Contemporanea*, New York, October
Gipe, Lawrence, 'L.A. Pop in the Sixties', *Flash Art*, Milan, October

1990

Selected exhibitions and projects
1990–92

1991
'The Times, The Chronicle, and The Observer',
Kent Fine Art, New York (group)
Cat. *The Times, The Chronicle, and The Observer*, Kent Fine Art, New York, text Douglas Blau

'The Contemporary Drawing: Existence Passage and the Dream',
Rose Art Museum, Brandeis University, Massachusetts (group)
Cat. *The Contemporary Drawing: Existence Passage and the Dream*, Rose Art Museum, Brandeis University, Massachusetts, text Susan Swoops

'For 25 Years: Gemini G.E.L.',
The Museum of Modern Art, New York (group)
Brochure, *For 25 Years: Gemini G.E.L.*, The Museum of Modern Art, New York, text Riva Castleman

1992
Book, *Vija Celmins*, A.R.T. Press, Art Resources Transfer, Inc., Los Angeles, interview by Chuck Close

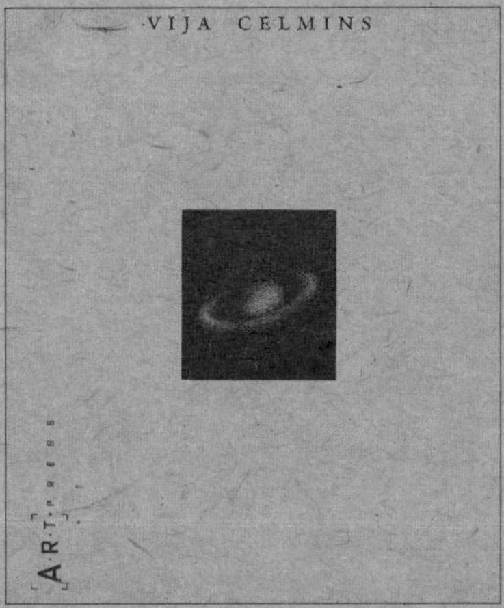

Cover, *Vija Celmins*, A.R.T. Press, Art Resources Transfer, Inc., Los Angeles

'Vija Celmins, New Paintings',
McKee Gallery, New York (solo)

'Vija Celmins Retrospective',
organized by the Institute of Contemporary Art, Philadelphia
Institute of Contemporary Art, Philadelphia, toured to **Henry Art Gallery**, University of Washington, Seattle; **Walker Art Center**, Minneapolis; **Whitney Museum of American Art**, New York; **Museum of Contemporary Art**, Los Angeles (solo)
Cat. *Vija Celmins*, Institute of Contemporary Art, Philadelphia, texts Judith Tannenbaum, Douglas Blau, Dave Hickey

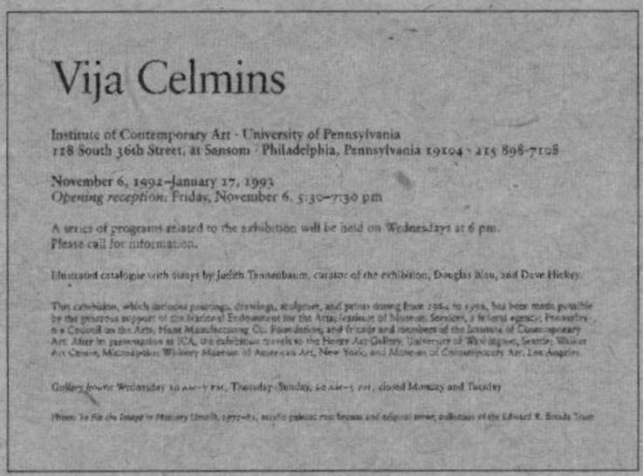

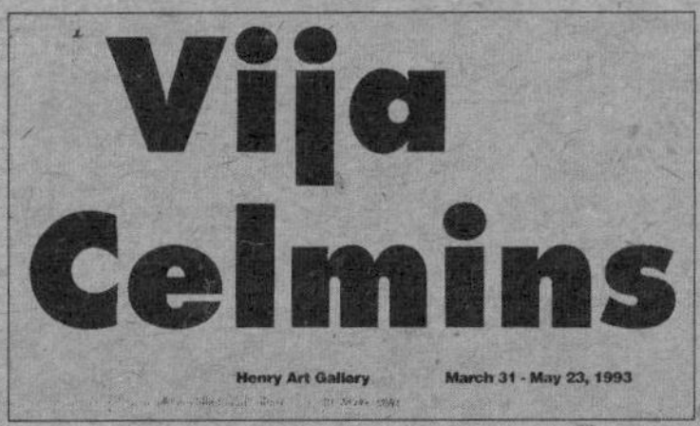

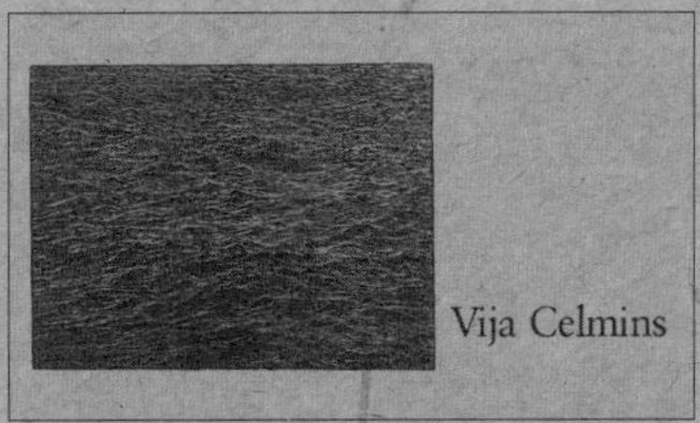

Selected articles and interviews
1990–92

Gerstler, Amy, 'Vija Celmins', *Art issues*, Los Angeles, November

1991
Schjeldahl, Peter, 'Past Perfect', *The Village Voice*, New York, 22 January

Sherman, Mary, 'Rose Exhibit Brings Drawings Back into Light', *The Boston Herald*, 22 March
Stapen, Nancy, 'Drawings at Brandeis Ask Profound Questions', *The Boston Globe*, 22 March

1992

Smith, Roberta, 'Seeing Infinity in Little Dots of White', *The New York Times*, 6 March
Schjeldahl, Peter, 'The Dearth of Painting', *The Village Voice*, New York, 25 March
Myers, Terry R., 'Vija Celmins', *Flash Art*, Milan, Summer
Liebman, Lisa, 'Vija Celmins', *Artforum*, New York, Summer
Heartney, Eleanor, 'Vija Celmins', *ARTnews*, New York, September
Kalina, Richard, 'Vija Celmins at McKee', *Art in America*, New York, September

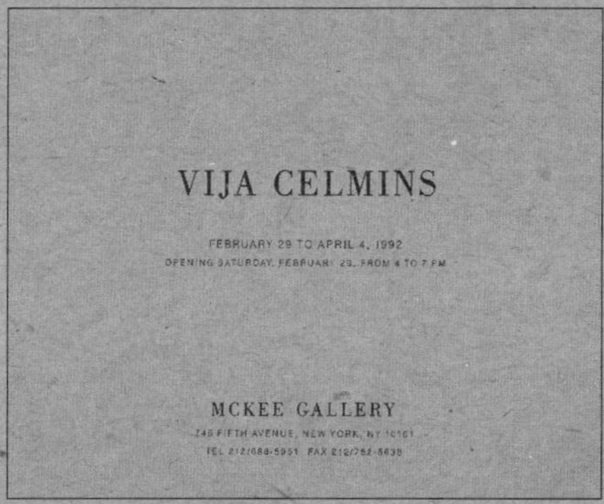

Sozanski, Edward, '2 in Exile from Their Homelands and Mainstream', *The Philadelphia Inquirer*, 22 November
Mangravite, Andrew, 'On the Nature of Space Heaters', *Welcomat*, Philadelphia, 16 December
Stein, Judith, 'Vija Celmins: Institute of Contemporary Art, Philadelphia', *ARTnews*, New York, February 1993
Cooke, Lynne, 'Philadelphia and Seattle', *Burlington Magazine*, London, March 1993
Lukac, Jenni, *Art Papers*, Atlanta, March–April 1993
Abbe, Mary, *Minneapolis Star Tribune*, 10 June 1993
Smith, Roberta, 'The Act of Seeing the Act of Creation', *The New York Times*, 17 September 1993
Larsen, Kay, *New York Magazine*, 4 October 1993
'Art: Passing Through', *The New Yorker*, 4 October 1993
Serraller, Francisco Calvo, 'El Pop domina la temporada neoyorquina', *El Pais*, 18 October 1993
Adams, Brooks, 'Visionary Realist', *Art in America*, New York, October 1993
Relyea, Lane, 'Earth to Vija Celmins', *Artforum*, New York, October 1993
Glueck, Grace, 'California Sensibility at "The Big Top"', *The New York Observer*, 25 October 1993
Zaya, Octavio, 'La trayectoria de Vija Celmins, en una gran muestra en el Whitney Museum', *Diario 16*, Madrid, November 1993
'Art Reviews', *Los Angeles Times*, 18 November 1993
Frick, Thomas, 'Vija Celmins', *Inside Moca*, Museum of Contemporary Art, Los Angeles, December 1993

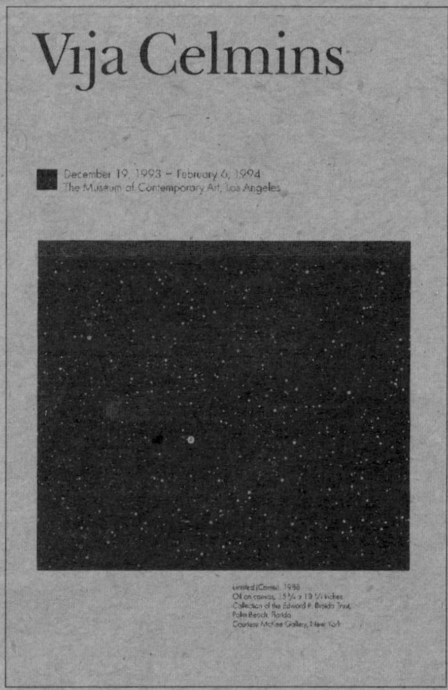

Selected exhibitions and projects

1992–94

1993

'Vija Celmins: Printed Matter',
University Gallery, Fine Arts Center, University of Massachusetts, Amherst (solo)

'About Nature',
Cleveland Center for Contemporary Art, Ohio (group)
Cat. *About Nature*, Cleveland Center for Contemporary Art, Ohio, texts Katherine Bowling, et al.

'Azur',
Fondation Cartier pour l'art contemporain, Paris (group)
Cat. *Azur*, Fondation Cartier pour l'art contemporain, Paris, texts John Ashbery, et al.

'45th Annual American Academy Purchase Exhibition',
American Academy of Arts and Letters, New York (group)

'Drawings: 30th Anniversary Exhibition for the Foundation for the Performance Arts',
Leo Castelli Gallery, New York (group)

Invitation card, 'Vija Celmins: Printed Matter', University Gallery, Fine Arts Center, University of Massachusetts, Amherst

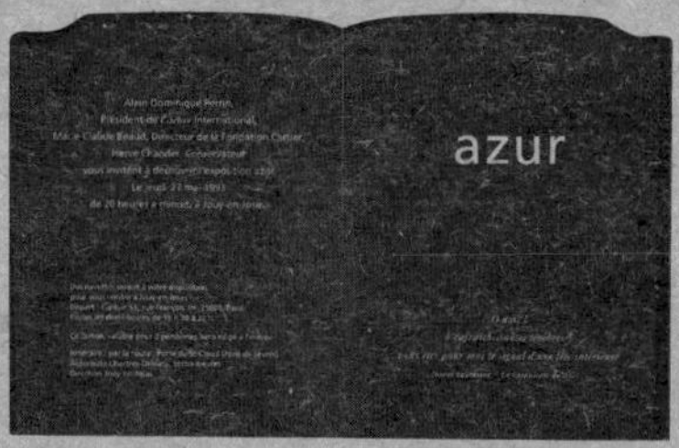

1994

'Vija Celmins: Prints, 1970–1992',
Cirrus Gallery, Los Angeles (solo)

'Love in the Ruins: Art and Inspiration of L.A.',
Long Beach Museum of Art, California (group)
Cat. *Love in the Ruins: Art and Inspiration of L.A.*, Long Beach Museum of Art, California, text Noriko Gamblin

Selected articles and interviews

1992–94

Morgan, Susan, 'The Beauty of a Long Attention Span', *Los Angeles Times Calendar Magazine*, 12 December 1993
Donohue, Marlena, 'Common Objects Made Special', *Daily Breeze*, Torrance, California, 17 December 1993
Knight, Christopher, 'The Profound Silence of Vija Celmins', *Los Angeles Times*, 21 December 1993
Knight, Christopher, 'It's Called Art Not Politics', *Los Angeles Times Calendar Magazine*, 26 December 1993
Lummis, Suzanne, 'Under Currents: Vija Celmins Ripples Dry Realism with Watery Abstracts at MOCA', *Downtown News*, Los Angeles, 27 December 1993
Young, Paul, 'Looking Hard', *Buzz Magazine*, December 1993–January 1994
Pincus, Robert L., 'Stunningly Seductive Forms Stick in the Imagination', *The San Diego Union - Tribune*, 2 January 1994
Rugoff, Ralph, 'A Thousand Points of Magic', *Los Angeles Weekly*, 28 January 1994
Kertess, Klaus, 'Seeing Stars', *Elle Decor*, New York, February 1994

Wagstaff, Sheena, 'Vija Celmins', *Parkett*, No. 32, Zurich
Knight, Christopher, 'Vija Celmins' Picture Planes', *Art issues*, Los Angeles, January–February

1993

Litt, Steven, *The Plain Dealer*, Cleveland, 3 April
Sparks, Amy, 'Plumbing Nature', *Cleveland Free Times*, 21 April

Domino, Christophe, 'Quand l'art se met au bleu', *Beaux Arts*, Paris, June

Pierce, Sarah, 'Space and Time: An Interview with Vija Celmins', *Q / A Journal of Art*, Spring
Jerry Saltz, 'Let Us Now Praise Artists' Artists', *Art & Auction*, April
'Vija Celmins, The Museums', *Art in America*, New York, Annual Guide, 1993

1994

Selected exhibitions and projects

1994–96

'Institute of Cultural Anxiety',
Institute of Contemporary Arts, London (group)
Cat. *Institute of Cultural Anxiety*, Institute of Contemporary Arts, London, texts Jeremy Millar, Francis McKee

1995

Fondation Cartier pour l'art contemporain, Paris (solo)
Cat. *Vija Celmins*, Fondation Cartier pour l'art contemporain, Paris, texts Vija Celmins, Robert Storr, Jeanne Silverthorne

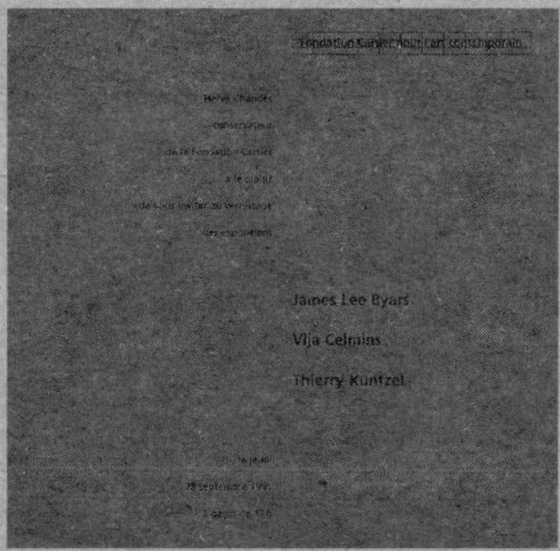

'About Place: Recent Art of the Americas',
Art Institute of Chicago (group)
Cat. *About Place: Recent Art of the Americas*, Art Institute of Chicago, text David Hickey

'Contemporary Drawing: Exploring the Territory',
Aspen Art Museum, Colorado (group)
Cat. *Contemporary Drawing: Exploring the Territory*, Aspen Art Museum, Colorado, text Mark Rosenthal

'American Academy Invitational Exhibition of Painting and Sculpture',
American Academy of Arts and Letters, New York (group)
Cat. *American Academy Invitational Exhibition of Painting and Sculpture*, American Academy of Arts and Letters, New York

1996

Receives American Academy of Arts and Letters Award in Art

'Night Sky Paintings & Drawings 1994–1996',
McKee Gallery, New York (solo)

'Vija Celmins: Works 1964–1996',
Institute of Contemporary Arts, London, toured to **Museo Nacional de Arte Reina Sofia**, Madrid; **Kunstmuseum Winterthur**, Switzerland; **Museum für Moderne Kunst**, Frankfurt (solo)
Cat. *Vija Celmins: Works 1964–96*, Institute of Contemporary Arts, London; Distributed Arts

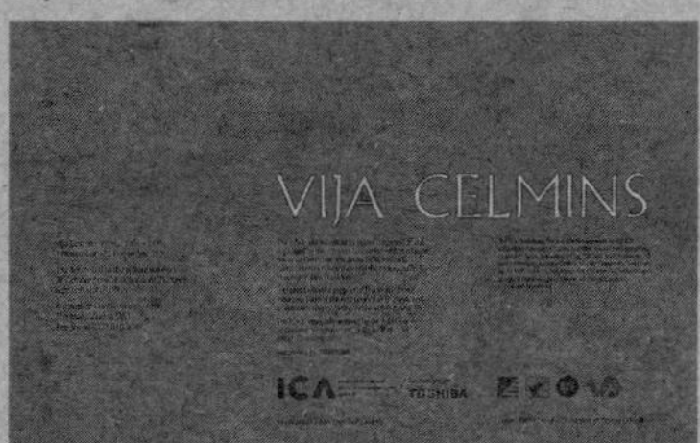

Selected articles and interviews

1994–96

Bemis, Mary; Recio, Belinda (eds.), *Nature Through Her Eyes: Art and Literature by Women*, The Nature Company, Berkeley

1995

Suchére, Eric, 'Vija Celmins', *ArtPress*, Paris, December

Princenthal, Nancy, 'Vija Celmins: Material Fictions', *Parkett*, No. 44, Zurich
Lewis, Jim, 'Night, Sleep, Death and the Stars', *Parkett*, No. 44, Zurich
Silverthorne, Jeanne, 'Vija Celmins in Conversation with Jeanne Silverthorne', *Parkett*, No. 44, Zurich
Shiff, Richard, 'Vija Celmins' Play of Imitation', *Parkett*, No. 44, Zurich

1996

Melrod, George, 'Openings', *Arts & Antiques*, Atlanta, February
Carter, Holland, 'Art in Review', *The New York Times*, 22 March
'Galleries: Uptown', *The New Yorker*, 8 April
Gibson, Eric, 'Vija Celmins: McKee', *ARTnews*, New York, June
Scanlan, Joe, 'Vija Celmins: McKee Gallery, New York', *frieze*, London, June–August
Princenthal, Nancy, 'Vija Celmins at David McKee', *Art in America*, New York, July

Grant, Simon, 'Exhibitions', *Guardian*, London, 26 October
Coomer, Martin, *Attitude*, London, November
Shiff, Richard, 'Realism of Low Resolution', *Apollo*, November
Feaver, William, 'Women's Work', *Observer*, London, 10 November

Selected exhibitions and projects

1996

Publishers, New York, texts James Lingwood, Neville Wakefield, Stuart Morgan, Richard Rhodes

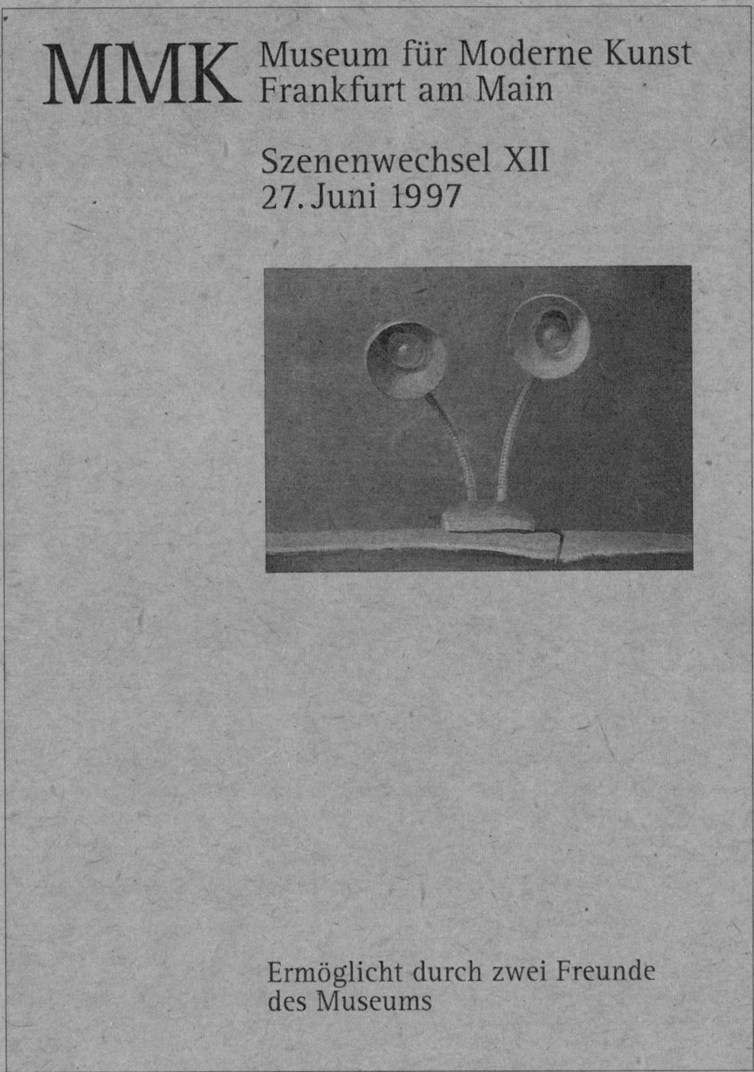

'About Photography',
Tokyo Metropolitan Museum of Photography (group)
Cat. *About Photography*, Tokyo Metropolitan Museum of Photography

'Views From Abroad: European Perspectives on American Art 2',
Whitney Museum of American Art, New York, toured to **Museum für Moderne Kunst**, Frankfurt (group)

Selected articles and interviews

1996

Dorment, Richard, 'Perfection in the Everyday', *Daily Telegraph*, London, 13 November
Coomer, Martin, 'Bare Necessities', *Time Out*, London, 13–20 November
Garner, Lesley, 'Art / Exhibitions', *Daily Express*, London, 15 November
Lutyens, Dominic, 'Vija Celmins', *What's On In London*, 27 November
Whitford, Frank, 'Vija Celmins', *Sunday Times*, London, 1 December
Cork, Richard, 'Dangerous Whispering', *The Times*, London, 3 December
'El Centro Reina Sofia muestra los cielos noturnos de las artist Lituana Vija Celmins', *ABC*, 20 January 1997
'Vija Celmins expone "cuadros impasibles"', *El Pais*, Madrid, 21 January 1997
'Vija Celmins exhibe en el Reina Sofia sus imagenes de la realidad', *El Mundo*, 21 January 1997
Alvarez Reyes, J.A., '"Outsider" del arte de su tiempo', *Diario*, Madrid, 21 January 1997
'Vija Celmins de lo contidiano a lo cosmico', *Bellas Artes*, Spain, 24–30 January 1997
Mebold, Adrian, 'Die Liebe zu Staub und Graphite', *Der Sandbote*, Germany, 4 April 1997
'Neue Malerei aus den USA', *Der Zurcher Oberlander*, Zurich, 17 April 1997
'Vija Celmins im Kunstmuseum Winterthur', *Weinländer Zeitung*, Germany, 17 April 1997
Berger, John, 'Penelope als Malerin', *Tages Anzeiger*, Germany, 18 April 1997
Mebold, Adrian, 'Sehnsucht nach den Sternen', *Der Sandbote*, Germany, 19 April 1997
'Gegenstande auf grauem Hintergrund', *Weinländer Zeitung*, Germany, 22 April 1997
Zwez, Annelise, 'Aus Allen Bildren fuhrt ein Elektrokabel', *Aargauer Zeitung*, Germany, 23 April 1997
Zwez, Annelise, 'Ein Stuck Unendlichkeit greidbar machen', *Berner Zeitung*, Bern, 26 April 1997
Zwez, Annelise, 'Steinwusten und Sternenbilder', *Schaffhaufer Nachrichten*, Germany, 26 April 1997
Scwitzler, Joachim, 'Gleich unter Gleichen', *Bischofszell Nachrichten*, Germany, 30 April 1997
Vogel, Sabine B., 'Die Oberflache der Sterne', *Kunstbulletin*, Kriens, May 1997
Mack, Gerhard, 'Die Herrin des Feuers', *St. Galler Tagblatt*, 10 May 1997
Mack, Gerhard, 'Als stunde die Zeit still', *Suddeutsche Zeitung*, Germany, 20 May 1997
Berger, John, 'Penelope as Painter', Insight Extra, *Tate Magazine*, London, Summer 1997
Schaufelberger, Peter E., 'Undendlich scheinende Tiefen', *Sudkurier*, Germany, 5 June 1997

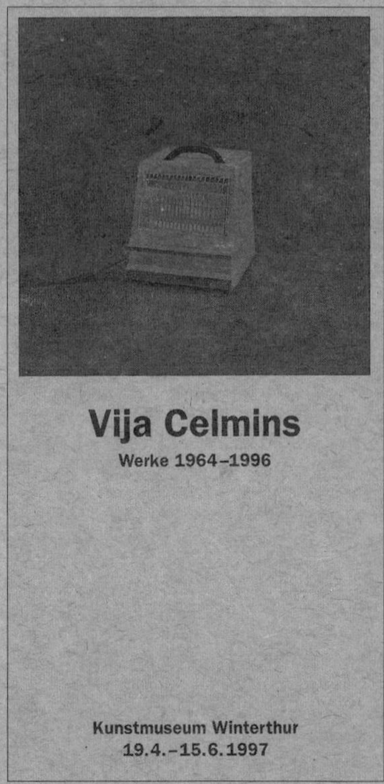

Silva, Arturo, '"Another" Art Exhibition at TMMP Goes beyond Traditional Boundaries', *The Japan Times*, Tokyo, 14 April

Rian, Jeff, 'Vija Celmins: Vastness in Flatland', *Flash Art*, Milan, Summer
Nelson, Robert S.; Shiff, Richard, (eds.) *Critical Terms for Art History*, University of Chicago Press

Selected exhibitions and projects
1997–99

1997
Receives Skowhegan Medal for Painting

Awarded John D. and Catherine T. MacArthur Fellowship

'Sunshine & Noir: Art in L.A. 1960–1997',
Louisiana Museum of Modern Art, Humlebaek, Denmark, toured to **Kunstmuseum**, Wolfsburg; **Castello di Rivoli**, Turin; **Armand Hammer Museum**, Los Angeles (group)
Cat. *Sunshine & Noir: Art in L.A. 1960–1997*, Louisiana Museum of Modern Art, Humlebaek, Denmark, texts Helle Crenzien, Lars Nittve

'1997 Biennial Exhibition',
Whitney Museum of American Art, New York (group)
Cat. *1997 Biennial Exhibition*, Whitney Museum of American Art, New York; Harry N. Abrams, New York, texts Louise Neri, Lisa Philips, et al.

'Heaven: Public View, Private View',
P.S. 1, New York (group)

'Birth of the Cool: American Painting',
Deichtorhallen, Hamburg, toured to **Kunsthaus**, Zurich (group)

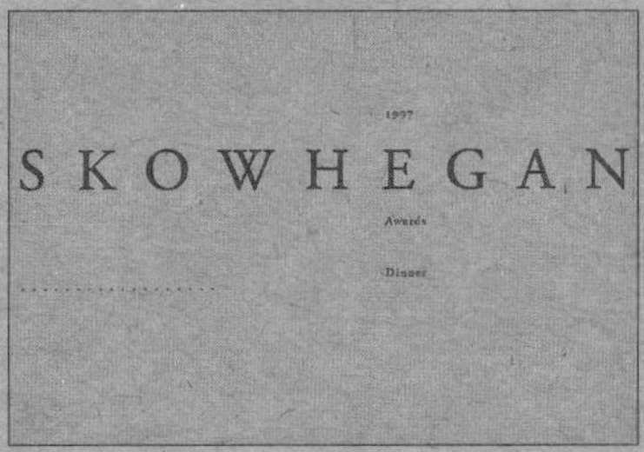

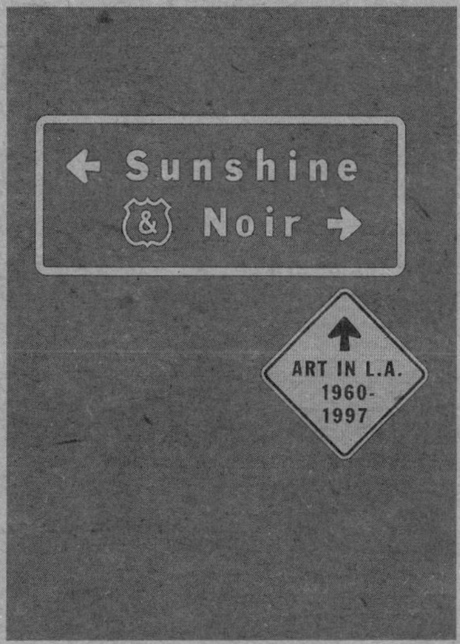

1998
'Terra Incognita',
Neues Museum Weserburg, Bremen, Germany; **Fondation Cartier pour l'art contemporain**, Paris (group)
Cat. *Terra Incognita*, Edition Braus, Heidelberg, texts Stephen Bann, Lynne Cooke, Michael Newmann

'Speed: Visions of an Accelerated Age',
Whitechapel Art Gallery, London (group)
Cat. *Speed: Visions of an Accelerated Age*, Whitechapel Art Gallery, London; The Photographers' Gallery, London, texts Jeremy Millar, Michiel Schwarz, et al.

1999
'Vija Celmins',
Anthony d'Offay Gallery, London (solo)

'Examining Pictures: Exhibiting Paintings',
Whitechapel Art Gallery, London, toured to **Museum of Contemporary Art**, Chicago (group)
Cat. *Examining Pictures: Exhibiting Paintings*, Whitechapel Art Gallery, London; Cornerhouse Publications, Manchester, texts Francesco Bonami, Judith Nesbitt

Selected articles and interviews
1997–99

1997

Honan, William H., 'MacArthur Foundation Chooses Grant Winners', *The New York Times*, 17 June

'Others On Stage at the Whitney Show', *The New York Times*, 9 March

Lord, M.G., 'New Visions of the Cosmos Now That It's Close at Hand', *The New York Times*, 29 June

Palmer, Laurie, 'Separated at Birth', *frieze*, London, May
Marcoci, Roxana; Murphy, Diana; Sinaiko, Eve (eds.), *New Art*, Harry N. Abrams, Inc., New York

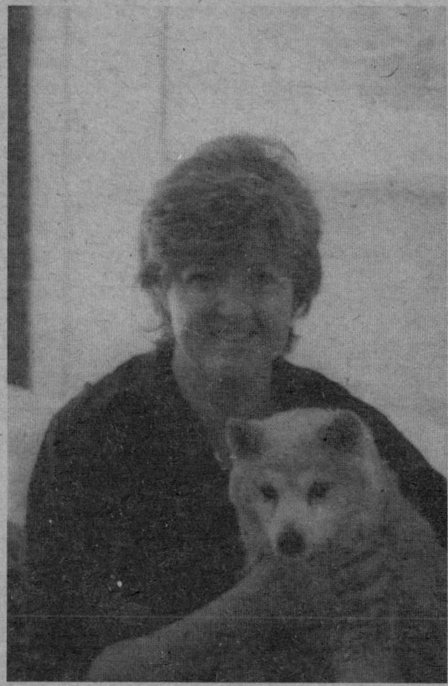
The artist with her dog, Zili, 1997

1998
Schiff, Hajo, 'Terra Incognita', *Neue Bildende Kunst*, Berlin, June–July

Coomer, Martin, 'Haste of Space', *Time Out*, London, 23–30 September
Searle, Adrian, 'It's a Blast', *Guardian*, London, 29 September

Wallach, Amei, 'Vision of the Void Behind the California Sun', *The New York Times*, 29 November
Prather, Marla F. (ed.), *History of Modern Art*, 4th edition, H.H. Arnason, Harry N. Abrams, Inc., New York
Salaman, Naomi; Simpson, Ronnie (eds.), *Postcards on Photography*, Cambridge Darkroom Gallery, England

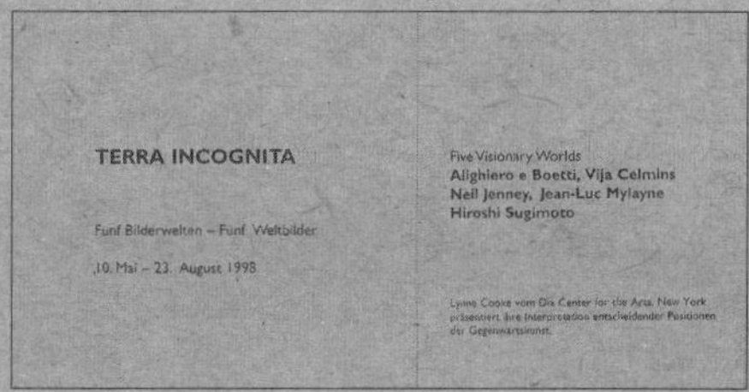

1999
Gayford, Martin, 'Exsquiste Miniatures from the Great Outdoors', *Sunday Telegraph*, London, 4 July
Kent, Sarah, 'Sky Writing', *Time Out*, London, 14–21 July

Patrick, Keith, 'Formal Dress', *Contemporary Visual Arts*, No. 26, London, 2000

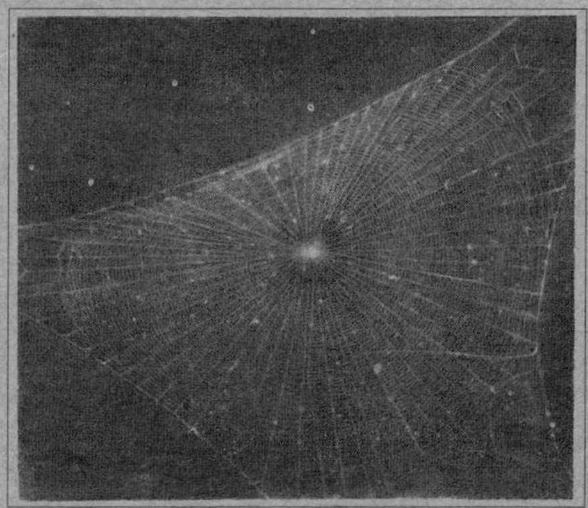
Invitation card, 'Vija Celmins', Anthony d'Offay Gallery, London

Selected exhibitions and projects

1999–2001

'Cosmos: From Romanticism to the Avant-garde',
The Montreal Museum of Fine Arts, Canada, toured to **Centre de Cultura Contemporania de Barcelona** (group)
Cat. *Cosmos: From Romanticism to the Avant-garde*, Prestel Verlag, New York, texts Jean Clair, et al.

'Regarding Beauty: A View of the Late Twentieth Century',
Hirshhorn Museum and Sculpture Garden, Smithsonian Institution, Washington, D.C., toured to **Das Haus der Kunst**, Munich (group)
Cat. *Regarding Beauty: A View of the Late Twentieth Century*, Smithsonian Institution, Washington, D.C., texts Neal Benezra, et al.

'The American Century, Art & Culture 1900–2000: Part II, 1950–2000',
Whitney Museum of American Art, New York (group)
Cat. *The American Century, Art & Culture 1900–2000: Part II, 1950–2000*, Whitney Museum of American Art, New York; W. W. Norton & Company, New York, text Lisa Phillips

2000
'Vija Celmins: Prints',
Cirrus Gallery, Los Angeles (solo)

'Celebrating Modern Art: The Anderson Collection',
San Francisco Museum of Modern Art (group)
Cat. *Celebrating Modern Art: The Anderson Collection*, San Francisco Museum of Modern Art; University of California Press, Berkeley, texts Neal Benezra, et al.

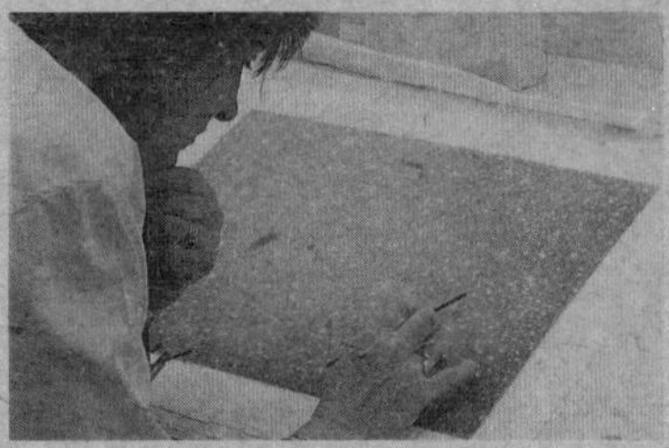
The artist, 2000

2000–01
Receives Coutts Contemporary Art Foundation Award

2001
'Vija Celmins: New Paintings',
McKee Gallery, New York (solo)
Awarded second place for best show in a commercial gallery, International Association of Art Critics (AICA)
Cat. *Vija Celmins*, McKee Gallery, New York, text Bill Berkson

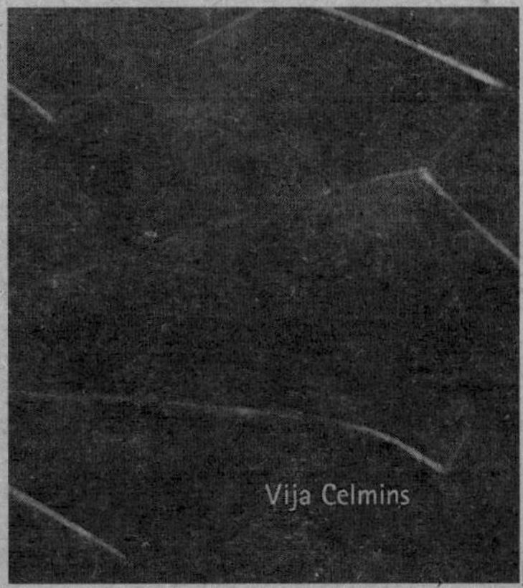

Cover, *Vija Celmins*, McKee Gallery, New York

Selected articles and interviews

1999–2001

Baillargeon, Stéphane, 'Jean Clair lance Cosmos aujourd'hui au Musée de Montreal', *Le Devoir*, France, 15 June
Leydier, Richard, 'Cosmos', *Art Press*, Paris, October

'Regarding Beauty, A View of the Late Twentieth Century', *Exhibitions*, Hirshhorn Museum and Sculpture Garden, Smithsonian Institution, Washington, D.C., October

Collier Hillstrom, Laurie; Hillstrom, Kevin (eds.), *Contemporary Women Artists*, St. James Press (The Gale Group), Farmington Hills, Michigan
Dave, Hickey, 'Best of the '90s', *Artforum*, New York, December

2000
Erickson, Karl; Falkowski, Andrew, 'Style Representation', *New Art Examiner*, Chicago, March

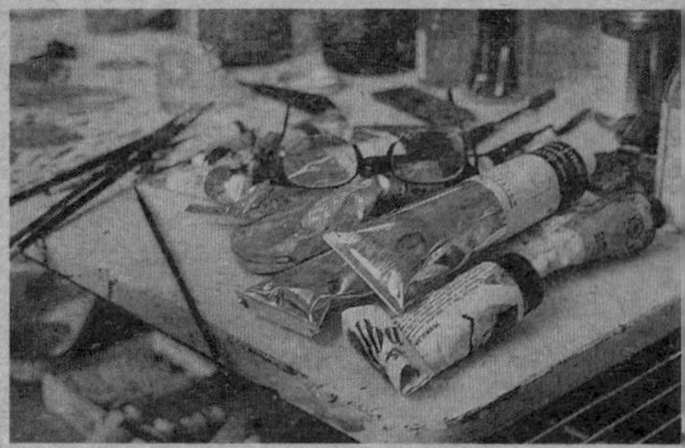

Rippner, Samantha J., 'Recent Acquisitions, A Selection: 1999–2000; Twentieth Century: Vija Celmins,' *The Metropolitan Museum of Art Bulletin*, New York, Fall
Fineberg, Jonathan, *Art Since 1940: Strategies of Being*, 2nd Edition, Harry N. Abrams, Inc., New York
Robertson, Jean; McDaniel, Craig, *Painting as a Language: Material, Technique, Form and Content*, Harcourt College Publishers, New York
Treasure from the Art Institute of Chicago, Hudson Hills Press, New York

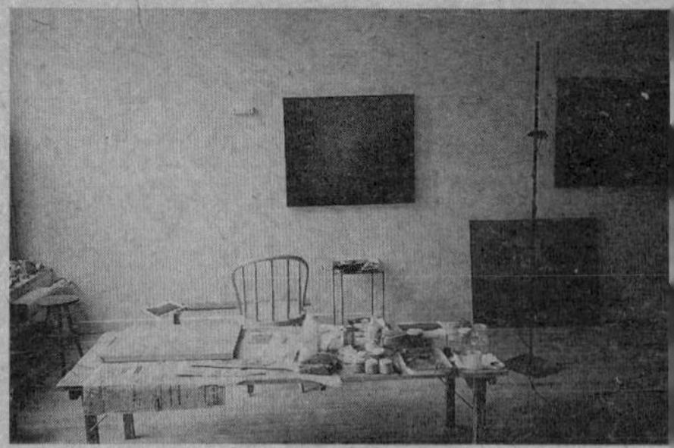
Artist's studio, New York, 2000

'Coutts Honors Contemporary Art', *Business Guide to Switzerland*, May–June

2001
Johnson, Ken, 'Vija Celmins', *The New York Times*, 1 June
Schjeldahl, Peter, 'Dark Star', *The New Yorker*, 4 June
Blair, Dike, 'Vija Celmins', *Time Out New York*, 14–21 June
Kerr, Merrily, 'Vija Celmins, Short List, Midtown', *The New York Art World.com*, Summer
Cohen, Mark Daniel, 'Vija Celmins: The Sublimity of Memory', *NY ARTS*, New York, July–August

Selected exhibitions and projects

2001–02

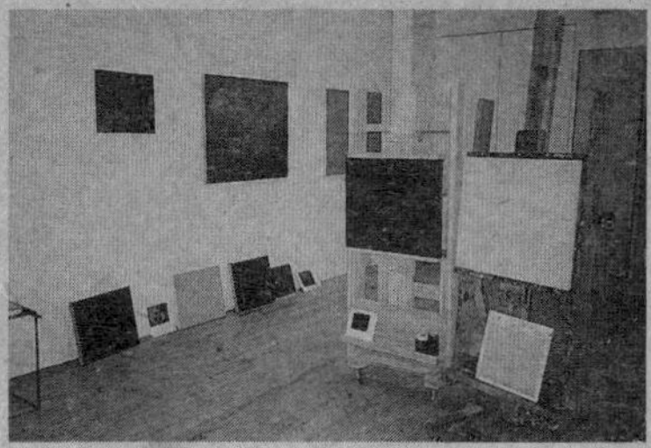

Artist's studio, New York, 2001

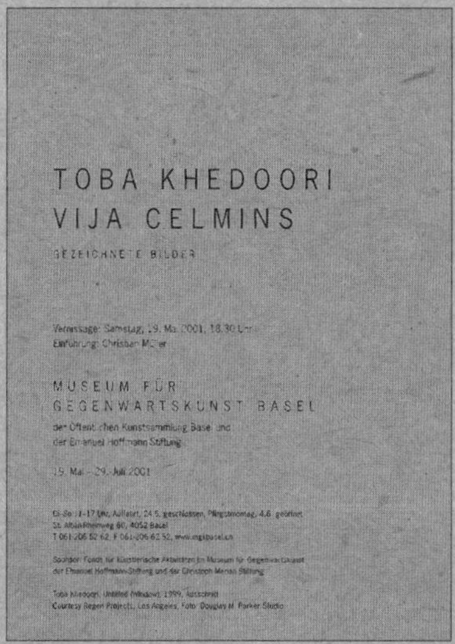

'Vija Celmins: Gezeichnete Bilder',
Museum für Gegenwartskunst, Basel (solo)
Brochure, *Vija Celmins: Gezeichnete Bilder*, Museum für Gegenwartskunst, Basel, text Iris Kretzschmar

Book, Donna De Salvo and Matthew Gale, *Giorgio Morandi*, (contribution by Vija Celmins), Tate Gallery Publishing Ltd., Millbank, London

Panel discussion, *Alberto Giacometti: An Artist's Panel*, The Museum of Modern Art, New York, 19 November

'Les années pop: Cinéma et politique: 1956–1970',
Musée National d'art Moderne, Centre Georges Pompidou, Paris (group)
Cat. *Les années pop: Cinéma et politique: 1956–1970*, Centre Georges Pompidou, Paris, texts Jean-Louis Comolli, Gérard Leblanc, Jean Narboni

'The Inward Eye, Transcendence in Contemporary Art',
Contemporary Arts Museum, Houston, Texas (group)
Cat. *The Inward Eye, Transcendence in Contemporary Art*, Contemporary Arts Museum, Houston, Texas, texts Lynn M. Herbert, Klaus Ottman, Peter Schjeldahl, Klaus Ottmann

2002
'Vija Celmins: Works from The Edward R. Broida Collection',
Museum of Fine Arts Houston (solo)

'The Prints of Vija Celmins',
Metropolitan Museum of Art, New York (solo)
Cat. *The Prints of Vija Celmins*, Metropolitan Museum of Art, New York; Yale University Press, New Haven and London, text Samantha Rippner

Lecture, *Vija Celmins: Prints and Drawings*, The Metropolitan Museum of Art, New York, 8 December

'Time to Consider',
The Arts Respond to 9.11, Deutsche Bank Lobby Gallery, New York (group)

'Whitney Biennial 2002',
Whitney Museum of American Art, New York (group)

Selected articles and interviews

2001–02

Zinnes, Harriet, 'Vija Celmins', *NY ARTS*, New York, July–August
Montreuil, Gregory, 'Vija Celmins, McKee', *Flash Art*, July–September
Kino, Carol, 'Vija Celmins at McKee', *Art in America*, New York, December

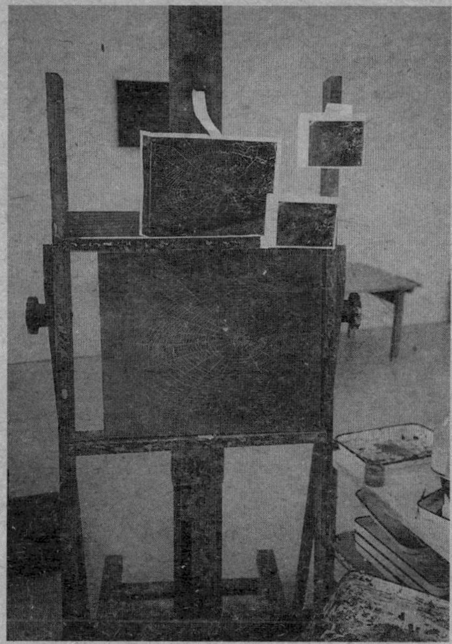

Artist's studio, New York, 2001

Livingstone, Marco, 'The Pop Years, Centre Georges Pompidou, Paris', *Artforum*, New York, May

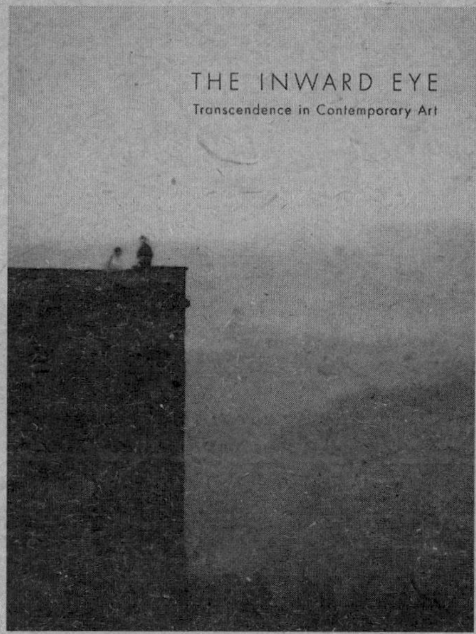

Siegel, Katy, 'Best of 2001', *Artforum*, New York, December
'If You Could Have Any Five Artworks For Your Home, What Would You Choose?', *frieze*, London, Tenth Anniversary Issue, November–December
Smith, Terry (ed.), *Impossible Presence*, Power Publications, The Power Institute, University of Sydney
Anderson, Maxwell L., *Whitney, American Visionaries: Selections from the Whitney Museum of American Art*, Whitney Museum of American Art, New York

2002

Glueck, Grace, 'With No Hidden Agenda, the Process Is the Point', *The New York Times*, 1 November
'Goings on About Town, Art, Museums and Libraries, Metropolitan Museum', *The New Yorker*, 4 November
Glueck, Grace, 'The Prints of Vija Celmins', *The New York Times*, 8 November
'The Prints of Vija Celmins', Exhibitions & The Collection, *Calendar, The Metropolitan Museum of Art*, November–December

Israel, Nico, 'Tribal Counsel', *Artforum*, New York, January

Selected exhibitions and projects

2002–05

Cat. *Whitney Biennial 2002*, Whitney Museum of American Art, New York; Harry N. Abrams, Inc., New York, texts Lawrence R. Rinder, Chrissie Iles, Christiane Paul, Debra Singer, et al.

'Tempo',
The Museum of Modern Art, New York (group)
Cat. *Tempo*, The Museum of Modern Art, New York; D.A.P., New York, texts Miriam Basilio, Paulo Herkenhoff, Roxana Marcoci

2003
'Celmins Prints',
Herron School of Art, Indianapolis (solo)

'Vija Celmins Prints',
Susan Sheehan Gallery, New York (solo)

Artist's book, *Vija Celmins: Drawings of the Night Sky*, Anthony d'Offay, London, texts Adrian Searle, Anne Seymour

Television programme, *Art:21 Art in the Twenty-First Century: Time*, Season Two, PBS, 15 September

Panelist, symposium, 'Unpacking Happiness', Mori Art Museum, Roppongi, Tokyo, 18 October

'Hyperrealismes USA 1965–75',
Musée d'Art Moderne et Contemporain de Strasbourg, France (group)
Cat. *Hyperrealismes USA 1965–75*, Musée d'Art Moderne et Contemporain de Strasbourg, France

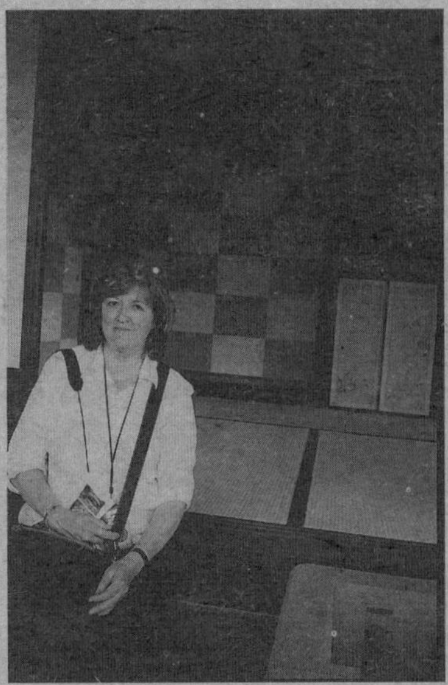

The artist on a visit to Japan, 2003

'Painting: From Rauschenberg to Murakami, 1964–2003',
50th Venice Biennale, Museo Correr (group)

'Happiness: A Survival Guide for Art and Life (Harmony)',
The Mori Art Museum, Tokyo (group)
Cat. *Happiness: A Survival Guide for Art and Life (Harmony)*', The Mori Art Museum, Tokyo

2004
UCLA Hammer Museum, Los Angeles (group)

2005
Hand-made book, The Museum of Modern Art, New York

2006
Centre Georges Pompidou, Paris (solo)

Selected articles and interviews

2002–05

Schjeldahl, Peter, 'Do it Yourself (Biennial Follies at the Whitney)', *The New Yorker*, 25 March
Gioni, Massimiliano, 'The Whitney Biennial: All the Small Things', *Flash Art*, Milan, May–June

Nickas, Bob, 'Multiple Voice', *Artforum*, New York, May
'AICA Picks Top Shows for 2000–01', *Art in America*, New York, February
Wolf, Sylvia, *Michal Rovner: The Space Between*, Whitney Museum of American Art, New York; Steidl Verlag, Göttingen

2003

Knight, Christopher, 'Mind's-Eye View of Nature, Vija Celmins' New Prints Explore the Artistic Side of Star-Gazing', *Los Angeles Times*, 24 January
Grand Street 71 'Danger', Grand Street Press, New York, Spring
Vogel, Carol, '20th-Century Masters Dominate Art Auction', *The New York Times*, 14 May
Larsen, Elizabeth, 'Vija Celmins Artist of the Eternal', *Utne, Arts Extra*, (Utne Reader), Winter

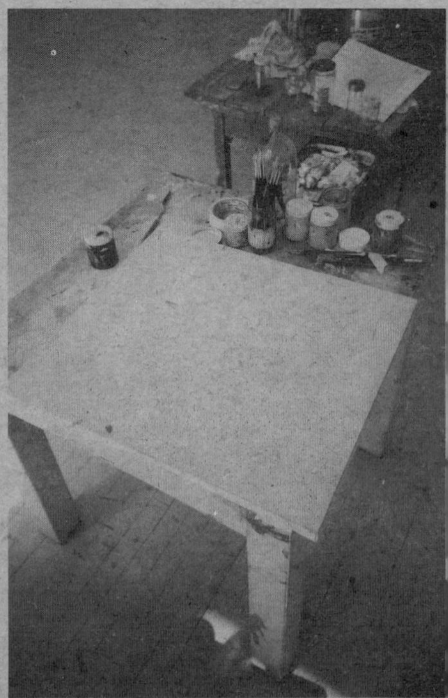

Artist's studio, 2004

Adams, Brooks, 'Visionary Realist', *Art in America*, New York, October 1993

Armstrong, Richard, 'Of Earthly Objects and Stellar Sights: Vija Celmins', *Art in America*, New York, May 1981

Armstrong, Richard, 'Vija Celmins', *Artforum*, New York, Summer 1983

Baker, Elizabeth, 'Los Angeles', *ARTnews*, New York, September 1971

Baker, Kenneth, 'A Landscape Beyond Reference Points', *The Christian Science Monitor*, Boston, 20 May 1983

Baker, Kenneth, 'Vija Celmins: Drawing Without Withdrawing', *Artforum*, New York, November 1983

Ball, Mandette, 'Vija Celmins: Objects and Illusions', *ArtWeek*, New York, 12 January 1980

Berger, John, 'Penelope as Painter', *Tate Magazine*, London, Summer 1997

Berkson, Bill, 'Spellbound', *Vija Celmins*, McKee Gallery, New York, 2001

Blau, Douglas, 'Solid Air', *Vija Celmins*, Institute of Contemporary Art, Philadelphia, 1992

Brenson, Michael, 'Vija Celmins', *The New York Times*, 2 December 1988

Close, Chuck, 'Vija Celmins Interviewed by Chuck Close', *Vija Celmins*, A.R.T. Press, Art Resources Transfer, Inc., Los Angeles, 1992

Cohen, Mark Daniel, 'Vija Celmins: The Sublimity of Memory', *NY ARTS*, New York, July–August 2001

Collier Hillstrom, Laurie; Hillstrom, Kevin (eds.), *Contemporary Women Artists*, St. James Press (The Gale Group), Farmington Hills, Michigan, 1999

Cooper, Dennis, 'Vija Celmins', *Artforum*, New York, February 1988

Cork, Richard, 'Dangerous Whispering', *The Times*, London, 3 December 1996

Crichton, Fenella, 'London: Vija Celmins at Felicity Samuels', *Art International*, Bogotá, June 1975

Domino, Christophe, 'Quand l'art se met au bleu', *Beaux Arts*, Paris, June 1993

Erickson, Karl; Falkowski, Andrew, 'Style Representation', *New Art Examiner*, Chicago, March 2000

Feaver, William, 'Women's Work', *Observer*, London, 10 November 1996

Fineberg, Jonathan, *Art Since 1940: Strategies of Being*, 2nd edition, Harry N. Abrams, Inc., New York, 2000

Frick, Thomas, 'Vija Celmins', *Inside Moca*, Museum of Contemporary Art, Los Angeles, December 1993

Gerstler, Amy, 'Vija Celmins', *Art issues*, Los Angeles, November 1990

Gibson, Eric, 'Vija Celmins: McKee', *ARTnews*, New York, June 1996

Glueck, Grace, 'The Prints of Vija Celmins', *The New York Times*, 8 November 2002

Haggerty, Gerard, 'Vija Celmins', *Arts Magazine*, New York, March 1988

Hazlett, Gordon J., 'Vija Celmins: A Reductionist by Nature', *ARTnews*, New York, February 1978

Heartney, Eleanor, 'Vija Celmins', *ARTnews*, New York, September 1992

Hickey, Dave, 'Vija Celmins: The Path Itself', *Vija Celmins*, Institute of Contemporary Art, Philadelphia, 1992

Johnson, Ken, 'Vija Celmins at David McKee', *Art in America*, New York, March 1989

Johnson, Ken, 'Vija Celmins', *The New York Times*, Friday, 1 June 2001

Kalina, Richard, 'Vija Celmins at McKee', *Art in America*, New York, September 1992

Kent, Sarah, 'Vija Celmins: Drawings', *Studio International*, London, July–August 1975

Kent, Sarah, 'Sky Writing', *Time Out*, London, 14–21 July 1999

Kertess, Klaus, 'Seeing Stars', *Elle Decor*, New York, February 1994

Knight, Christopher, 'Vija Celmins, Newport Harbor Art Museum', *Artforum*, New York, March 1980

Knight, Christopher, 'Vija Celmins' Picture Planes', *Art issues*, Los Angeles, January–February 1992

Knight, Christopher, 'The Profound Silence of Vija Celmins', *Los Angeles Times*, 21 December 1993

Knight, Christopher, 'It's Called Art Not Politics', *Los Angeles Times Calendar Magazine*, 26 December 1993

Knight, Christopher, 'Mind's-Eye View of Nature, Vija Celmins' New Prints Explore the Artistic Side of Star-Gazing', *Los Angeles Times*, 24 January 2003

Kozloff, Max, 'Vija Celmins', *Artforum*, New York, March 1974

Kutner, Janet, 'The Visceral Aesthetic of a New Decade's Art', *Arts Magazine*, New York, December 1976

Larsen, Susan, 'A Conversation with Vija Celmins', *LAICA Journal*, Los Angeles Institute of Contemporary Art, October–November 1978

Larsen, Susan, *Vija Celmins: A Survey Exhibition*, Fellows of Contemporary Art, Los Angeles, 1979

Larson, Kay, 'Prints for the Present', *New York Magazine*, 28 November 1983

Lewis, Jim, 'Night, Sleep, Death and the Stars', *Parkett*, No. 44, Zurich, 1995

Leydier, Richard, 'Cosmos', *Art Press*, Paris, October 1999

Liebman, Lisa, 'Vija Celmins', *Artforum*, New York, Summer 1992

Lingwood, James, 'Picture of the Facts', *Vija Celmins: Works 1964–96*, Institute of Contemporary Arts, London; Distributed Arts Publishers, New York, 1996

Lippard, Lucy, *Pop Art*, Praeger Publishers, New York, 1966

Livingston, Jane, 'Four Los Angeles Artists', *Art in America*, No. 5, New York, September–October 1970

Lord, M.G., 'New Visions of the Cosmos Now That It's Close at Hand', *The New York Times*, 29 June 1997

Marcoci, Roxana; Murphy, Diana; Sinaiko, Eve (eds.), *New Art*, Harry N. Abrams, Inc., New York 1996

McCann, Cecile, 'Los Angeles Artists', *ArtWeek*, New York, 9 December 1972

Montgomery, Cara, 'West Coast Report', *Arts Magazine*, New York, September 1973

Montreuil, Gregory, 'Vija Celmins, McKee', *Flash Art*, July–September 2001

Morgan, Stuart, 'The Hard Way', *Vija Celmins: Works 1964–96*, Institute of Contemporary Arts, London; Distributed Arts Publishers, New York, 1996

Morgan, Susan, 'The Beauty of a Long Attention Span', *Los Angeles Times*, 12 December 1993

Muchnic, Suzanne, 'Fellows Get Shows on the Road', *Los Angeles Times*, 24 December 1979

Myers, Terry R., 'Vija Celmins', *Flash Art*, Milan, Summer 1992

Nelson, Robert S.; Shiff, Richard, (eds.) *Critical Terms for Art History*, University of Chicago Press 1996

Palmer, Laurie, 'Separated at Birth', *frieze*, London, May 1997

Perlmutter, Elizabeth, 'A Hotbed of Advanced Art', *ARTnews*, New York, January 1976

Pierce, Sarah, 'Space and Time: An Interview with Vija Celmins', *Q / A Journal of Art*, Spring 1993

Plagens, Peter, 'Exhibitions in Los Angeles', *Artforum*, New York, March 1970

Plagens, Peter, *Sunshine Muse: Contemporary Art on the West Coast*, Praeger Publishers, New York, 1974

Prather, Marla F. (ed.), *History of Modern Art*, 4th edition, H.H. Arnason, Harry N. Abrams, Inc., New York 1998

Princenthal, Nancy, 'Vija Celmins: Material Fictions', *Parkett*, No. 44, Zurich, 1995

Princenthal, Nancy, 'Vija Celmins at David McKee', *Art in America*, New York, July 1996

Ratcliff, Carter, 'Vija Celmins: An Art of Reclamation', *Print Collector's Newsletter*, New York, January–February 1984

Relyea, Lane, 'Earth to Vija Celmins', *Artforum*, New York, October 1993

Rhodes, Richard, 'Vija Celmins, Painter', *Vija Celmins: Works 1964–96*, Institute of Contemporary Arts, London; Distributed Arts Publishers, New York, 1996

Rian, Jeff, 'Vija Celmins: Vastness in Flatland', *Flash Art*, Milan, Summer 1996

Rippner, Samantha, *The Prints of Vija Celmins*, Metropolitan Museum of Art, New York; Yale University Press, New Haven and London, 2002

Rugoff, Ralph, 'A Thousand Points of Magic', *Los Angeles Weekly*, 28 January 1994

Russell, John, 'A Remarkable Museum Debut', *The New York Times*, 28 July 1980

Russell, John, 'The Sea and Stars as Seen by Vija Celmins', *The New York Times*, 18 March 1983

Scanlan, Joe, 'Vija Celmins: McKee Gallery, New York', *frieze*, London, June–August 1996

Schjeldahl, Peter, 'The Dearth of Painting', *The Village Voice*, New York, 25 March 1992

Shiff, Richard, 'Vija Celmins' Play of Imitation', *Parkett*, No. 44, Zurich, 1995

Silverthorne, Jeanne, 'Vija Celmins in Conversation with Jeanne Silverthorne', *Parkett*, No. 44, Zurich, 1995

Silverthorne, Jeanne, interview, *Vija Celmins*, Fondation Cartier pour l'art contemporain, Paris, 1995

Smith, Roberta, 'Seeing Infinity in Little Dots of White', *The New York Times*, 6 March 1992

Smith, Roberta, 'The Act of Seeing the Act of Creation', *The New York Times*, 17 September 1993

Searle, Adrian, *Vija Celmins: Drawings of the Night Sky*, Anthony d'Offay, London, 2003

Seymour, Anne, *Vija Celmins: Drawings of the Night Sky*, Anthony d'Offay, London, 2003

Smith, Terry (ed.), *Impossible Presence*, Power Publications, The Power Institute, University of Sydney, 2001

Solomon, Elke M., *Vija Clemins*, Whitney Museum of American Art, New York, 1973

Stebbins, Theodore E., *American Master Drawings and Watercolors*, Harper & Row, New York, 1976

Stein, Judith, 'Vija Celmins: Institute of Contemporary Art, Philadelphia', *ARTnews*, New York, February 1993

Storr, Robert, *Vija Celmins*, Fondation Cartier pour l'art contemporain, Paris, 1995

Suchére, Eric, 'Vija Celmins', *ArtPress*, Paris, December 1995

Tannenbaum, Judith, 'Vija Celmins: Holding On to the Surface', *Vija Celmins*, Institute of Contemporary Art, Philadelphia, 1992

Vogel, Sabine B., 'Die Oberflache der Sterne', *Kunstbulletin*, Kriens, May 1997

Wagstaff, Sheena, 'Vija Celmins', *Parkett*, No. 32, Zurich, 1992

Wakefield, Neville, '"Temps Morts"', *Vija Celmins: Works 1964–96*, Institute of Contemporary Arts, London; Distributed Arts Publishers, New York, 1996

Wallach, Amei, 'Vision of the Void Behind the California Sun', *The New York Times*, 29 November 1998

Westfall, Stephen, 'Vija Celmins', *Arts Magazine*, New York, June 1983

Whitford, Frank, 'Vija Celmins', *Sunday Times*, London, 1 December 1996

Wholden, Rosalind G., 'Los Angeles', *Arts Magazine*, New York, December 1964

Wortz, Melinda, 'New Editions', *ARTnews*, New York, March 1976

Wortz, Melinda, 'Autobiographical Erasers', *ARTnews*, New York, April 1980

Young, Paul, 'Looking Hard', *Buzz Magazine*, December 1993–January 1994

Zinnes, Harriet, 'Vija Celmins', *NY ARTS*, New York, July–August 2001

Public Collections

High Museum of Art, Atlanta
The Baltimore Museum of Art
Fogg Art Museum, Cambridge, Massachusetts
The Art Institute of Chicago
Modern Art Museum of Fort Worth, Texas
Mount Holyoke College Museum of Art, South Hadley
Los Angeles County Museum of Art
Centro Cultural, Mexico City
Walker Art Center, Minneapolis
Newport Harbor Art Museum, California
Metropolitan Museum of Art, New York
The Museum of Modern Art, New York
Whitney Museum of American Art, New York
The Oakland Museum of Art, California
Orlando Museum of Art, Florida
Centre Georges Pompidou, Musée national d'art moderne, Paris
Fondation Cartier pour l'art contemporain, Paris
Philadelphia Museum of Art, Pennsylvania
Carnegie Institute, Museum of Art, Pittsburgh
San Francisco Museum of Modern Art
National Aeronautics and Space Administration (NASA), Washington, D.C.
National Gallery of Art, Washington, D.C.
Kunstmuseum, Winterthur, Switzerland

List of Comparative Images

page 19, **René Magritte**
Time Transfixed
The Art Institute of Chicago

page 19, **René Magritte**
Personal Values
San Francisco Museum of Modern Art

List of Illustrated Works

page 124, **Bikini**, 1968
page 14, **Burning Man**, 1966
page 50, **Burning Plane**, 1965
page 72, **Clouds**, 1965–69
page 18, **Comb**, 1969–70
page 92, **Desert Surface #1**, 1991
page 93, **Desert Surface #2**, 1992
page 33, **Double Galaxy (Coma Bernices)**, 1974
page 88, **Drawing Saturn**, 1982
page 56, **Explosion at Sea**, 1966
pages 64–65, **Fan**, 1964
pages 52–53, **Flying Fortress**, 1966
pages 12–13, **Freeway**, 1966
page 31, **Galaxy # 1 (Coma Bernices)**, 1973
page 134, **Galaxy (Cassiopeia)**, 1973
page 11, **German Plane**, 1966
page 69, **Gun with Hand #1**, 1964
page 119, **Heater**, 1964
page 126, **Hiroshima**, 1968
page 137, **Holding onto the Surface**, 1983
page 120, **Hot Plate**, 1964
page 15, **House #1**, 1965
page 17, **House #2**, 1965
page 40, **Hubble #1**, 1998
page 41, **Hubble #2**, 1998
pages 42–43, **Hubble #3**, 1998
page 47, **Lamp #1**, 1964
page 128, **Letter**, 1968
page 86, **Long Ocean #1**, 1973
page 74, **Moon Surface (Luna 9) #1**, 1969
page 75, **Moon Surface (Surveyor I)**, 1971–72
page 90, **Moving Out (Star Field II)**, 1982
page 35, **Night Sky #2**, 1991
pages 36–37, **Night Sky #5**, 1992
page 96, **Night Sky #6**, 1993
page 97, **Night Sky #7**, 1995
pages 142–43, **Night Sky #12**, 1994–95
page 136, **Night Sky #16**, 2000–01
page 24, **Night Sky #17**, 2000–01
page 141, **Night Sky #18**, 1994–95
pages 105, **Night Sky #18**, 1998
pages 100, 102–03, **Night Sky #19**, 1998
pages 130–31, **Ocean: 7 Steps #1**, 1972–73
page 32, **Ocean Surface Woodcut 1992**, 1992
page 121, **Pan**, 1964
page 16, **Pencil**, 1968–70
page 62, **Pink Pearl Eraser**, 1966–67
page 62, **Pink Pearl Eraser**, 1966–67
page 62, **Pink Pearl Eraser**, 1967
pages 70–71, **Pistol**, 1964
page 125, **Plane**, 1968
page 58, **Puzzle**, 1965–66
page 4, **Soup**, 1964
page 89, **Star Field I**, 1982
page 91, **Star Field III**, 1983
page 57, **Suspended Plane**, 1966
page 49, **T.V.**, 1964
page 66, **Time Magazine Cover**, 1965
pages 27, 28–29, **To Fix the Image in Memory I-XI**, 1977–82
page 19, **Train**, 1965–66
page 9, **Truck**, 1966
page 35, **Untitled #2**, 1994
page 140, **Untitled #9 (For Felix)**, 1994–95
page 95, **Untitled #10**, 1994–95
pages 80–81, **Untitled (Big Sea #1)**, 1969
page 32, **Untitled (Desert-Galaxy)**, 1974
pages 138–39, **Untitled (Divided Rectangle)**, 1986–87
page 84, **Untitled (Double Desert)**, 1974
page 85, **Untitled (Large Desert)**, 1974–75
pages 76–77, **Untitled (Moon Surface #1)**, 1969
page 132, **Untitled (Ocean with Cross #1)**, 1971
page 133, **Untitled (Ocean with Cross #2)**, 1972
page 79, **Untitled (Ocean)**, 1968
page 44, **Untitled (Ocean)**, 1968
page 30, **Untitled (Ocean)**, 1969
pages 82–83, **Untitled (Ocean)**, 1990–95
page 85, **Untitled (Regular Desert)**, 1973
page 135, **Untitled (Snow Surface)**, 1977
page 20, **Web**, 1992
pags 112–13, **Web #1**, 1998
page 21, **Web #2**, 2000–01
page 108, **Web #3**, 1999
pages 22–23, **Web #3**, 2000–02
page 111, **Web #8**, 2004
page 59, **WWII Puzzle Toy**, 1965
page 123, **Zeppelin**, 1968